The Least of These

Mary Van Cleave

The Least of These
Stories of Schoolchildren

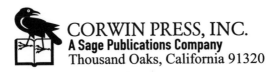

CORWIN PRESS, INC.
A Sage Publications Company
Thousand Oaks, California 91320

For information address:

Corwin Press, Inc.
A Sage Publications Company
2455 Teller Road
Thousand Oaks, California 91320

SAGE Publications Ltd.
6 Bonhill Street
London EC2A 4PU
United Kingdom

SAGE Publications India Pvt. Ltd.
M-32 Market
Greater Kailash I
New Delhi 110 048 India

Printed in the United States of America

Library of Congress Cataloging-in-Publication Data

Van Cleave, Mary, 1937-
        The least of these : stories of schoolchildren / by Mary Van
    Cleave.
            p.   cm.
        ISBN 0-8039-6200-2 — ISBN 0-8039-6201-0 (pbk.)
        1. Socially handicapped children—Education (Elementary—United
    States. 2. Education, Urban—United States.   I. Title.
    LC4091.V35   1994
    371.96'7—dc20   94-31984

This book is printed on acid-free paper that meets Environmental Protection Agency standards for recycled paper.

94 95 96 97 98 10 9 8 7 6 5 4 3 2 1

Corwin Press Production Editor: Marie Louise Penchoen

Contents

Acknowledgments

I could not have written this book without unstinting support from Mary Kinnick. From first to last she believed that the children's stories needed to be told and, when my confidence and direction ebbed, was always there to say the one right thing that set me writing again. No one has believed in *The Least of These* more than Mary has. Much credit also goes to Nancy Porter who came by one day and found the manuscript spread out all over the dining room table with a wastebasket near at hand. She gathered it up, took it home, and, with insight and kindness, read through at least two more drafts. Thanks to Marilyn Richen and Claudia Peabody; they listened to me talk about the book for months on end, read the manuscript thoughtfully, were patient during the discouraging times, and celebrated when the writing was going well. And to the women of "The Flight of the Mind," I give my hearty thanks for welcoming me and for showing me how empowering a writing community can be.

I extend deep gratitude to Margaret Marsh, Vince Welch, Peggy Lyons, and Ruth Williams. We have worked beside each other for many years and have lived together the experiences that the book describes. These remarkable teachers have shown me the meaning of courage and friendship, and they teach me every day what is possible. The entire staff, as well as the families, of Kelly School have been a source of constant inspiration, not only for my writing but also for my work as a principal. I am indeed blessed.

And a final word of thanks to Bill Greenfield for taking the trouble to read the manuscript and for introducing me to the wonderful people at Corwin Press.

I did not know until now how many spirits gather round to help in the making of a book.

About the Author

Mary Van Cleave is the principal of Kelly Elementary School in Portland, Oregon. She received her bachelor's degree from Willamette University, her master's degree in liberal studies from Reed College, and her doctorate in English from the University of Oregon.

During her 30 years as an educator, she has been a high school English teacher, an evaluation and budget specialist, a middle school assistant principal, and an elementary principal. She is active in a variety of professional organizations and has served as president of the Portland Elementary School Principals' Association.

Her greatest satisfaction, however, grows from the day-to-day pleasures and challenges of working beside her staff and families to create a school that truly belongs to children, especially children who face the rigors of poverty and violence on a daily basis. Toward that end, she has encouraged restructuring efforts, initiated many innovative family involvement projects, begun an extensive "Arts Partners" program in conjunction with Young Audiences, and has opened the doors to over 100 community volunteers and mentors—all the while seldom missing lunch duty or traffic patrol.

And, in the odd quiet morning when her head is clear, she writes.

To Tom, Amy, and Ted,
the children I first loved.

I
The Children
of
September

1

Marilyn Wallace backs out of the driveway just before 7:00 a.m. the day after Labor Day, the first day of school. She drives through her neighborhood with its bungalows and Tudor houses built in the '20s and '30s. Pots of bright geraniums crowd porches, and lawns are lush even after the August heat. The sun is just high enough nearly to blind her until she turns away from this cozy, close-in neighborhood. In a few more blocks, she joins the Interstate traffic and in 10 minutes is tracing the perimeter of the city. The habit of the drive lulls her out of her opening day nervousness, and the sun pouring through the car windows reminds her of the morning that "boils, pure gold" in "Pippa Passes." It strikes her as odd that people quote, "God's in His Heaven—/ All's right with the world!" oblivious to the irony. It has been a long time since she's talked about Robert Browning with anyone.

As she settles into the drive, a stand of small birch trees in the distance catch her eye, and she is reminded of how much is "right with the world." She wonders if Jane Reed will do her tree project again this year. Jane is such a good teacher, one of the best at James Madison School, one of the best anywhere. Images from 2 years before flood Marilyn's thoughts. It was a day as warm as today, even though a few dry leaves scuttling across the grass and the thinning light signalled that summer had modulated to fall. It was also the opening event of "Project Adopt a Tree." Jane is forever fierce about this project. She's angry about the drug users who own the park at night and on weekends, and she's determined to reclaim it—at least part of the time. So, early in the day, when the druggies are sleeping it off and when she can keep an eye out for anything suspicious, she takes her second graders out to *their* park. The very first week of school she begins telling the children how each of them will find and adopt their own "most wonderful tree in the whole park."

That September day 2 years ago was "Finding Day," and Jane asked Marilyn to come along. Jane and the children walked in pairs holding hands across two tight lines. A new girl, still shy and unsure, didn't have a partner, so Jane walked with her carrying a plastic wastebasket. "No talking 'til we get to the park," she called out to her small parade.

When they got to the middle of the park, Jane coached them into a semi-circle of three rows. Before the children sat down, she told them to inspect the grass around them. As part of Jane's routine each child brings along a plastic glove. "If you see something that could hurt you or someone else, put on your plastic glove and pick it up. Bring it over, and put it in this waste basket that I'm setting down right here." The children scavenged cigarette butts, empty potato chip bags, and candy wrappers, but no broken bottles or used needles that morning. As the 29 children sat on the grass, Marilyn scanned their faces. Jane's class was crowded, but, in the spaciousness of the park, there didn't seem to be too many.

Jane took center stage. Marilyn can still see her there, wearing her purple and green wide-striped T-shirt, neon purple sandals, and iridescent earrings with a wide green loop inside a larger purple one. Her room key dangled like an oversized charm from a purple coil bracelet.

"OK. You guys say you don't know how to pick your tree. Well, you just watch Mrs. Reed pick *her* tree. Brandon, you got your eyes on me? That's good! Just keep 'em there and don't move your body 'til I say so. That goes for *every* body. Now watch! I'm going to find my tree. I know it's here." Jane stretched her arms out at her sides, swayed in a circle, and closed her eyes while she intoned, "Treeee. Treeee. Whoo are you? Wheere are you?" The children tittered, not used to a teacher with a flair for comedy.

Jane opened her eyes. She took three steps toward a maple already touched with red. "No, no, not you. You're beautiful, but you're not *my* tree." She raised her hand to shield her eyes from the sun while she gazed at a graceful flame ash. She shook her head slowly. "Not quite, luv. Not quite." She closed her eyes again. "Oh treeee, oh, treeee, where are you?" she chanted. She opened them and started walking toward a young birch. "Is it you? Are you the one?" She stretched her arms out, broke into a slow, exaggerated run, and stopped short in front of the birch. "Oh yes," she sighed. "Yes. You *are* lovely." She patted its trunk. "Your black and silver bark is the most beautiful of any tree's. And your leaves are like feathers. You must love the fall when you wear your golden garments. Oh, my lovely birch, may I have the honor of kissing you?"

Marilyn smiles to herself remembering how the children broke out in a single guffaw. Jane took no notice. She put her arms around the small tree, kissed it, and then rested her cheek against its trunk. "Yes, little birch, I think we're made for one another." She turned back to the amazed children. "I hereby formally adopt this little birch as my one and only tree."

Then Jane broke character and, brushing tiny black particles from her cheek and the front of her T-shirt, gave the children their directions. "You got the idea? Now, I want you to take it nice and slow. You need to look at the trees, touch them, talk to them. You gotta get into this. Trees are shy; they won't talk to you if they think you're going to make fun or hurt them. But, if you're really, really respectful, they'll speak to you. Not the way you expect. They won't say, 'Hi, Chris, how y'doin' today?' or anything like that. You'll just get a big feeling. Then you'll know that you've found your very own tree. Now, when I say 'Begin,' you can start your search. Today we'll just find our trees and look at them *really* hard so that we can remember who they are when we come out tomorrow. Tomorrow will be 'Naming Day.' OK. Ready?" The children all nodded. "Begin!"

Just to test the limits, two or three boys ran hard down to the foot of the hill and back again. Jane kept her eye on them, making sure they didn't notice. Several of the girls and a couple of boys began to mimic Jane, becoming less and less self-conscious as the magic of play took over. Others watched until finally all the children were drawn under the spell of the sun and the trees.

All except for a slender child who wandered off alone. She sat on the roots of an elm so old that it must have been a large tree long before there was a park here. She pulled her knees up against her chest and tucked her head between them. Marilyn remembers she could not see her face, only tawny ringlets all matted and tangled, which—with washing and brushing—would have gleamed gold in the morning sun. The child and the old elm gave each other no comfort. Jane walked over, sat down beside her, and leaned in close. The child began first to look at Jane and then to nod her head. After a few minutes, Jane got up and stretched her hand down. The little girl took it and let Jane give her a pull up. Hand-in-hand they began walking toward a nearby tree.

Late the next afternoon, Marilyn met Jane coming down the hall lugging an armload of booklets. "Journals for the kids. This morning they drew pictures of their trees for their covers, and I've been putting them together so that they can start writing in them." All of Jane's students would be writers—and poets—before the year was over.

"I love this project, Jane," Marilyn said.

"Me too," Jane agreed.

"Once they got started, the kids sure had a good time yesterday."

"Yeah, and it just gets better and better as they get more into it."

"Who was the little girl sitting over by the elm?"

The pit of Marilyn's stomach tightens as she recalls Jane's words. "Oh, that's Star. She was in Susan's room last year. You remember. Susan was always complaining about her. She wasn't getting her consonants. Her mother wouldn't come in for a conference. Susan thought she might be a hooker from the way she looked and the hours she kept. I guess her mother's out of the picture now, though. Star says she's with a 'friend' in Florida. Sounds like Star is living with her father. I'm not exactly sure what the situation is. It's hard to get her to say much."

Marilyn shook her head. "Yeah, she sure looks like things are rough. Did she find a tree?"

"We walked all through the park. Then she asked if she could share mine. You know what she said? 'It's better to have two parents.'" Jane's eyes filled with tears.

"Poor kid. You've got your work cut out for you, Jane."

"Yeah, I know. I just want to bundle her up and take her home." Marilyn wonders to herself how many times she's heard Jane say that.

Almost every day for the next month, Jane and her children trooped out in pairs to their trees. They talked about them. They drew them. They wrote about them. And, as their journals grew fat, the children learned their tree's history, its botany, and its poetry. Whenever the class went out, Star was beside Jane. They laughed lightly, as easy and relaxed as a mother and daughter enjoying family small talk. They had fallen into this habit of lazy chatting because Star had begun to come early in the mornings so that Jane could brush her hair before the rest of the children got there.

Marilyn still carries the image of Star walking beside Jane, her curls blowing lightly about her face, her eyes squinting against the late October sun as she looked up at the teacher she loved.

Nearly lost in her reverie, Marilyn is forced into the moment by the sudden slowing of the cars ahead. She glances up to her left at the homes sitting high on the hillside. The people who live in them have proud views both of the city to the west and the mountains to the east. She drops off the Interstate into a tangle of intersections and traffic lights, passing a field choked with dry grass, waist-high thistles and dusty Queen Anne's Lace. All traces of her silver-lined musings vanish as she confronts the hard reality of her other neighborhood. She passes a forgotten house and an empty store front. The Wishing Well Antique and Junque Shoppe takes up the rest of the block. A faded "For Rent" sign painted on cardboard hangs indecisively over the narrow stairway that separates the Antique from the Junque sections of the store. The building's second story has been vacant ever since a small alternative school went elsewhere or maybe nowhere.

Now that she is back on surface streets, Marilyn keeps different company. The powerful foreign cars, the snappy new vans, and the "semis" that streak along the Interstate have not taken this exit. She waits at a stoplight among old American-made cars and pickups sporting mud flaps with nudes in silver silhouette. Windows are rolled down so that the talk shows and the hard rock on the other drivers' radios drown out hers. Marilyn switches off Bob Edwards who is interviewing students at a Chicago racially mixed high school about their attitudes toward each other. She isn't very interested anyway. Or, more correctly, she resents this school's getting recognition and presumably help when her own efforts to find funding have been mostly a matter of going up blind alleys.

She can feel how hot the day is going to be, and already she objects to the tyranny of her pantyhose. As she leans against her seat belt to look at herself in the rear view mirror, the waistband of her three-year-old madras skirt pulls, and she wishes she'd lost weight this summer. The rest of her outfit is as ordinary as her skirt—a tailored white linen blouse, seed pearls and earrings to match, navy blue flats with thick soles ordered out of a catalog. She wears almost no makeup, having decided a couple of years ago that it only makes matters worse for women over fifty. Her short brown hair fast going to grey is nearly dry. She brushes through it with her hand. This is the last time today she will look in a mirror.

The light changes, and she makes a habitual turn. The gas station on the corner has an early customer. She has seen this pickup and trailer for hauling lawn mowers and other yard equipment here before and speculates that whoever owns it must have steady work at least 9 or 10 months of the year. The men at the service station move slowly as they talk around their cigarettes. No one seems to mind waiting or to be in a hurry to get anywhere.

Next to the service station is Slippery Sue's Tavern. Nudes stencilled in black dance on either side of the doorway, arms lifted toward a faded rainbow that arches between them. The men who drive the pickups by day come to Slippery Sue's by night. Women come here too. The sign on the door promises male strippers on Thursdays. A Saturday night brawl which led to a fatal shooting was the lead story on a slow Sunday for TV news a couple of weeks ago. This is about the only kind of publicity the neighborhood expects.

An adult bookstore boasts it is "Open 10 til Midnight Every Day of the Year." Two more taverns take up the other side of the street. One of them is already open, true to its sign — "Day Lounge. Open at 7. Don't Drink n Drive. Never Abuse Drugs." A fan sitting in the doorway lightly blows the curtain on the window of the open door. The scrawl on another sign reads, "Bathrooms for Customers Only." A thin, tired-looking man walks through the doorway into the dark of the tavern. Marilyn looks down at her car clock which runs 4 minutes fast — 7:17.

An abandoned movie theater on the corner hints of a time before the heavy traffic of Interstate approaches dealt the ailing neighborhood its fatal blow. A woman sits cross-legged against the boarded-up ticket booth. Her face is lined deeply; her pale eyes are wary. A bed of stuffed garbage bags nearly engulfs her. She is dressed altogether in bright blue — hat, sweater, long dress. Only her high-top black basketball shoes interrupt the color scheme. She has shoved a grocery cart piled with the odds and ends of her life up against a wall once reserved for posters of Gary Cooper and Barbara Stanwyck. It occurs to Marilyn that the woman might be no older than she is.

She notices that this morning no U-Hauls or pickups piled with mattresses, kitchen tables, and toys are moving along the streets. People have finished their before-school moves. Will all the moving mean more children? We could lose as many as we gain, she thinks. She remembers the overloaded fourth grade classes — all at 28. Please, no more fourth graders, she pleads to no one in particular.

Now Marilyn is in residential terrain dominated by apartments with "Vacancy. No Deposit" signs and houses with crumbling front porches and broken windows. Before World War II, this sunny land was given over to strawberry fields. A few solid old houses scattered here and there suggest that once they presided over farms on the city's edge. Old people still tend them defiantly in the face of encroaching decay. Their gardens spill over in harvest profusion— squash, corn, tomatoes, green beans. The reassuring bounty asserts itself in the midst of desolate apartments and shanties.

Marilyn has never been in the well-kept houses because these are not where her children live. She catches a glimpse of a small shack sitting far back on a lot where there is no grass, only packed dirt and derelict cars. A woman kneels in the doorway, arms around a child of two or three. An older boy stands a little behind. This madonna lingers long enough in her imagination for Marilyn to form a whisper of an impression that the family is Latino. She wonders if the boy will enroll this morning. Every year more Latino, Southeast Asian, Russian, Romanian, and Black American children come to Madison School. This year, about a quarter of its 500 students will be minority children.

In another two blocks the school claims the landscape. It is a handsome place put up in the early '50s, a one-story brick-and-wood, U-shaped structure built to do its job and to last a long time. Forty years later, Madison still holds its reputation as one of the best school buildings in the city. The two acres of its grounds are well planted. Ever since Harry Schneider came to teach at Madison 36 years ago, he has seen to it that the graduating class plants a tree or a shrub. Marilyn enjoys walking around with him while he tells her the stories that go along with the plantings. The courtyard between the wings of the building blooms wild in March with hundreds of daffodils naturalized from three dozen bulbs Mr. Schneider planted 20 years ago. As much as everyone admires the courtyard, his favorite is the plum tree which stands by the front door. It explodes into a glorious pink every April, and then puts on hard, little fruit that the children throw at each other and at the school's windows all summer long. The tree is dry and tired now, and a few of its leaves are beginning to fall.

The children have a playground with enough room for them to roam freely, though it would seem more like a place for children if asphalt were not poured over so much of it. The playground butts up against a baseball field and the park that has been taken over by the druggies.

The parking lot is already comfortably full. Chuck, the head custodian, has been here since 6:00. He will leave at 2:30 when Gus, the toothless old evening custodian, comes in. Florence, the school cook, came at 6:30 to start breakfast. The secretary, Rose, is getting out of her car. She is loaded down with a fan, her lunch bag, and a jug of iced tea. In another couple of weeks, most of the teachers will be coming at 8:00 or a little later, but this morning even the old-timers have first-day jitters. All of the teachers drive to Madison School from other parts of the city just as Marilyn does.

Marilyn takes her usual shortcut to the office—through the back door and across the cafeteria into the front hall. Chuck hasn't turned on the lights in the cafeteria yet, and the room is still and stifling from being closed up over the long weekend. The smell of fresh wax hits her as she walks through the cavernous darkness toward the light. Chuck has been herding his huge polisher up and down for days, snapping at Marilyn for getting in his way. She stands for a moment looking down the main corridor, savoring the mirror shine on the old, rich maroon tile.

The walls of the entryway are clean this morning, bereft of the jumble of forgotten notices that multiply through the year. The showcases have bright displays—one with new library books and words printed large enough to be read halfway down the hall proclaiming, "We Are a Family of Readers at Madison School." Another cabinet boasts a collection of dinosaurs saved from last year; yet another one is filled with art prints and the promise of a new art curriculum. Chuck comes around the corner and waves at Marilyn as he turns on the rest of the lights.

"Mornin', Ms. Wallace. Seen the graffiti out around the music room? I already called downtown about it. They'll send out a crew when they can, but they're awful busy this morning. Damn kids went crazy all over town. They got to get off the gang graffiti 'fore they do our stuff. No more get it painted out and somethin' else is back. This time it's bad."

"What a way to start out. And you had everything looking so good. Makes you sick, doesn't it?"

Chuck shrugs. "Yeah, kinda. But what can you do? Can't have someone here 24 hours a day."

"True," Marilyn agrees. " I'll go out and take a look."

"You aren't gonna like it," Chuck calls after her as she goes into her office. She unlocks her closet, puts in her purse, locks the closet again and pockets the keys. She's always aware of the "great grand master" she carries. After years of being so conscious of her keys, she's fallen into the habit of handling them—out of boredom, out of nervousness, sometimes as a way of letting people know that she's the one in charge.

She shoves her lunch in her bottom drawer with forgotten sacks, crumbs, and aspirin. Taking a vase from the bookshelf, she gets water from the workroom on the other side of the outer office. She stuffs in the ruby chrysanthemums fresh from her garden, pulls their stems apart just enough to look as if they have a reason for being in the vase, and sets them on the corner of her desk.

As Marilyn hurries through the halls, she glances quickly into doorway after doorway. Several classrooms are already open, and she hears the hum of fans coming from inside. The teachers are trying to banish the stale heat from the weekend before today's heat begins to accumulate. Built into the wall beside each door is a small glass-framed case with a slit at the top to slip in a piece of paper.

Estelle Douglas, in her 37th year of teaching, has not changed her frame's picture in the three years Marilyn has been the principal at Madison. She looks at the small girl with a head of blond ringlets wearing an orange dress and leaning forward to water a patch of daises with a silly watering can. At the bottom of the picture, spidery calligraphy spells out "Miss Douglas, Grade 3" on yellowed paper.

Grace Johnson, Grade 1, has cut autumn leaves out of construction paper and has printed her name in big green block letters. A clipboard hangs below the frame for parents to check off how their child will get home from school—"bus," "walk," "go to baby-sitter," "parent will pick up," "brother or sister will pick up."

Marilyn stops at Jane Reed's door. Jane will be one of the last teachers to check in. She works late in her room long after her second graders have gone home and is often still there when Marilyn returns to school for 7:00 meetings, so she seldom comes in early. A cartoon face fills this frame—big smile, exaggerated teeth, tousled hair, bright red glasses, pencil behind her ear, and the words "Hi, I'm

Mrs. Reed. Who are you? Let's get to know each other!" Lucky children, Marilyn thinks.

She smells a cigarette. Nan Smith is in the boiler room having a smoke before the day begins. Marilyn sticks her head in the door, "Hi, Nan! Here we go, ready or not!"

Nan looks up with a wide grin. "You said it!" Nan is 38 and has been the school counselor since she was 23. The generations are short in this neighborhood, so she remembers when many of the parents were students at Madison; she's been in their houses and knows their lives from the inside. Everyone calls her Nan or, once in a while, Nan Smith, but never Ms. Smith. Nan's red hair hugs her chin in a blunt line while the top of her head is cropped so that it stands up giving a faintly punk effect. Three small, bright earrings run along the side of her left ear, and a silver stick woman dangles from her right. Dense freckles cut a swath over her nose and cheekbones, then scatter across the rest of her face. Nan is on the short side and has the build of a goalie. This morning she is wearing a jeans skirt that stops mid-thigh, pink work-out anklets, white tennis shoes, and bright pink lipstick that's a surprise against her summer tan.

"Chuck says there's a new batch of graffiti out on the music room, so I'm going out to have a look." Marilyn and Nan are too used to each other to bother with small talk.

Nan shakes her head and bats her hand downward toward the floor in disgust. "Geez. Not on the *first* day!"

Marilyn is on her way again almost before Nan finishes. She turns into the intermediate wing. Lil Wagner's frame says "Welcome to Grades 3/4 from Your Teacher, Mrs. Wagner." Bright paper balloons, each with a child's name on it, cover her door and all the wall space around it. Marilyn smiles as she imagines the warm welcome Lil will give her children this morning.

Corine Conrad teaches next door to Lil. Corine has used her frame to get a head start on explaining the rules: "Keep hands and objects to yourself," "Raise your hand before talking," "Follow instructions." Marilyn glances through the window. Individual desks are arranged in careful rows, each desk piled high with workbooks. The daily schedule and a list of pages to be completed by the end of the day are on the board. Those children are going to have a long year, she thinks. She passes Mr. Schneider's room. His frame contains a picture of an American flag with 48 stars.

2

Marilyn pushes open the heavy side doors. A low concrete block building squats on the asphalt behind the school, hidden from the view of neighbors and passing motorists. She stops short. Two six-foot female torsos loom above her—huge females, thigh to neck, no heads or arms or feet. The red-brown spray paint that gives them form is in curiously tasteful contrast to the cream walls of the building. One torso wears a lacy belt with dangling garters attached to nothing. Three or four locks of pubic hair cascade onto its thighs. The other form has no decoration, just an arrow running diagonally from its vulva down to the circled word *pussy*. Pendulous breasts dangle strangely to the sides of the torsos' chests. "School Sucks" is sprayed off to the right as a belligerent non sequitur.

Marilyn wishes for her own can of paint and the clarity of physical work to get rid of the contamination she feels. A sense of foreboding laps around her. For the moment, the torsos seem to matter more than all the work she and the teachers have put into getting ready for the new school year.

As she stands in the hot sun, Marilyn struggles to reclaim the cool mornings last June when she and a few teachers sat together trying to wrestle their hopes into words and phrases to live by. She tries, but she can't remember the ideas that seemed so powerful just a short time ago. Slowly, they begin to return: Try to make our school feel like a *family*; create classroom environments that *nurture*; treat children with *respect* and expect them to *respect* themselves and others; understand that children will feel safe and strong if they have clearly established and consistent *boundaries*; have *faith* that, given the right conditions, children can accomplish more than anyone might imagine. But, in this moment, Marilyn is face-to-face with the reality that these words embody frail hopes, hopes that have faded quickly in the strong sun of the first hour of this first day.

Marilyn remembers the more practical work of the summer—assigning children to classrooms, hammering out schedules, coming to agreements about who does what duties when. Will this work have any more staying power than philosophy? She'll be lucky if the elaborate structures of careful planning support them as far as Halloween.

She thinks of the children. How many of the 500 will come this morning? Many will straggle in over the next weeks as their families settle into spots they are renting for now, houses they're sharing with friends, or driveways where relatives let them park beat-up station wagons and vans. Others will come only after an adult in the house notices it's September or gets tired of the children's nagging about wanting to go to school. Marilyn's standard line is "We can count on the first heavy rain to bring in the last of them." By the first of October, most of the children in the neighborhood will have come to school. By Thanksgiving, a number will have gone somewhere else, and others will take their place. Forty percent of the children who start the year at Madison will not be there in June.

Three years ago, after Marilyn was suddenly transferred to Madison from Lincoln School in an upper-middle-class neighborhood across town, she felt as if the children's needs would overwhelm her. But, little by little, she began to see that many of them were thriving. They came to school, played on the playground, ate breakfast and lunch in the large cafeteria, began to feel at home in their classrooms, realized their teachers cared about them—even loved them, and they learned. As she watched the children, Marilyn started to realize how much they could teach her about the human spirit. She began to have faith in their resilience.

What Marilyn does not know is whether she and her staff can make *enough* difference in the children's lives. The test scores from last year came out in the newspaper a few days ago. Once again, Madison's were among the lowest. Marilyn knows that the parents won't ask about the scores; she suspects many of them can't read, let alone read the newspapers. She also fears that they don't expect anything different. In any case, most of them would be more likely to blame themselves than the school.

But the teachers *do* read the newspapers and that worries Marilyn. She doesn't want them to become so discouraged they give up on the children or so self-critical they begin to doubt themselves. She tried to talk about the scores in the opening staff meeting last week.

The teachers sat in chairs around tables pulled together in a large rectangle. They had had their coffee and rolls; Marilyn, sitting on the edge of a table, had introduced the new teachers and had spent longer than she intended on administrative details. Now she was uncomfortably aware that everyone was anxious for her to finish. There were bulletin boards to put up, tables and chairs to arrange, textbooks to unpack, and supplies to bring up from the storeroom.

She fingered her keys as she waited for the teachers to stop their talking, waited to discover how she could put words to her feelings. It had been easier in June when she sat with Jane and Lil, Nan, Marge, and other sympathetic teachers. Now she was nervous with Estelle, Susan, Corine, Mr. Schneider, and those who either disagreed with her or sought to live comfortably in the neutral wasteland between the two groups. Finally, the group noticed that she was waiting and, little by little, began to fall quiet.

"You've read the newspapers, so you know about our scores."

Mr. Schneider raised his hand. "Well, you know Marilyn, the tests came at a really bad time last spring. We didn't have enough time between spring vacation and the tests to finish teaching the material."

Corine nodded in agreement. "That's right. There was no way we could get through. Not with these kids. They can't remember anything for more than a couple of weeks."

"Please don't think that I'm blaming anyone," Marilyn hurried to say. "You're all teaching as hard as you can. We have a fine staff. There's not a better one in the city." She saw the teachers' faces relax, their shoulders drop, and heard a few sighs of relief. This was just going to be another pep talk.

"But . . ." She turned over her keys. A flicker of worry crossed some of the faces. "But the fact remains that we're not getting the results we want. The last thing I want to do is place too much emphasis on test scores. They don't begin to tell the whole story. I know it's not just scores you think about." She needed to draw the teachers in. "You're worried about all the conditions that keep the children from learning." She saw Nan nod. She glanced at Lil for support. Corine's face was stony. Estelle was staring at the ceiling.

Marilyn swallowed and plowed ahead. "It seems to me that if something isn't working we usually do either one of two things. We repeat what we've been doing, only we do it longer or harder—like drilling multiplication tables or getting hung up on phonics and spelling." A couple of teachers exchanged looks. They already knew Marilyn's position on phonics, and they didn't like it. Marilyn moved her keys from one hand to the other. "Or we do something new, and then, as soon as that doesn't seem to be working, we try the next hot approach. I don't know about you, but it's making me tired. Sure, you could fine-tune your curriculum, you could go to more workshops, and we could spend months analyzing our test data. But I just don't have a lot of hope that, even with all that effort, we could make much difference in those scores." Marilyn looked at Jane. Jane was tapping her left hand against the palm of her right hand close to her body in silent applause. Marilyn felt her courage come back.

"We have some other things to do first. We need to make the children as secure as we can. We need to see who they are—what they like and don't like, what their strengths are. Let's give them a school where they can get their hands on things, get involved in projects that answer the questions they have about their world. Let's let them talk to us and to each other."

Marilyn was picking up speed. She had stopped being afraid of what the teachers might be thinking in the joy of saying what she believed. "I don't care about the test scores. I *really* don't care. What matters is that the children have a school where they feel safe and secure and loved, where they feel as if they have something to contribute, where they feel their own worth. If we can work together to create that kind of environment, they'll learn everything we want them to learn—and more."

"Let's make a pact not to worry about the test scores for three years. Let's begin talking about the kind of school we need to create for our children and for ourselves. Let's break new ground. What do we have to lose? The only way we have to go is up, so let's try to go up 'our way!'" She suddenly ran out of words. "I've kept you too long. You have a million things to do in your classrooms, so go to it! Here's to a good opening! And a good year!"

Marilyn gathered up her papers, and the teachers pushed back their chairs. Jane walked out the door with Marilyn. "Boy, what a speech! It gave me the shivers. Do you really think we could do it?"

Marilyn smiled. "I want to believe that we could. But it would be hard."

"It *would* be hard," Jane agreed. "But I'm game."

As she gazes at the sun-washed wall, Marilyn begins to feel self-conscious about talking that way in the staff meeting. She feels as exposed as the torsos. She overstated her case; she was too passionate. She is afraid that her words will come back to haunt her. She has opposed some of the teachers, and she knows full well that when she opposes them, even in the mildest of ways, they match her and more. She can imagine what they're saying:

"Ms. Wallace doesn't think test scores matter. She wants us to let children play and roll around on the floor and do what they want to. That's not teaching. We know how to teach. That's our job."

"I'll bet she's going to try to make us stop using worksheets. How are students ever going to master skills without plenty of drill and practice?"

"And did you hear what she said about discipline? It sounds like she doesn't want any rules. Can you imagine the chaos? Nobody would ever learn anything."

"I've asked for a new set of encyclopedias for two years now. The newest one in the library is 10 years old. How does she expect students to do research projects without encyclopedias? We'll never get them ready for middle school if they can't even do reports."

The talk reverberates in Marilyn's mind. It's fear, she thinks. They're afraid they're wrong but even more afraid to change. They're paralyzed. But not all of the teachers are like that. A good number of them move Marilyn to humility when she listens to them talk about teaching or watches them working with the children; most give an honest day's work. And there are a few who eat out her insides and keep her constantly on guard, for they are as cunning as wounded animals riveted to their need to survive. Even with all the cordiality of the new year, Marilyn knows the old struggle will surface about the time the first head cold begins to make its way around school.

She comes back into the moment with a rush of anxiety. They'll be looking for me. I need to find Rachel and tell her about this mess, she thinks. Rachel Hamilton is the golden music teacher whom Marilyn hired only 2 weeks ago. Marilyn can imagine Rachel in a cream-colored silk blouse and pearls, bending gracefully to bow her violin. She cannot imagine her standing on the hot asphalt, squinting at the torsos, struggling to fit them into her fantasy of sitting in a circle, clapping and singing among happy children.

For a bare second, Marilyn can't see when she steps back into the hall. She almost bumps into Rachel whose honey hair is pulled back and up, tied with a blue ribbon. Rachel has four or five song books in one arm, a tambourine in the other hand. Her mouth is slightly open and small drops of perspiration bead her upper lip.

"Oh, Rachel. I've just been out looking at your building. There's nasty graffiti painted all over the east wall." The reply of her blank look says that Rachel doesn't have the faintest idea what Marilyn is talking about. "You're thinking about your first class, aren't you?" Marilyn asks gently. Rachel nods. "Well, listen, Rachel, try not to get upset about the wall. The physical plant crew will be out just as soon as they can to paint it out."

Rachel tries to focus on what Marilyn is saying. "OK. Thanks." The two walk through the door to confront the wall. Rachel stops, draws in her breath, and whispers, "That's awful!"

"It's pretty bad," Marilyn confirms.

"Does that happen a lot?"

"Not too often. We mostly get it when the weather's nice."

"Who did it?" Rachel presses as if the older woman must have some certain knowledge.

"I don't know. Probably some teenagers mad about school starting today."

"Will they catch them?"

No, Rachel, Marilyn thinks to herself. The police aren't going to waste their time on a little graffiti around a school. But she says, "I don't know. I hope so."

Rachel has already jumped to another question. "What will I say to the children?"

"Just see how it goes. If they ask about it, tell them that you don't like it either. You can explain that some men will come soon to paint over it and say that it's really important for all of us to take good care of our school because it is a beautiful school and we are proud of it." Rachel watches Marilyn intently, almost mouthing the words, trying to get them just right. "Keep your ears open, too. The fifth grade boys usually have a handle on what's going on in the neighborhood. Let me know if you hear something." She pauses. "Listen, don't let this spoil things for you, Rachel. This your first day of teaching. Make it a good one."

"Thanks, Ms. Wallace, I will," Rachel promises.

"Marilyn!" Marilyn calls over her shoulder.

"Marilyn," Rachel returns with an nervous giggle.

3

Every morning Florence makes coffee, plugs in the water for tea, and puts out rolls or coffee cake, sometimes toast and peanut butter. Teachers sign in, unlock their doors, empty their tote bags, and go down for breakfast. Some carry plates back to their rooms; others sit around tables in the staff room, reading the paper or visiting in predictable clusters.

This morning, though, the staff room is empty except for Tom Campbell, the gym teacher. Tom has come early every morning for 20 years. He sits by himself studying the sports page, his coffee cup all but hidden in his large hand. Tom played good baseball in his time, but he is tired now and bored from his years among the women who dominate the school. Marilyn depends on his steadiness and is comfortable with him. This morning she doesn't take the time to sit down or ask who he thinks will be in the World Series because she needs to see how things are going next door.

Even on rainy days, light from the bank of high windows facing east gives the cafeteria a sunny feeling. Last year the 5th graders fit a "to scale" red dinosaur on one wall—except for a few feet of its tail that wound around the corner. A deep stage with faded maroon curtains runs the width of the wall opposite the windows. Marilyn nags Chuck about the cast-off furniture that gathers along with dust on the stage and about the cardboard boxes that multiply at the back door. Chuck never claims knowledge of the stuff on the stage and always reminds her that the night man breaks down boxes for pick-up on Wednesdays. As the prerogative of being head custodian, Chuck leaves just as much work for Gus as he can.

The cafeteria overflows on nights of the fall open house, the winter music program, and the spring carnival, and people stand along the walls and in doorways. These comings together remind Marilyn that many of the children have adults in their lives who love them, a reality she sometimes forgets as she moves among the emergencies that so often claim her attention.

Even though school doesn't start for another 45 minutes, the room is already filling. Marilyn stops at the doorway to watch the scene. Rose has claimed the side farthest away from the kitchen for registering new children, and Florence manages breakfast and lunch tickets on the other side.

The children are still taking their bearing on the day. Most of them get a free breakfast, and many didn't have much for dinner the night before. Florence does right by them this morning—big sticky buns, oranges, white and chocolate milk. A few parents who have come with younger children quietly watch. Every so often, a mother tells her older child to share some food with a pre-school brother or sister. A clutch of fourth and fifth graders are checking the class lists tacked up on a portable bulletin board—more to see which friends are in their class than to find out who their teacher is. Every now and then a sudden yelp of "Aw Right!" punctuates the sleepy breakfast quiet. The group of list readers will grow as more children finish breakfast, but, for now, eating has priority.

When they have finished, the children queue up in front of the little table where Florence presides over lunch tickets. She is already barking: "Aw right, you kids. You 'member what Florence wants you to do? You want breakfast? Line up right here by the kitchen door. You want a lunch ticket? Line up behind Florence's table like you did last year. You big kids, you help the little ones. They don't know what to do. That's right. OK. Let's go!" Marilyn winces. Florence has a huge voice and a frame to match, and she frightens the first graders. By the time the children are in second grade, they know she means no harm.

Nan is already in the cafeteria, moving among the tables, leaning over to greet the children one-by-one. Her grin and her laugh tell them how much she has missed them. She has questions: "Are you guys still living in the same place?" "Dad home yet?" "How's your mom's job?" "How'd your little sister's operation go?" She sits down on the bench beside Amy to probe a little farther. Third-grade Amy is very small, her dark brown eyes seeming to take up her whole face. Marilyn filed two child abuse reports on Amy last year.

The other children have a hard time being patient. "Hi, Nan!" "Nan, come over here!" "Guess what I did this summer, Nan?" She continues to listen to Amy's story while she waves and says, "Yeah.

I'm coming. Just want to see what's going on with Amy here." Nan never stops grinning, never stops scanning the room.

As she gets up, a boy comes up from behind and puts his hands over her eyes. "Guess who?"

"Cory?"

"I'm almost as tall as you," Cory declares as he drops his hands. Their red hair makes them seem as if they could be mother and son.

"You sure are, Cory. Great haircut you've got! Your mom let you have a tail, huh?" She gives Cory a little sock on the shoulder and walks over to the table where the fifth graders are sitting.

She wants to make sure that she touches base with Joey, a tall, blond boy with eyes as hard and as blue as lapis. His good looks and athletic ability could easily make him the most popular boy in school, but Joey is more interested in raw power. Nan wants to check out the rumor that his mom has left and that his dad is out of work and trying to take care of Joey, his 7-year-old brother, a 3-year-old brother, and a little sister who's 18 months old. The rumor is not a rumor.

When Marilyn sees the children again each September after the 2½ months of summer, she is struck by how beautiful they are. Standing there in the doorway, she feels greedy, as if she can't look at them long or hard enough. She's glad to see that Leticia and La Shanda are back. They are cousins, both in second grade, whose mothers share an apartment. Marilyn has gotten to know Lillian, Leticia's mother, because she picks up the girls every day after her shift at the K-Mart warehouse. Lillian told Marilyn last year that they had come to this neighborhood because she could afford the rent and because the gangs weren't out here.

Leticia's hair is in braids all over her head, each one finished off with a bright barrette—red, yellow, blue, pink, lavender, or white. She and La Shanda are talking happily. Last year Leticia had three or four crying spells a day, and Marilyn wonders if she will cry as much this year. La Shanda, on the other hand, rarely shows emotion and seldom talks. Her skin is a dark olive and freckles cavort across her face. There's a poise and knowing about her that makes her seem older than her years.

Marilyn draws a deep breath and moves into the cafeteria among the children. A few of them notice her and begin to nudge and poke each other. She gives a small wave intended as a greeting but not an invitation. It doesn't work. Sylvia gets up and runs over, "Hi, Ms. Wallace. I missed you a lot. What were you doing all summer?"

"I was here at school getting ready for you to come back. It was really quiet around here without all of you or any of the teachers."

Sylvia finds this information puzzling. She can't imagine an empty school. "Well, who *was* here?"

"Mostly just Chuck and Gus. They had to clean the whole school. They moved the furniture out of every room and scrubbed and polished all the floors. It was a big job!"

"Yeah!" Sylvia agrees.

"What did you do this summer?"

"I helped my mom. And I read a lot. She made me. She wasn't ever off my case. So I read 64 books. Lots of them were long ones too."

Other children have spotted Marilyn now and get up from their table to come over to hug her and to tell her the news. She enjoys the fuss.

She looks across the room to see Eddie standing alone. He's in third grade this year. His face is red from the heat of his black imitation-leather jacket. He stands with one shoulder against the wall, the other dropped, hands in his pockets. Eddie is wiry and strong for his size. As Marilyn approaches, his intense blue eyes and brown-blond hair remind her of a young James Dean. "Hi, Eddie. Did you have a good summer?"

"Yup." He speaks softly—sometimes, like this morning, in monosyllables and sometimes in torrents punctuated with quick, shallow pants as if he doesn't want to breathe deeply for fear the words will choke him.

"Glad to be back?"

"Nope."

"Y' do anything special?"

He hasn't looked at Marilyn until this question. Without changing his flat, soft tone, he says, "Mitch took me and mom and the baby on a haul."

"Did you like that?"

"Yup. I got to ride in the cab. It's got beds and a refrigerator and a TV and everything." Eddie stifles a smile.

" You like Mitch, don't you?"

"He's OK."

Marilyn knows Eddie won't let her pry any further. "Did you have breakfast yet?"

"Nope. I was waiting for the line to go down. I don't like all those grabby pigs."

Marilyn has been thinking about Eddie off and on all summer. She wonders whether he will do better with Lil. He had a terrible year in Estelle's room last year. In the spring Marilyn asked Lil to be Eddie's teacher this year. She listened quietly while Marilyn explained the difficulties with Eddie, and then said, "I think I can work with him."

Lil will have a split class of third and fourth graders. Besides Eddie, she'll also have three or four other children with major problems and probably one or two more that Marilyn doesn't know about because either they're new to the school or they haven't attracted much attention yet. Marilyn hopes she has not asked too much by giving Eddie to Lil.

Rose comes up. "We need you over here. There's a mom trying to register her girl. Says the school last year wanted to retain her. I didn't think you'd want me to assign her."

As she walks back toward the registration tables with Rose, Marilyn takes in the crowd. Christine Bailey, the Chapter 1 services teacher, and Marge Friedman, the Special Ed teacher, are helping Rose. Christine won't begin working with the remedial children until next week, so she has extra time this morning. Marge will have to leave in a few minutes to meet the bus that brings her students. At least 35 children are waiting to register. "How's fourth grade?" she asks.

"Not good. We're even up to 29 in Wagner's room," Rose answers grimly.

Marilyn groans and shakes her head. "We're in trouble. Don't give Lil any more. She already has way too many for a split. And keep Conrad low if you can." Marilyn puts children in Corine's class as a last resort.

She notices a child and his mother sitting on one of the benches. Something makes her stop. "Hi, I'm Marilyn. I'm the principal. You're new this year, aren't you?" The woman nods. Marilyn bends down to talk to the little boy. "What's your name?"

The little boy stands staring at her; then his mouth begins to move. Finally, sounds come. "C-Cody."

"Hi, Cody. Are you going to be in first grade?" Marilyn almost never misses when she makes one of these guesses. Cody nods.

"Are you kind of frightened today?" Cody nods vigorously this time.

"I know. First days are hard, but I think you'll like this school. Everybody is nice, and we have lots of fun here. You'll get to learn to read, too."

Cody smiles, but he doesn't look reassured. His mother speaks for him: "He was real excited about school starting. That's all he's talked about. But he's shy, so it's kinda hard for him this morning."

Rose glares impatiently. She doesn't have time to wait around for small talk. Rose Martin has been at Madison for as long as Mr. Schneider. Principals usually don't stay long at Madison, so she has seen seven or eight of them come and go. She likes Marilyn no better than the rest, probably not as much, and, after 3 years, she still isn't used to working for a woman.

Marilyn follows Rose back to the table that she's commandeered for the morning. A large-boned woman sits on the bench holding a baby; an equally large, strong-looking girl and a younger boy stand beside her. Marilyn sits down beside the woman. "Hi, I'm Marilyn. I'm the principal." She looks up at the girl. "What's your name?"

"April."

"Hi, April. You have a pretty name."

"I'm supposed to be in second grade."

"You are? Where did you go to school last year?"

Unsure of how to answer this question, April turns to her mother. "Well, we moved around some last year. She started out in Taft, and we were in Bakersfield for awhile. Then we came up here and she went to . . . What was the name of that last school, April?"

"Highland Park," April offers.

Marilyn has the picture. "I didn't get your name," she says, looking at the woman.

"Mrs. Stevens."

"Hi. What's your first name?" Marilyn asks.

"Cheryl." She smiles.

"And the baby's? Your little boy's?

"Autumn and Cliff."

"Is your baby about 10 months?"

"No. Everybody thinks that, but she's just 7. Big for her age."

"Rose tells me last year's teacher recommended April have another year in first grade."

"Yeah, here's the report card. You can see what she wrote."

Marilyn takes the report card and glances over it—lots of checks for "Needs improvement." At the bottom the teacher wrote, "April is a nice girl. She tries hard and is liked by her classmates. She was only in my class from mid-April to June. During that time, she was absent for 19 days. She is behind in her reading. She knows most of her consonants but doesn't know any of her vowels. She only knows her math facts through five. I recommend that she repeat first grade."

Marilyn looks at Cheryl and April.

"April, is it all right with you if your mom and I talk about what grade to put you in with you right here?"

April nods.

"Is that all right with you, Cheryl?"

"You bet," Cheryl says.

" OK. Cheryl, how do you feel about retaining April?"

"Well, if that's what she needs, I guess it'd be all right." Cheryl hesitates and then adds, "But she don't want to stay back, and I don't want her to feel like she's dumb or anything." Another, longer pause. "That happened to me. I had to do second grade twice."

"How was that for you?" Marilyn asks.

"Not so good. I was big like my girls. It's OK for a boy to be big. Like Cliff. He don't mind, but it's hard for girls. The other kids teased me bad. I never did catch up."

"What's your situation right now, Cheryl?"

"Good. Lots better. My husband just came up, and he got a job—night attendant at the service station over on 128th." Marilyn nods in recognition. It's the station she drives by every day on her way to work. "He don't like shift work, but it's a start. We rented our own place last month."

"Does it look like you'll be staying all year?"

Cheryl nods. "Yeah. That was the idea. We wanted to get somewheres where April and Cliff—he starts kindergarten—could stay the year. I don't like having to pull them out of school."

"No, no of course you don't." Marilyn hurries to agree. "You had a lot of moves last year, and it looks like April missed some school. Those two things could explain why she's behind."

"Yeah, she missed out on school. I'll admit to that. After we got up here, I was alone. It just seemed like we was sick an awful lot. Sometimes I needed her to stay home and help me with the little ones, especially right after Autumn was born. That was a pretty hard time."

"I'm sure it was. Well, it looks like it's going better for you now. If you think you're more settled and if you think it's the right thing to do, I'd like to put April in second grade. But it'll be really important for her to come to school every day."

"She'll be here," Cheryl says solemnly.

April nods in agreement. "I can come every day."

"Great!" Then Marilyn asks, "Could you read to her every day and have her read to you?"

Again Cheryl nods, "Sure." She sounds doubtful.

Every time Marilyn asks this question, she feels uneasy. Of course she'll agree to help, but can she? Marilyn wonders. She doesn't want to put Cheryl on the spot. "And we'll watch her here too to be sure that she gets extra help."

"Thanks. Thanks a lot," Cheryl says, relief spreading through her words. April mirrors her mother's relief.

"I think you'd like it better in second grade than in first, April. Your teacher's name will be Mrs. Reed. She's a very nice teacher."

Rose has been listening to all of this. "You want me to put her in Reed's room then?" Marilyn nods, and Rose bends to her paperwork. "Second grade's getting awful full." That is Rose's way of telling Marilyn that she thinks she made the wrong decision.

Marilyn tries to shake off Rose's disapproval. "When you finish filling out the forms, you can walk April down to class," she tells Cheryl. "Her room is 106. You just go out that door and down the hall."

4

It is nearly time for class to start, so Marilyn goes out into the congestion of the front hall to direct traffic. Joey comes up to her, "There's a little kid out front crying. I tried to tell her to come in, but she won't. She's scared."

"Thanks, Joey. I'll check it out." That's Joey, Marilyn thinks. One minute he's giving some other kid a bloody nose, and the next minute he's taking care of a little girl.

A tiny girl stands over by Mr. Schneider's plum tree. Marilyn squats in front of her, puts one hand on either side of her waist, and begins to talk to the child. Slowly she calms down enough to tell Marilyn that her name is Julie and that she is in first grade. "My mommy stopped the car. She told me to get out. She had to go to work. She couldn't wait. She said to go on in by myself. Somebody will help me. But the big kids were all around, and I didn't see nobody who helped. I want to go home. I want my mommy," she sobs.

A few minutes later Marilyn is walking back from taking Julie to Grace Johnson's room, making a mental note to check on her at lunch. She sees a woman coming toward her and, in this first flash of impression, understands that she will get to know her well. She is tall and very thin, her face strongly beautiful. Her dark hair falls to her shoulders. Her thighs strain against faded jeans, and the muscles in her arms and neck carry the same tension. Marilyn can't make any sense of the woman's gait—a fast kind of dancing, bouncing, up-and-down walk. *Cat on a Hot Tin Roof* flutters through her imagination.

"Are you the principal?" the woman asks. Her voice is deep and raspy. She moves close enough for Marilyn to smell the tobacco on her clothes.

"Yes. Hi. My name is Marilyn. What's yours?"

"Mona. Mona Lassiter. I went to this school." She is sucking in air as she talks. "You wasn't here then, but I went here from kindergarten on. I had Mr. Schneider when I was in eighth grade. You don't go to eighth grade any more?"

Marilyn shakes her head. "No, only to fifth."

"That's too bad. I don't think them middle schools are good for kids. Part of why I moved back in the neighborhood was so's Nathan could have Mr. Schneider. He's a teacher who won't put up with nothin'. Nathan needs that kind of teacher. Know what I mean?"

"Is this Nathan?" Marilyn asks, looking at the boy beside Mona. He cocks his head toward the older woman, his eyes both questioning and challenging her to "do something about it."

Marilyn returns his gaze. "Are you in fifth grade, Nathan?" He simply stares at her. His shirt is two sizes too big and does nothing to hide his shoulder bones. He's all bone—wrists, ankles, skull so defined that his face seems more like a sculpture than a real boy's. He will probably be a large, rangy man one day, but at age 10 his head is strangely out of proportion to his slight body. A shock of black hair falls over his high forehead. His prominent nose is finely chiseled; a wry smile plays about his thin, tight lips making his face seem old. Nathan's brown eyes are set far back in his skull beneath heavy eyebrows, behind long, thick eyelashes. He watches and waits.

"I've had a lot of trouble with him. You wouldn't believe it. He's making me crazy. He's diabetic. Real bad. Can't keep him under control. You know what I mean? Mr. Schneider is a hard teacher. He can control him. Otherwise, I'm just . . ."

Marilyn interrupts Mona midsentence. People are milling around, and a couple of teachers are standing close by looking impatient.

"I need to find out a little more about Nathan. Can you two wait for just a few minutes?"

Mona pulls back. "You aren't going to tell me he can't go here?"

"No. No, I just want to find out more about him and what he needs. OK?"

Mona rubs her hand along her cheek and jaw while she stares Marilyn up and down. "Yeah, OK. I guess so. You want us to wait?"

"Please. You start filling out the registration forms, and I'll come and get you in just a few minutes."

"I was afraid you wasn't going to take him. Yeah, I'll get that stuff done and wait for you. He can start today, can't he?"

"You bet. I'll be right in."

As Mona and Nathan start toward the cafeteria, the teachers close in. "We don't have free and reduced lunch lists yet. They were supposed to be in our boxes this morning." Marilyn knows that Rose is too busy to find the lists, so she goes into the office and starts rummaging through the piles of paper on Rose's desk. She hurriedly makes copies, hands the teachers theirs, and starts stuffing boxes with the rest of them.

While she's at the teachers' boxes, Marilyn scribbles a note to Mr. Schneider asking him to stop by to see her so that she can fill him in on his new student. Then she goes back into the cafeteria to find Mona and Nathan. She's decided that she wants to talk with Mona alone, so she takes Nathan over to Nan. The sooner Nan gets to know this guy, the better, she thinks.

She walks with Mona into the quiet of her office, and they sit down in the two side chairs in front of Marilyn's desk. She waits a couple of seconds trying to form a question, but none is needed. Mona starts in. "You're gonna have problems with this kid. Boy, are you! You wouldn't believe what it's like with him."

Mona sits on the edge of her chair, bouncing her foot, chewing gum, and looking around as if she expects Nathan to burst through the door at any second. She tries to explain their life. Nathan's acute juvenile diabetes was diagnosed when he was just over a year old. Mona describes how difficult it was taking care of him as a baby. She talks about "I," and her only references to "we" include only Nathan. Just as Marilyn decides that Nathan's father doesn't figure in their lives, Mona tells a story about him:

"Nathan's father kidnapped him when he was 3. Took him out in the desert. He had him there for almost a week. No insulin, no nothin'. Hiding out. Nathan freaked. He thought he was going to die. Three years old. I'll never forgive that man. I was scared spitless."

"Does Nathan see his father now?" Marilyn asks cautiously.

"Yeah. He don't live too far. Most of the time, he don't show up when he says he's going to. Nathan don't like him much, but he *is* his father." Mona's expression grows thoughtful and her foot quiets. "Sometimes he says he wants to go live with his dad, but I don't think he means it." She pauses. "Naw, he don't mean it." She starts tapping her foot again. "There's times I wish he would."

"Like what times?"

"When he steals stuff from the neighbors. Or at the mall. People get totally pissed at him, and then I gotta talk them out of it. He's a real klepto, and I'm sick of it."

"Are you getting any counseling?" Mona nods and explains that the juvenile authorities got involved when Nathan tried to steal a

Walkman, a portable TV, and a camcorder from an electronics store all in the same day. He was referred to Children's Services, and the counselor there had in turn referred him for intensive work.

"He's got a psychologist. He's going to have Nathan start with a psychiatrist. That guy knows Nathan's got problems, I mean *big*. I think they want to send him somewhere to live."

"Residential treatment?" Marilyn asks.

"I can't afford nothin' like that. No way."

"I don't think that you'd have to pay if Children's Services recommends it, Mona."

"I would if I don't give them custody. And I ain't never gonna let the State take him away from me." She is sucking in air again. She gets up and paces around the room. Mona whirls. "Don't you go start trying to talk me into that. You don't know what I know about *those* people."

Marilyn does know not to push. "Well, let's just talk about Nathan and school for now," she says calmly.

Mona lets the subject drop. "He's smart. Really smart." Marilyn nods in acknowledgment, but right now that isn't what she's worried about.

"I'd like to get permission for Nan, our counselor, to talk to Nathan's psychologist. Do you remember Nan? Was she here when you went to school here?"

"Naw, I don't think so. We didn't have nothin' like a counselor when I was here. Just tough teachers. But that'd be good if she talked to him."

"OK. I'll have Nan call Children's Services and talk to Nathan's counselor. He'll give you a release form to sign, and then the two of them can work together. That'll help us a lot."

Marilyn asks Mona about her move back to the neighborhood. She explains that she'd been moving a lot, but that she thought it was hard on Nathan, so she made up her mind to come here, close to her mother, and stay put. Mona would talk longer, but Marilyn sees people waiting in the outer office. Besides she doesn't know what more she could learn today that would make a difference. Nathan is here, and she will just have to wait to see what it will be like with him.

Rose is back in the office. The crowd in the cafeteria has thinned enough for her to leave Christine to finish up. She glances at Marilyn. "Jolene's been waiting to talk to you for half an hour. She's in the workroom copying a flyer to send home. Wants to know if it's all right with you." Rose is curt, still out-of-sorts with Marilyn over putting April in second grade.

Jolene Ferguson is the PTA president. She grew up in the neighborhood and has one child, Stephanie, who is 10. Jolene is 27, no younger than most of the other mothers at Madison. Her wrists and ankles are as delicate as a child's. Today she is wearing white patent heels with a sunburst of multicolor sparkles on the toes, a melon-colored blouse, and a white polyester skirt. Jolene spends most of her time at school. Last winter, when she was out of furnace oil, she came every day and helped with whatever needed doing until her husband got paid, and they could get oil. Then she wasn't there for a few weeks. Jolene comes to school because it gives her a place to be, but she also comes because she cares about the children. "These kids—a lot of them—don't have anything to hold on to. They have trouble in their lives," she tells Marilyn. "We got to be there for them."

Marilyn leans her arm on the jamb of the workroom door. "Hi, Jolene. Want to talk for a minute?"

"Yes, please. If you have time."

"Sure do." They go back into Marilyn's office and settle in the same side chairs that Mona and Marilyn had used a couple of minutes before. Jolene's feet don't quite touch the floor. From her angle, Marilyn can see five or six pink slips on her desk and wonders if anything important is waiting there for her.

She turns to Jolene, hoping this won't be a long conversation. She has to be careful with Jolene. She's shy and her feelings get hurt easily.

"What's up?"

"Well, I want to know if we could send a flyer out for the candy sale today? We really need to get some money, or we won't be able to do all our projects like we promised."

"You think we've got the best candy company?" Marilyn asks.

"Un-huh. That salesman is really nice. He wants to work with us. Do you think it will be all right to have the assembly next Friday?"

"Could we get by without having a kickoff assembly? The kids get all excited, and they always think they're going to win one of the big prizes. Then, when they don't, it's so hard for them." Marilyn comments as casually as she can.

Jolene can't mask her disappointment. "Oh, but it's fun to try. They really get a kick out of it."

Marilyn should have known better. Jolene likes the kickoff assembly as much as the children do. Still, Marilyn's not quite ready to let go of her request. "You know, when we get the children all hyped up like that, they forget that they're not supposed to sell door-to-door. The older children can probably take care of themselves, but I worry about the little ones."

"You got a point." Usually Marilyn can appeal to Jolene on this argument.

"But that's their parents' job to look after them. You know, the company won't guarantee a minimum profit if they can't do an assembly."

"I know," Marilyn concedes. "Well, how about this, Jolene. What if we left the kindergarten children out? They really are too young to understand what's going on, especially so early in the year."

"Yeah, that'd be all right. How about we have the assembly next Friday?"

"Sure. Let's do it the last 20 minutes before school is out." Marilyn suddenly realizes that time is getting away from her. She gets up and moves around to sit at her desk chair.

"OK. I sure hope we make money. We really need it this time."

Marilyn leafs through her phone messages as Jolene talks about how much they need to raise money and then, hoping to bring the conversation to a close, changes the subject. "That's a pretty blouse you're wearing."

Jolene giggles. "Thanks. People give me all my clothes. I don't never buy anything new. I don't need to. There were some real nice things in this last bunch. Well, I got to go finish running off the flyer and get it to the teachers."

Jolene leaves, and Marilyn is alone in her office for the first time this morning. It's large enough for her desk, a small conference table, and the two side chairs. When she moved into it 3 years ago, she threw out 10 garbage cans of old reports and files that the retiring principal had left behind. On the second morning of her clean-out, Florence walked into the office. "You want a suggestion?"

"Sure," Marilyn answered, not wanting to alienate someone as powerful as the cook after only one day.

"Well, you should put the desk over here, not all shoved off in the corner like it is now." Florence strode to the middle of the room, spread her arms to show Marilyn where the desk should go—at an angle in front of the windows facing the door.

"You like that idea?" Florence asked.

Before Marilyn could get in a word, Florence was on one end of the desk shoving it into its new position. She stood back to survey her work. "Now, *that* looks friendly."

Marilyn likes where Florence put her desk. It's easy to catch someone's eye and beckon people in without making a fuss. The walnut desk and the heavy, simple conference table are old school issue, scratched and stained from 40 years of use. During the dead days of summer—when the teachers are gone and the phones have stopped ringing—she climbs around putting prints ordered from museum catalogs on the high walls and arranges and rearranges the chairs. But she never touches the desk. That's Florence's business.

Marilyn has filled the wide window sill that runs the length of the wall behind her desk with plants—African violets, a fern, an old begonia. Gus stopped his dust mopping one afternoon to say, "You can sure tell this is a woman's office."

"How's that, Gus? How can you tell?" Marilyn asked, genuinely curious.

"Oh, all them flowers and pictures and just the way you got things set out."

"Do you like it?"

"I guess it's all right. If you like that kind of stuff, it's pretty nice. Lot to dust, though."

Marilyn smiled and decided to take his assessment as a compliment. "Thanks, Gus."

Marilyn sorts through the pink slips. Frank Renshaw, her boss, has called. From the way he looks and talks, it seems as if it has been a long time since he was happy. Marilyn thinks that it might have been as long ago as when he was a pilot in World War II. The only pictures on his office walls are of fighters, and his whole persona changes when he occasionally forgets himself and begins to tell war stories. It isn't hard to imagine him as once having been tall, thin, and movie-star handsome, but now he is bald and his belly strains against his shirt buttons and spreads over his belt.

Marilyn puts Frank's slip at the bottom. He wants to know what her enrollment is, and she won't be able to give him a good count for awhile yet. Whenever she talks to Frank, she feels as if she's done something wrong. He likes straight answers, simple solutions, and no problems. She gives him long answers, complicated solutions, and doesn't always fall into line. So, whenever she can, she waits to call him until she feels as if she knows exactly what she's doing.

Two of the slips have names she doesn't recognize but prefixes from the neighborhood. She calls. Both are mothers of first graders who have heard that the children never have enough time to eat and that they have to throw away their food without finishing it. Marilyn reassures them that the teachers in the lunchroom try to see to it that the children have plenty of time and explains that sometimes the little ones are so excited on the first day that it's hard for them to eat. She asks the children's names and tells the mothers she'll check on them herself at lunch. Marilyn is used to this conversation.

Then she calls Pam McBride, the principal at an inner-city school. Pam's neighborhood is as poor as Marilyn's and her test scores are as low; but, unlike Madison, Jackson School has almost entirely minority students. After a little wait, Pam comes on the line.

"Hi, Marilyn. How's your opening?"

"About the same as usual. We're still getting children into classes. Hope I didn't pull you away from something important."

"Naw. I'm glad for the break. How're your numbers looking?"

"I think they're OK. I don't have my count yet, but it feels like we're up. How about you?"

"I think we're down. Way down. We only registered about 10 this morning. I don't know what's going on. It's weird."

"Don't you think they'll wander in?"

"I sure hope so. If it stays like this, I'll lose a teacher."

Marilyn and Pam will spend the next month worrying about their numbers—up or down, it's hard. Either way, they'll have to juggle children and teachers, and no one will be happy about it.

"Sometimes I think it's October 15 before we do any real teaching. Everybody just sits on pins and needles, and nobody starts anything until we get the classes balanced," Marilyn says.

"I know it. Well, if you have any extra kids, send them my way, will you?"

"I've got a few I could send you right now if you want them."

"Thanks anyway. I have enough of those already. How're you feeling, Marilyn? Are you ready for the year?"

Marilyn laughs. "I'm just letting it roll over me, taking one thing at a time and trying not to get knocked down. And you? How are you?"

"I'm tired. School hasn't even started, and I'm tired. It feels like I'm just walking in place. No, worse. I'm falling behind. Did you hear about Gloria?"

"Gloria? No."

"She just walked into the superintendent's office and resigned last week. Said she'd opened school for 19 years—guess she was one of the first woman principals in the district. She figured that was about 4 years too many and, if it was all the same to him, she'd just as soon someone else did it this year."

"What a way to go out! What do you think happened?"

"I heard her say last year that the way the district, the parents, and the teachers treated the principals, they might just as well line 'em up and shoot 'em. She'd just had enough. That's all."

Marilyn notices Mr. Schneider standing in the doorway and hurries her conversation with Pam to an end. They're used to these kinds of endings, so no apologies are necessary.

"You wanted to see me?" Mr. Schneider asks. "My students are in music, so I've got a few minutes. Hope they don't give the new music teacher a hard time. She sure looks young."

"Doesn't she? I think they'll like her, though. You were out by the music room?" Mr. Schneider nods.

"Has the work crew gotten there yet?"

"They just pulled up when I was dropping off my class. Do you ever wonder how much money the district spends painting out graffiti?"

"I don't even want to think about it, Harry." Marilyn laughs and gets down to business. "Thanks for stopping by. I wanted to talk with you about one of your new children."

"Nathan?"

Marilyn nods and begins explaining. The rest of her day will be no different from these first couple of hours—too crowded for her to know much about what she is thinking or feeling. She will see to that later as she is driving home or in the evening quiet, maybe just before she goes to sleep. School has started.

II

Star:
The Lost Child

5

The last week of September, children are still trailing in almost every day. Marilyn knew in August that the intermediate classes would get up to 32 and 33. She called Frank three times trying to get approval to add a section. "You'll just have to see what you have when school starts. I'll help you out then, if I can." School started, and she had 20 more students than projected. She called Frank again. "Families move around a lot in the first couple of weeks. Hold your horses, Marilyn."

Marilyn's hands turn cold every time she has to ask a teacher to take another child. And it's not just that new students are enrolling. Marge Friedman wants to know if she can mainstream a couple of students into Jane Reed's room for part of the day. Marge knows Jane is overloaded, but she also knows that her room is so rich and Jane so accepting that she can't *not* ask. Marge will ask the other two second-grade teachers to mainstream only as a last resort. Harriet Fletcher is absent almost as much as she's there, and Janice Low teaches a worksheet curriculum. Marilyn doesn't want to put any of Marge's children in their classes either, but she cringes at the unfairness of Jane's having to take even more students while Harriet and Janice have only 24 or 25. It's not just the children who suffer from bad teachers, she thinks.

Last week Estelle Douglas came to see Marilyn on behalf of the teachers' union. "There's growing concern about the large classes," she said. She wanted to know "by when" she could tell the members what Marilyn planned to do about it.

Marilyn called Pam McGuire. "What *I* plan to do? What makes them think that this is *my* doing?"

"You're just the nearest target. Don't expect it to be reasonable."

Marilyn kept up the complaint. "Why not? Why can't I expect it to be reasonable? I'm so tired of always being caught in the middle between the union and downtown.

"It's part of the job description, m'dear." Marilyn realized that Pam was not going to be a soft shoulder today. Her enrollment was still below what she needed to keep from losing a teacher and having to reassign teachers and students. She would probably lose her music teacher too.

Late yesterday afternoon, Frank had called Marilyn to tell her she could add half a teacher and that, first thing in the morning, he wanted a written justification for how she would use the teacher. She tried to write the memo at home last night and ended up walking the floor instead, so she had come in at 7:00 this morning, thinking she could get it out of the way in the early quiet.

But her anger at Frank won't go away. The help he offers seems almost more trouble than it's worth. I can't make a new class with half a teacher, she thinks. And besides, even if Frank gets this memo today, he'll sit on things for another couple of days. By the time he sends the paperwork to personnel and budget, I'll be lucky to see a new teacher in a month.

After three or four false starts, she wanders over to the cafeteria and is instantly annoyed with Joey and Florence. Florence has been letting Joey earn extra food by coming early to work on the cafeteria line and to wash tables after the other children have finished breakfast. Marilyn appreciated Florence's suggestion when she made it. They all know that Joey's dad is having trouble managing his food stamps and that Joey, who is growing fast, is always hungry.

The arrangement between Joey and Florence works most of the time, but some days he won't stay behind the counter. Instead he roams through the cafeteria playing hot shot for all the young ones. "Joey! You're not supposed to be in here. You need to go back to the kitchen," Marilyn tells him. Joey stands there looking straight at her. "Now." He turns and begins a slow saunter in the direction of the kitchen.

Marilyn is about to go after him to hurry him up when some children run up, urgency written all over their faces. She follows them out to the front door where Julie has just thrown up. Marilyn is trying to help her and keep other kids from stepping in the vomit when Joey comes up and says, in the loudest possible voice, "What's a matter? Somebody barf?"

"Joey! Get out of here. You're no help right now," she says, not feeling her teeth clench.

"Aw, come on! I was just trying to see what's going on."

"Joey, *leave.*"

Joey stands there.

"Now!"

"Well, what's the matter with *you* this morning? You get up on the wrong side of the bed?"

Marilyn straightens from picking up Julie's things and, holding the little girl's backpack in one hand and guiding her by the shoulder with the other, finds Joey blocking her way.

"Joey!" There's a mother's whine in her voice. "Go sit in the office. Right now! I've had it with you. I'll see to you in just a minute."

"That's stupid! I don't need *you* to see to *me*." Joey shoots back as he goes into the office and slams into one of the chairs across from the counter.

On the way back to the workroom to help Julie wash her hands and face, Marilyn tells Rose to ring for Chuck to clean up the vomit before the children come in from outside and track it all over the hall. Julie begins to throw up again, this time hitting Marilyn's hands and the sleeve of the navy blue wool blazer she is wearing for the open house tonight.

Marilyn washes Julie off and settles her on the cot. She stops at the sink in the workroom and dabs at her sleeve with a paper towel, leaving brownish flecks all along the cuff. Then she looks for Joey. He isn't sitting where she put him. Instead, she finds him washing tables in the cafeteria. "I thought I told you to wait for me."

"I'm working for Florence."

"Joey, when I ask you to do something, you're supposed to do it."

"I didn't do anything wrong."

"You didn't do what I asked you to."

"If you'd let me, I coulda helped. I knew where Chuck was. I coulda got him for you."

She is beginning to see Joey's point. He hadn't meant to be rude. Her voice softens. "Yeah. You could have. You were trying to help, weren't you?" Joey just looks at her. He isn't going to give her an inch. "I took it wrong. I didn't like the way you were talking. Joey, when I'm in the middle of something like that, I don't have a lot of patience."

"You were hot all right."

"Sometimes I just don't have time to stop and work things out with you. If I ask you to go somewhere and wait for me, you need to do that. OK?"

"Yeah. I guess. But I could of been helping Florence." Marilyn searches for a response that will be honest without compromising her authority when she senses someone behind her. She turns around and almost bumps into Rose.

"I need you." The expression on Rose's face and the tone of her voice adds "Now!" They walk a few steps away from Joey. "Star Williams is back. There's a kid in the office with her, saying he's her guardian. He wants to register her for school. I figured you'd want to handle it."

Marilyn stops in her tracks. The dispute with Joey, the children's breakfast chatter—everything fades.

6

Marilyn's head is a blur of vignettes from September 2 years ago when the fragile little girl in Jane's second grade showed such promise of blossoming. Now Marilyn's mind races from the memory of Star exchanging loving smiles with her teacher—her protector and friend—to another afternoon that same fall. It was the last hour of the day, and she had just started a "to do" list for the next day when she heard Rose get up from her desk. A woman stood at the front counter while Rose studied a piece of paper. The woman alternated between drumming her fingers on the counter and looking back over her shoulder at a man standing in the doorway. Rose edged toward Marilyn's office, and, recognizing the signal, Marilyn walked out to stand beside her. "This is Star Williams' mother. She wants to take Star with her," Rose explained as she handed Marilyn the crumpled paper.

The woman was as tall as Marilyn imagined Star would be one day, deeply tanned, very thin and very dirty. She wore a loose-fitting sweatshirt that had long since lost its color, ragged jeans, and tennis shoes with no socks. Once her hair was as golden as Star's, but now it was a sick brown, caught with a rubber band at the nape of her neck. "I'm Marilyn Wallace, the principal."

"Yeah? Well, I need to take Star out of school. That paper's from the court. Says I have custody."

Marilyn took a deep breath. "Will you come in and sit down while I take a look at this and see what's going on?"

"Why d'ya want to do that? It's all right."

"Maybe it is, but I need to be sure," Marilyn said, then added, "For Star's sake." She turned, walked to the door of her office, and stopped to wait for the woman.

"Hey, I'm her mother. Right?"

Marilyn nodded.

"Where do you get off telling me what's right for my daughter?"

Marilyn moved on into her office, sat down in one of the side chairs, and motioned for the woman to come in and sit in the other one. "Now, let's see what this says." Marilyn took a long time reading the court order so that she could think. The only sound in the room was the woman's sniffing.

"It gives me custody of Star. See. That's what it says." Her hand shook as she leaned over in her chair to point at the paper.

"You're Wanda?"

"Yes. Wanda Williams." She let go of the chair arms, and her shoulders dropped a little.

"But Star hasn't been living with you for awhile?"

"I had to go out of town, so her dad's been taking care of her." She scooted toward the edge of the chair. "But it was just a temporary arrangement 'til I could take care of some business." She drew a long sniff.

The 2-year-old court order appeared to give Wanda full custody of Star. "Let me just make a phone call to see what the status is of this order. Would you mind waiting outside for a couple of minutes?" Wanda looked doubtful, but she got up and went out to the row of chairs across from the counter. Marilyn dialed the School Police. "This is Marilyn Wallace from Madison. Will you run a check on a court order dated 8/12/87 giving a Wanda Williams custody of a child named Star Williams?"

While she held, Marilyn watched Wanda and the man. He paced back and forth in front of the counter and finally established himself in the doorway of the outer office, his bulk nearly blocking it. He had long, curly, black hair and an unruly beard. His red and black plaid flannel jacket hung open over a torn T-shirt, and his beltless jeans rode low on his hips. "We can't hang around here all day. Make her give you the kid. You're her mother," he snarled. Wanda tried to quiet him down, but he only grew more agitated. "Can't you just go get her?"

A voice came on the line. "Ms. Wallace? That order looks like it's still in effect. It's the most recent thing we've got on the computer for Star."

"You sure?"

"It looks that way."

"Is there an open file on her with Children's Services?"

"The file was closed in December of '87."

Marilyn hung up slowly. She got up and went to the door of her office. "Wanda, can I see you for a minute?"

"You don't have to go back in there, babe. That woman's just going to try to pull something on you," the man said.

Wanda looked at Marilyn and then at him. "I'll be right back."

She came in but wouldn't sit down. "It looks like things are OK," Marilyn said. Her hands were as icy as her voice. "I'll go down to Star's class and bring her to you." Wanda looked nervous.

"Just tell me where her room is. I'll go get her myself."

Marilyn's voice was shaking now. "No. You wait here. I'll be right back." Marilyn pushed through the doorway of the outer office, past the man. She brushed his arm, and he pulled back. "Hey, what's going on here?" he demanded. The smell of whiskey was unmistakable. She clutched her keys tightly and walked on as if he weren't talking to her.

She didn't look back and felt relieved not to hear his footsteps behind her. When she stepped into the buzz of Jane's classroom, the children were sprawled all over the room—on all fours, on their stomachs, cross-legged, snuggled in pairs—reading to each other. As Marilyn picked her way among the children, Jane looked over and saw her. "Aren't they wonderful?" Marilyn acknowledged Jane with a smile and a nod but with none of the usual small talk.

"I need to see Star. Her mother's in the office with a custody order. She wants to take her."

Jane's smile evaporated. "I don't think her mother's supposed to have her."

"Are you sure? How do you know?"

"I don't *know* . It's just an impression."

"Let's talk to Star. Where is she?"

Star was sitting in the reading corner with her back to them, her head bent close to Abigail's. As she turned a page of *Mother Night,* Abigail looked toward her friend and ran a hand slowly down her arm in absentminded affection. Jane walked over to them. "Abigail, may I read the next page to you? Ms. Wallace needs to talk to Star."

Marilyn put her hand on Star's shoulder. "Let's go over here, Star." Marilyn took a corner behind Jane's desk. "Star, honey, who are you living with right now?"

"My dad."

"How long have you been staying with him?"

"I don't know. Since summer. Why?"

"Well, your mom's here to see you." Star shook her head frantically.

"No! She's not supposed to see me. My dad got the judge to say that she had to stay away."

"Star, are you sure about this?"

"You can ask my dad. Call him. He's at Slippery Sue's. The number is 555-5978. He's always there after lunch. But I *can't* go with my mom."

"OK, honey, I'll check things out. You want to go back and read to Abigail now?" Of course she didn't, but she went over and sat back down.

Jane looked up. "Now I need to talk to you for a minute, Mrs. Reed." The women moved back to the corner. "I think you're right, Jane. This could get nasty. You better keep all the children inside the room and lock your door."

"Are you serious? What's going on?"

"I don't know. The man her mother has with her is scary. He might try to come looking for Star."

"School's out in another half an hour. What should I do? I shouldn't dismiss Star, should I?"

"No. Keep her with you until I can get back to you. You just sit tight."

"OK. This must be awful for Star." Marilyn heard the tears in Jane's voice.

Marilyn still remembers the sound of Jane's closing the door and locking it after her. Even after 2 years, she can see the man coming down the hall toward her, careening from classroom to classroom in a wide zigzag. As he looked into each window, he pounded the door with the heel of his hand. Wanda was just behind him. She tried to grab his arm to get his attention, but every time she did, he shook her off. "Come on, Rod. Come on. This ain't the way to do it. Stop. Please stop," she pleaded.

When Rod saw Marilyn, he strode to meet her. "Where in the fuck is the kid?"

"She can't go with you. I've still got some questions about things. Come on back to the office and let's see if we can get them cleared up."

"No way. There's no way we're going back in there with you. You got it? We've had enough of your bullshitting. We want Star right now. You hear?"

"I'm not going to release her to you until I'm sure that Wanda has custody." Marilyn moved her keys from one had to the other. She tried to make her voice as quiet as she could in the unconscious and futile hope that Rod would stop shouting. A couple of teachers had already opened their doors to see what was happening, quickly closing them again.

"What d'ya mean?" Wanda asked. "You saw the paper. You called. I've got my rights. She's my daughter and I want her. Where is she?" Wanda sniffed deeply and rubbed her nose on the sleeve of her sweatshirt.

"I'm not going to tell you."

Suddenly Rod seemed to change his mind. "Let's get outta here, babe. We don't have to take nothin' off the bitch. You hear that, bitch? We don't have to take a damn thing off you." He turned and started lumbering back down the hall toward the front door. Wanda looked at him, back at Marilyn, and then followed him. Marilyn stayed close until they went out the door. They stood talking on the sidewalk. It looked as if they were arguing.

She walked back into the office. "Rose, get Nan up here right now." Marilyn went behind her desk, picked up her phone, dialed the School Police, and then turned to watch Wanda and Rod through the window. "This is Marilyn Wallace. I've got a disturbance out here—a custody problem. A real belligerent man and a woman. Can you send a car?"

"Will do. Where are they now?"

"Standing out front on the sidewalk."

"You think they'll stay put long enough for a car to get there?"

"I don't know. Maybe I can hold them. How far away is a car?"

"Probably 15 minutes."

Nan came in as Marilyn lowered the phone. "Go over to Slippery Sue's. See if Star's father is there. Find out what the situation is. Does he have custody or what?"

Just as Marilyn began to explain, Rose came in. "Susan called down. Those two were looking in her window like they were trying to find someone."

"Jesus Christ. They're crazy. I'll go see."

Marilyn's expletive gave Nan a clearer picture than any explanation could have. "I'm on my way," she said.

Marilyn spotted Wanda and Rod at the far end of the building down by the kindergarten rooms. She wasn't thinking anymore. She was imagining Melanie Crawford taking her children to play on the patio just outside their room and the man trying to grab one of them. She broke into a run. By the time she got to Rod and Wanda, she was out of breath. "You need to leave this area."

"What'cha mean, lady? This is a free country, and this is public property, ain't it? We have a right to be anywhere we want to. We have a right to see Star. Don't tell us what to do, lady." The stench of whiskey was stronger, and Marilyn noticed a bulge in his jacket pocket. He's got a flask, she thought.

She wasn't afraid any more. "I'm telling you that you are trespassing. Leave now." Her voice didn't seem like her own.

"Come on, Rod. Come on." Wanda began to move out toward the sidewalk in front of the school. She didn't look at Marilyn.

"Don't do it, babe. Don't let the bitch scare you. We have our rights." But he followed Wanda. "Come on, let's get outta here." They both started across the street. They were off school grounds now, and Marilyn knew that they were out of her jurisdiction. They walked toward the corner, and she followed, not knowing why or what she would do. She just knew that she had to watch them.

"Hey, what'cha doing?" Rod half lunged at Marilyn. She stood her ground.

"I just want to be sure that you don't try to take Star until I have better information."

"Leave us alone, lady." Rod moved into the intersection, and Wanda went to stand near him, shivering in the warm afternoon. Rod was looking down the street away from the school. From their talk, Marilyn figured out that friends had dropped them off and that they were waiting for a pickup. They couldn't leave. They were trapped.

The threesome fell silent for a little while as Rod paced up and down in the street. Then he wheeled. "You get outta here, lady! You'll scare off our friends. You hear? You get outta here!" Marilyn remained silent. A few seconds passed—maybe a minute. It seemed longer.

"What'cha doing?" Rod wanted to know. She didn't answer.

"You tell me, bitch. You tell me what'cher doing!" Rod took a couple of steps toward her.

"I'm just trying to make sure that no one is hurt. That Star is safe."

"You'll be the one gets hurt, bitch. *You'll* be the one." A long pause. "Who d'you think you are, anyway? You're just a fucking bitch. You think you're hot shit. You can't tell me or anyone else what to do. I know your kind. But in the end, you can't do anything about me. I'm right here in your face, and I'm going to stay right here." He jammed his hand into his right pocket. "You get outta here."

Marilyn felt a shiver of fear. She wanted to walk slowly across the street and down the sidewalk in front of the school, then turn, walk up to the front door, and calmly go into the building. Just as she took her first step, a heavy white car pulled around the corner. It came to an abrupt stop in the middle of the street, and two young officers had begun to get out before Rod realized what was happening.

"You goddamn, fuckin' bitch! You called the cops. Goddamn it!"

One of the officers was at Rod's side in a flash. "OK, buddy. We're going to have a talk. You go on inside, Ms. Wallace. I'll be in when we get through with this guy here."

On the way back in, Marilyn realized that school would be out in 10 minutes. She headed straight for Jane's room. Nan caught up with her halfway down the hall. "You find him?" Marilyn asked, barely looking at Nan.

"He was there all right. Drunk, but he knew what was going on. Says he just got custody in September and that there's a restraining order out on Wanda and her boyfriend. According to what Star's dad says, the guy just got out of prison. He and Star's mom are strung out."

"Damn computer. Nothing's ever current. The School Police are out there talking to them right now. Dad didn't say he was coming down or anything?"

"He's too drunk to go anywhere."

"And he's the best Star's got right now."

"Looks like it." Nan shook her head.

"Listen, Nan. Let's get Star. Can you keep her with you until I call you?"

"Sure thing."

Trying not to make any noise, Marilyn turned the handle of Jane's door. It was still locked. She unlocked it with her master, and she and Nan went in. Jane was just putting down *Wind and the*

Willows, and the children's faces were as relaxed as if they were waking up from a nap. Star was sitting at a table with five other children. She was the only child who noticed that the two women had come into the room. She looked closely at Marilyn and then at Nan, trying to read their faces. Marilyn gave her what she hoped was a reassuring smile. At that moment, Jane saw them.

"OK, kids. Time to get ready to go home. Pick up all around your table. Make sure that everything is put away, put your chairs on the table, get your coats and papers, and line up." Marilyn walked over to Jane. Nan sat down at Star's table and began talking with the children.

"What's the deal?" Jane asked.

"You were right about Star's dad. I think things are OK for now, but just to be sure, Nan is going to take Star down to her office 'til the kids get cleared out. Stop by on your way back from loading the bus, and I'll tell you what I know."

"Is she going to be all right?"

Marilyn shrugged. Jane wanted to know more, but they both knew that they couldn't talk then. Marilyn started back to the office, leaving Nan behind to bring Star along. One of the officers was waiting for her. "We had to take that guy into custody. The backup car's taking him downtown right now. Did you know he was packing a firearm?"

Marilyn shook her head. "I thought it was a flask."

A look of incredulity spread over the officer's face, but he chose not to comment. "How long were you out there with him?"

"I don't know. A few minutes. Not long."

"Ms. Wallace? I wouldn't confront guys like that if I was you. You never know. You need to be careful."

"Yeah, I know. What about the little girl?" Before the question was out, Marilyn realized that he wouldn't know. Before he could open his mouth, she asked him a question that he could answer: "When do you think Rod will be released?"

"Oh, I'd be surprised if they even hold him overnight. They'll book him and he'll be out on the streets in 4 or 5 hours. Unless they got a warrant out on him for something else."

"That's what I thought. Listen, I think you'd better take Star into protective custody for the night."

A few minutes later, Nan, Jane, and Marilyn watched Star walk down the sidewalk with the officer and climb into the patrol car. She carried her tree journal and a hand puppet that Nan had given her for company. Jane wept softly. Nan said, "Well, I'll see you guys. If you need me, try the boiler room. I need a cigarette. Bad!"

Jane and Marilyn walked back into her office, and Marilyn took a handful of tissue out of the box sitting on the edge of her desk and put it into Jane's hand as they sat down.

"I should have taken her home with me." Jane sat crying for a little while; then she blew her nose. "She's really a wonderful little girl." She began to talk in a tumble. "I can't get her to do her math. She's way behind, really low. I just don't think she has the concentration for it. Her reading's good, though. I don't know why Susan was so upset about her. But what you should see is her writing! She's worked out an imaginary world where she's the mother taking care of her little girls. She's named them and can tell you what each one looks like, how each one is naughty in a different way. She buys them beautiful dresses, combs their hair, lets them dress up and put on makeup, takes them to movies, buys them presents." Finally, Jane's talking wouldn't sustain her any longer, and she began to cry again. "What's going to happen to her, Marilyn?"

"Don't know. I suppose she'll be back with her dad by tomorrow."

"You don't think they'll put her in a foster home? She'd really be better off in a good foster home." Marilyn shook her head. "So she should be back in school in a couple of days?"

"I think so."

"Well, I'd better get back down there and put my room together. Let me know if you hear anything."

Marilyn remembers sitting there, thinking how much she envied Jane for being able to cry. Marilyn has forgotten the last time she cried—not when the grandmother who loved her so much died, not when her father died, not during the long years when her marriage was sick and dying. Then she shook her head to gather herself and began to thumb through the stack of papers on her desk. She looked at the yellow tablet with the beginning of a "to do" list. Pulling the tablet toward her, she couldn't think of what to write next. She put her pencil to the page anyway. Only then did she notice that her hand was shaking too hard to write. She put down her pencil and leaned back in her chair with her eyes closed.

Slowly she realized how tired she was. And afraid. Rod could have shot her. Or one of the teachers. Rose. A child. She felt the heaviness of grief—Jane's, Nan's, hers. There was so little hope for Star. Even if Rod and Wanda went to jail, or got too far lost in their drugs to care, or left town for some reason or other, all that would happen would be that Star would be left with her dad who spent every afternoon at Slippery Sue's. The grief began to give way to the love that she and Jane and Nan shared. She sighed deeply. If Star came back to school, they would try to create a haven for her where they would watch after her. But it would be a small and flimsy haven. It wouldn't be enough. Marilyn opened her eyes. She'll slip away from us in the confusion of all the other children and the chaos of her own life, she thought.

An hour later, Marilyn stuffed the still unfinished list and the day's unread mail in her briefcase. The light was still on in Jane's room, but she didn't stop. There was nothing more to say tonight. On the way home, she was glad for the radio trivia—a cut in the county library budget, traffic reports, tomorrow's weather. She halfway decided not to do her paperwork after all. Maybe she would read for awhile and go to bed early. Maybe she would just have a couple of glasses of wine and skip the reading.

As fall deepened toward winter that year, Jane stopped Marilyn more and more often to describe something that had happened with Star. Once Jane came back into the room from checking on the noise in the boys' bathroom to find Star curled up inside Jane's coat closet sucking on the back of her index finger. Star was almost always sucking on something—her finger, her hair, the house key she wore around her neck, pens and pencils. If another child said something to her she didn't like, she crawled under the table. Once Jane even found Star wedged into the tiny space of her locker. She also wanted to sleep. She fell asleep when Jane played a tape or a film or while she read to the children. Whenever there was a quiet time, Star sucked or hid or slept.

Late on a Friday afternoon, Marilyn was lonesome for Jane. Most of the classrooms were dark and locked, so Marilyn made her way down the hall more quickly than usual. When Marilyn walked into the room, Jane was standing by the window where Fred's cage sat. "Hi, how's Fred?" Marilyn asked.

Jane picked up the orange and white guinea pig. "Oh, he's such a cutie-pie. Aren't you, Freddy ?" She lowered him back into his cage and gave him one more pat. "There you go, boy. You're all fixed up." Then she turned to Marilyn, "What's up?"

"Nothing much. Just wandering. Guess I can't face the mess on my desk," Marilyn sat down on one of the children's chairs. Jane came and sat across the table from her.

"I'm glad to see you. I'm really worried about Star. She's so snarly these days and she's saying odd things."

"Like what?"

"Yesterday, she was sleeping again during free reading. I woke her up and tried to ask her why she was so tired all the time. She looked right at me and said, 'You'd be tired, too, if you had to get up in the middle of the night and take showers.'"

"Oh, God, Jane. You don't think she's being sexually abused?"

Jane shook her head and shrugged. "I don't know. She's totally clammed up. I sure wish I could be a fly on the wall in that house. Something's going on."

On Monday morning Nan, Jane, and Marilyn talked. They decided that Nan should interview Star to see if she would disclose anything and that they should let her caseworker know what they suspected. But they decided not to make an official report unless Star gave them something to go on. If a male officer in uniform came to interview her, she'd be too frightened to say anything. For the time being, Nan and Jane would keep notes about everything they thought might help build a case. Marilyn looked at the other two women, "And in the meantime, we're leaving Star to deal with God-knows-what the best way she can."

"That's about it," Nan summed up as she got up to go about the day's business. Jane made herself busy in the outer office going through her mail. Marilyn sat at her desk and wondered if she had let Jane and Nan down.

The women's fears were lost as the days folded into winter break and the blur of the holidays. The first day back in January was quiet and dull. Marilyn fought her lethargy all morning as she enrolled children who had moved into the neighborhood over vacation. At midmorning Jane came into the office. "Marilyn. Have you seen the absentee list yet?"

"Not yet. I've been up to my ears getting the new kids to class."

"Well, Star's absent."

"I think there are a lot of kids out today, aren't there? People haven't figured out that school's started again, and there's flu around."

"Star's never out. Never."

Star was still absent 3 days later, and Jane wasn't going to wait any longer. "Marilyn, I'm going over to Slippery Sue's after school. I'm going to find Star's dad and see what's going on. This just isn't right."

Marilyn felt guilty about not offering to go with Jane, but she just didn't have the energy or the determination to walk into the fetid dark of that tavern and poke around for Star's father. Jane, on the other hand, was not to be deterred. Just as Marilyn was getting ready to go home, Jane burst into her office. "She's gone, Marilyn. Her mother and that man grabbed her over vacation. Her dad doesn't know where she is. Thinks probably they've gone back to Florida. He doesn't care. Said she was getting to be too much of a handful. Now what do we do?"

"There's not much we can do. I'll talk to the caseworker in the morning, and she can alert Florida, but you know that this'll be a real low priority with them."

"You mean we're just going to let her go like that?"

"Honest to God, I don't know what else we can do, Jane," Marilyn said, feeling miserable from the pressure Jane was putting on her and wanting the conversation to end.

The rest of that year went by without their hearing anything. And another year passed. Every once in a while, a long-legged winsome child would remind Marilyn of Star, and she would wonder where the little girl was or remember standing out on the street corner with Wanda and Rod on that afternoon 2 years ago.

7

Star has changed in the last 2 years, 9 now instead of 7 and, in clear but inexplicable ways, no longer a child. She is as thin as before, and she's grown tall—only an inch or two shorter than Marilyn. Her hair is darker but still the beautiful brown-gold that Marilyn remembers from the fall day in the park. Star's navel peeks above the waistband of tight jeans, and little walnuts of breasts press against a cropped tank-top that reveals two or three inches of midriff. The toss of her head and the way she moves suggest a woman's sensuality. It is her face, though, that sends a shudder through Marilyn. Black eyeliner and mascara give grotesque emphasis to hazel eyes that register nothing. A very young man stands beside her looking uncomfortable.

"Hi, Star. I'm really glad to see you. Mrs. Reed and Nan will be, too. We've missed you." Marilyn feels an impulse to hug the girl, but Star's manner warns her off. "Are you going to go to school here this year?" Star nods. "Let's go in my office. We can talk better in there."

The young man sits uneasily. "I'm gonna be Star's guardian. I gotta sign the papers for her to start school."

Star answers the question Marilyn has not asked. "My mom died. Randy and Debbie were in Florida with me and my mom and our friends. They wanted to come back here, and they said I could come too. We tried to find my dad. But he's in jail, so that didn't do me no good. Randy and Debbie said I might as well stay with them." She pauses for a moment, then—talking to herself as much as to Marilyn—adds, "We'll get jobs, and we'll do OK. I was modeling in Florida."

"What kind of modeling?" Marilyn asks. Star shrugs.

"How did your mother die, Star?"

"Drugs. She got into them awful bad."

"I'm sorry."

Star shrugs again. "That's the way it goes."

"Where's Rod?"

"I dunno. He split a long time ago. Before my mom died. He was pretty mean."

52

"I'm glad you're coming back to school. Where are you living?"

Star and Randy exchange glances, then Randy says, "We got our van right now 'til we find someone to move in with me and Debbie or get some money ahead for rent. We got some details to work out, but we thought Star should be in school, and she liked it here. So we brought her over."

"Well, let's have you fill out the forms so we can get her in class. I'll hold her paperwork until you can let me know your permanent address. Please tell Rose as soon as you have it." Technically, Marilyn can't enroll a child who doesn't have a permanent address in the Madison attendance area, and neither Star nor Randy could appreciate the risk she is taking by letting Star come to school. The district defines "permanent address" as, at the very least, having a rent receipt or a utility bill. In practice, technical definitions don't work well. And so Marilyn enrolls children who live in cars or in tents or in someone's driveway, or whose mother has left them with a friend for overnight and still hasn't come back for them a month later.

She lets those names stay on the rolls for the official attendance count on October first and prays the computer doesn't pick them up as having invalid addresses. If it does, she's in trouble with Frank. At best, she'll have to drop them. That means she has two choices. She can make them leave the school, or she can keep them as phantoms who never appear on class lists or are registered in the computer. If she carries them, she can't count them to earn her full allocation of teachers or her allocation for operating expenses, so classes will be large and supplies and field trips stretched thin.

And the teachers will have to be her co-conspirators and not report to the union that they have uncounted students in their classes. This year, with the classrooms as crowded as they are, Marilyn can't imagine that the pact will hold for long. Until the first time one of the phantoms tells Estelle Douglas to "go fuck herself"? Until Corine Conrad has 10 students with head lice? Until Susan Parrish is exhausted from the flu? Until Marilyn reminds Harriet Fletcher that she has been late for duty three times in a week?

But, even with all the risks, Marilyn can't bring herself to send Star away. "Let's see. You're in fourth grade now, aren't you?" She looks at her fourth-grade class lists. Twenty-nine in Lil's split class, 30 in Marcia Bannister's, and 29 in Corine's. It will have to be Corine. "Mrs. Conrad will be your teacher, Star. I'll walk down to her room with you. Thanks for bringing her in, Randy."

"Sure thing. See ya after school, kiddo."

When Marilyn opens the door, Corine looks up from reading out of a teacher's manual saved from a textbook adoption that has been out of use for 8 years. She stands by the chalkboard, and the children sit at desks arranged in tight rows except for one that is pulled up in front of the oak teacher's desk. Corine is a year or so over 40. An occasional grey strand interrupts black hair that she wears in a short pageboy. A few freckles run across the bridge of her nose and high along her cheekbones. Her eyes are a warm amber, but she is not quite pretty. The clothes-conscious teachers such as Susan Parrish and Melanie Crawford don't like Corine. They make fun of the pills on her wool and acrylic plaid skirts and laugh about her hand-crocheted vests all in the same pattern but in different colors and her Naturalizer pumps—black, navy, and brown for fall and winter, bone for spring. Melanie and Susan avoid sitting with Corine at lunch and rarely include her in their gossip. And Corine chooses to make no overtures toward them.

Marilyn meets Corine's long look. "I've brought you a new student, Mrs. Conrad."

"This room is already overcrowded. I have no more desks." The pitch of Corine's voice gets higher. "I really don't believe that I should have to take another student, Ms. Wallace." Marilyn wants to put her arm around Star, but she stands stiffly out of easy reach.

"Shall we talk about it at lunch, Mrs. Conrad?" Marilyn and Corine have danced this dance before. Corine knows that she has no choice, so she lets the request stand. Marilyn looks around the room. "If you let Star use this desk for now," Marilyn says pointing to the desk in front of Corine's, "I'll ask Chuck to bring you in another one." Corine nods. "Let's pull it over closer to the other desks," Marilyn suggests.

"I prefer to leave it where it is," Corine replies.

Instead of walking straight back to her office, Marilyn goes out the back door to the empty playground and takes the long way around the outside of the building. Once outside, her usual fast pace slows. As she walks and thinks, she stops every now and then to pick up a piece of paper or a bit of broken glass. Even with Chuck's huge vacuum, shards of smashed beer and whiskey bottles from weekend parties glint in the sun.

In Marilyn's first year at Madison, Corine was trying to get off on a good foot. She sometimes left a shiny Almond Roca candy on Marilyn's desk. She surprised Marilyn by talking about the details of a short marriage many years ago. Ten years later Corine is as freshly angry with her husband as if he had left only last week. "The man gambled. He was always at the races—dogs, horses, it didn't matter. He forged my name on loans to pay off his gambling debts. When he didn't pay, they'd go after me. Do you know how humiliating that is—to have your wages garnisheed? I ended up losing everything."

The way Corine used to talk always left Marilyn with the impression that this husband must have been abusive as well. Something had to have happened to make Corine's need to punish the children as great as it is. Maybe she never finished punishing her husband. Or her father. Marilyn wonders what happened to Corine and is convinced that she has her own terrible story.

Mothers come often to complain to Marilyn that Mrs. Conrad is mean. When she asks them if they will write down their complaints or give her permission to tell Corine what they have told her, they hesitate and then refuse. "Everyone has to have a bad teacher sometime," they say. Marilyn knows what they mean, but she is furious with herself for acquiescing to this point of view and for finding herself agreeing with the mothers. Pain should not be justified on the basis of familiarity. To the mothers' credit, they are afraid they will only make things worse for their children by subjecting them to Corine's reprisals. And Marilyn has no doubt that they have reason to be afraid.

Corine threatens to break boys' arms for throwing paper airplanes, to smash their knuckles for pencil fighting; she grabs girls' cheeks and pinches them to make the girls look at her and promise not to pass notes; she puts children in the corner for hours at a time. Marilyn has heard these stories over and over, but whenever she goes into Corine's room, the children are working quietly at their desks, heads bent over their worksheets while Corine watches. Everything is under control. Marilyn shivers in the tomblike room and leaves as quickly as she can.

Corine is already tense and hinting to other teachers that Marilyn has intentionally loaded her class with behavior problems. She won't like Star out-of-hand because she's her 30th student, and, when she begins to understand what Star's life is like, she will not be able to override her disgust. Marilyn decides to look for a chance to transfer Star to Lil or Marcia's room when one of their students moves. She calculates that Corine will be all right with Star for a week or two because Corine likes girls better than boys. Marilyn wonders how long it will take for Susan to fill Corine in on her version of Star. She hopes that the mutual dislike between the women will keep the news from spreading too fast. It's not even October, Marilyn thinks.

Rose looks up in surprise when Marilyn comes in from the opposite direction. "I took a swing around the building to check for glass. It's not bad," Marilyn says as she empties her handful of debris in the workroom garbage can.

Even after her walk, she has a hard time settling in to her work. She has a long list of chores to get done for the open house, and she still hasn't finished Frank's memo. She is finally printing it when she hears Rose ask, "What's the matter, Nathan?" in a half-tired, half-frustrated voice.

"I don't feel good. I want to test my blood sugar."

"OK. Come on back." Nathan comes around the counter and heads back to the workroom where his blood sugar kit is stored. Rose shakes her head as she watches him, and the women's eyes meet long enough for Rose to act on her impulse to talk.

"Do we really have to let him test his blood sugar any time he wants to?" Marilyn nods. "He just uses that as an excuse to get out of class. Mr. Schneider always gives a spelling test about now. He's already been down here three times this morning."

"You're right, Rose. I'll talk to the nurse the next time she's here—maybe get Mona and the nurse together to see if we can come up with a better plan. The way it is now, we're all going crazy."

"That's for sure." Rose sighs and lifts herself out of the chair. Marilyn hears her settle back at her desk. Nathan sticks his head in the door. "It's OK, Ms. Wallace."

"That's good, Nathan. Now you get back to class and take that spelling test." She shakes her head as she signs his pass back to class. She marvels at how long a tether Mr. Schneider, who is not a patient man, has given him. Having both Nathan and Joey in the same class would be hard for even the long suffering.

Marilyn spends the rest of the day making Chuck and Rose's lives miserable over tidying up for open house. The teachers have been working as hard as she has all week, coming early and staying late, getting everything ready for the parents. Most of them will spend another hour or two in final preparations after school and then make a quick trip home to change clothes. Marilyn doesn't go home. She knows from many years of open houses that people will come early.

About 5:30 she gets a bologna sandwich that Florence put in the staff room refrigerator for her. She intends to make do with that, but then remembers Florence's stash in the kitchen and goes in to rummage for a big peanut butter cookie. She promises herself that tomorrow she'll stay away from sugar, a promise she makes virtually every day.

In the tiny bathroom on the other side of the office, she brushes and straightens her navy blazer, arranges a silk scarf with crimson and blue flowers around her neck, brushes her hair and puts on fresh lipstick—somehow managing to do all of this without exactly looking in the mirror. When she locks her purse back in the closet, she changes from her flat shoes to conservative pumps.

She walks out into the deserted main hall. Gus is working in some far corner of the building, and the teachers have not yet begun to come back. She walks slowly through the building for a last look. She unlocks each classroom door and steps inside. All of the rooms are empty except for Jane's.

"I wish I'd known you were here. I would have brought my sandwich down and eaten with you."

"I was going to call you to see if you wanted to go out for something, but then I thought we'd better not. So I just ate some crackers and cheese and changed in the girls' bathroom."

It would not have raised as many eyebrows if they had been seen eating together in the classroom as in a nearby restaurant. Marilyn and Jane try to keep it a secret, but the fact is that they are old and good friends. When Marilyn moved to Madison, Jane followed the next year. But they are careful, not wanting to heighten suspicions that they are friends and thus violate the code that separates principals from teachers. Whenever Marilyn walks down to Jane's room, she stops at two or three other teachers' rooms on the way so that it looks as if she's just touring around. If Jane comes into Marilyn's office, they keep the door open and sit within plain view. If anyone looks their way, Marilyn calls for them to "Come on in."

They also send sealed notes back and forth making arrangements to go to dinner at out-of-the-way restaurants. On these evenings they talk about their frail mothers who live across the country, exchange stories about their childhoods, trade novels, give each other advice about clothes, and fall into gossip.

"Your room looks wonderful," Marilyn tells Jane.

"Thanks. It's always sort of a mess, but I think it's OK. The kids really were the ones who decided how they wanted it to look. They're pretty pleased with it."

"They should be." Marilyn pauses. "Guess what?" Jane looks at her. "Star's back."

"She's back?" Jane's surprise and pleasure quickly fade into concern. "Is she all right?" Marilyn tells Jane the little that she knows about the last 2 years of Star's life. "Poor kid. God, can you imagine everything that's happened to her in her 9 years?"

"I don't want to."

"I'll talk to Corine in the morning, see if she'll let Star come down and work with my kids some."

"I'm sure she'll let you have her all you want." The two women smile at each other. "Say, how's April doing?"

"Good. Really better than I thought."

"Do you think she's OK in second grade?"

"Definitely. She was kind of slow at first, but now she's really grabbing hold. And she hasn't been absent yet. I really do think they just had a bad year last year. You know, she's not real cute—she's so big and all, but I like her. Sort of reminds me of myself when I was her age."

"I was worried about putting her up a grade."

"I know you were, but she would have been miserable in first. You did the right thing."

As Marilyn walks back to her office, she feels happier and easier for having had a few minutes with Jane. She lingers a little while in the library feasting on the beautiful books and stops to enjoy the displays in the hall. She feels the expectancy everywhere.

8

Mr. Schneider sets up in the front hall, signalling that that people will soon be arriving. He has been at every school event within memory, sitting behind a little table with a large garbage can beside him. He arranges 8 or 10 cans and boxes of food on the table for advertising purposes. As people come through the door, many of them stop and hand him a can or a package, and, with a formal nod, he says, "Thank you very much. Your contribution will go to a family who has more need than you do." By Thanksgiving, Mr. Schneider will have collected enough food and gotten enough donations to make food baskets for 15 or 20 families.

Marilyn walks through the crowded hallways largely unnoticed or, if she is noticed, unacknowledged. And being the odd woman out, she is free to study the people who have come tonight. The children no longer surprise her as they did during her first few months at Madison. But the adults still do. The men wear jeans and cowboy boots, flannel shirts or old T-shirts, and—almost always—a baseball cap. Their hair is long and many have moustaches and beards. The tattoos on their arms have been there since they were teenagers— roses, girls, USMC. One man has a home-done tattoo of a marijuana leaf on the inside of his forearm. The men look tired and as if they want a cigarette.

Many more women than men are here tonight. They push babies in strollers, and a couple of them have their toddlers in harnesses. Like the men, they wear jeans and tattoos, T-shirts or loose-fitting tops. Marilyn tries not to bully them with small talk or to engage them in conversations they don't invite. But she feels awkward not talking so she stops beside a woman who is standing just outside one of the classrooms.

"Hi. Thanks for coming tonight." The woman looks at her without saying anything. "What do you think of the school? Is everything all right here?"

The question surprises the woman. She hesitates. "Yeah. You got good teachers here. It seems like they really want to help the kids.

Teachers deserve a lot of respect. Too bad some kids don't know that. Their parents neither."

She notices another woman close by and can't help but stare at the buttons hanging from her T-shirt. One says "We'll get along fine as soon as you realize I'm God." Another one says "Different Shit/ Different Flies." Marilyn decides not to try to strike up a conversation with her.

"Mrs. Wallace?" She hears someone call, and turns around to see Cheryl Stevens pushing a stroller with Cliff and April coming along behind. "Hi, Mrs. Wallace. I wanted to tell you that April's doing good in Mrs. Reed's class. You was right about Mrs. Reed. She's nice. April likes her a lot."

"I'm so glad. You know, I was just talking to Mrs. Reed, and she told me how much she likes April. She says April's coming along just fine in her reading, too."

"I know it. And she likes to read. I think she's going to be all right now."

They move on down the hall toward Jane's room, and Marilyn goes back to taking in the people around her. A woman leans over a stroller to push a bottle in her baby's mouth, her hair falling forward to hide her face. Marilyn can't remember seeing a mother at Madison nurse her baby. The women's voices are husky from smoking, and the way they carry their bodies makes them seem older than they are. Many are overweight, some so much so that their bellies spread over wide thighs and their breasts fall to their waists. Other women are thin, not the kind of expensive thin the mothers at Lincoln School had; the kind of thin bred from childhood gymnastics, swimming lessons, and balanced diets; the kind of thin maintained by memberships in athletic clubs and the pleasure of expensive wardrobes. No, these women have the thin of poor nutrition, frequent illness, smoking, and—all too often—drugs.

Marilyn watches the women with their daughters. Many of them already have old eyes and mouths, and, in ineluctable ways, are becoming their mothers. These little girls will be grandmothers before they are 40.

The parents do not greet each other or stop to visit as they pass in the halls. They may live next to one another in apartments or in small houses on one of the neighborhood's unpaved streets, but they have no easy small talk to share. They do not know each other, and they are not likely to make each other's acquaintance tonight, certainly not at school where they remember feeling out of place when they were children and where they feel no different tonight.

Still, they have come. They crowd into the classrooms and sit in small chairs while their children show them the work in their folders, explaining each project in the elaborate detail of child talk. A clump of three or four parents surrounds each teacher waiting to ask questions. Marilyn always urges parents in newsletters and flyers not to use open house as a time to talk individually about children, to wait until parent conferences, but they can't help it; they have to ask just one question. The teachers expect as much and are gracious about being put on the spot. Marilyn watches the parents listening to their children explain a shoebox microcosm painstakingly constructed with clay and toothpicks that depicts a scene from a favorite story, sees the smiles of pride as they look at a particularly nicely written page from a journal or a math paper marked 100%, watches them watch their children. They love them, she thinks, and they want the best for them. It's just . . . She doesn't finish her thought.

As people are leaving, she walks down the hall close behind a man and his 5-year-old son. When he gets to Marilyn's door marked "Principal," he stops and bends down to talk directly to his little boy. "See that. That sign says 'Principal.' Do you know what that is?" The little boy shakes his head. "That's where you have to go when you're bad."

She knows that she should go up to the man and the little boy, introduce herself, talk to them, change his mind, but she is suddenly shy.

It takes a week before Corine begins talking about Star around the lunch table. "There's something wrong with that girl. You should see the boys—they go around her like bees after honey. They can't stay away from her. She knows too much."

Almost every day, Star hangs around school long after the rest of the children have abandoned the playground for TV or video games. The clothes she wore in Florida are too thin for the cold, rainy weather that has set in. When the middle school boys come to skateboard under the play shed at 4:30 or 5:00, Star is often still there. She hangs around watching them and talking to them. For three weeks or so, Randy and Debbie eventually come screeching up in their old white van with its primer-red front fender. "Hey, Star, come on. We ain't got all day." She scrambles in, and they drive away leaving a fart of exhaust behind. But as the days pass, Randy and Debbie come later and later. Often Star gets tired of waiting and goes off into the neighborhood with the boys. When Randy and Debbie come, they do not bother to look for her. Sometimes they don't come at all.

There is frost in the mornings now. Marilyn usually waits for the children in the front hall or the cafeteria when they come in for breakfast. In fun, they try to rub the backs of their hands against her cheeks. She laughs and takes their cold hands between her warm ones. She notices how smooth they are and how faint their small veins. And she remembers how the large blue veins of her grandmother's hands both fascinated and repelled her and how once she was unable to imagine that her hands would ever become like her grandmother's.

As cold as it is, children still wear thin T-shirts. For several weeks, Marilyn has been putting reminders in the newsletter that it is time for jackets and caps, but she suspects that almost no one reads it. First, the children would have to get the newsletter home along with all the rest of their stuff. Then, someone at home would have to read it. Marilyn doesn't like to admit that many of her reminders are not at all friendly. They often have to do with the bureaucracy's being able to say that parents were notified in case a problem comes up. As much as she wishes it weren't so, Jane is right when she points out that Marilyn hasn't existed in the system for over 20 years without becoming a bureaucrat herself. Like it or not, she can depend on Jane to tell the truth.

One especially chilly morning, little Sylvia comes up to Marilyn as she stands by the front doors. "Come here, please. I want to show you something." Sylvia takes Marilyn by the hand and leads her down the hall to the Lost & Found table. Every school has a place where sweaters, jackets, caps, mateless mittens, and an occasional sock or tennis shoe pile up after recess. What is unusual about Madison's Lost & Found is that clothes don't stay there for more than an hour or so before relieved children claim them. Once in awhile, though, a jacket is still lying on the table after a couple of weeks. "You see this coat? It's been here a long time. What I think is we should leave the clothes here for 1 week, and, if no one comes to get them, we should give them to the needies."

"That's the best idea I've heard in a long time, Sylvia!" Then Marilyn looks straight at the wide-eyed girl. "Sylvia, do *you* have a jacket?"

"Oh, yes. A real nice one. It's blue and lavender. Nan got it for me."

Nan and Jolene are both busy trying to get children outfitted for the winter. Nan asks all the neighborhood organizations—the Fire Bureau, the local businessmen's association, foundations—and follows up on every lead she gets for donations. Jolene searches for used clothes at yard and rummage sales. Marilyn figures that between them, Nan and Jolene find 75 jackets every year.

Along with the change in the weather and the jackets and caps come head lice. Right after school starts one morning, Lil Wagner calls Rose to say that Eddie is "itching his head something awful" and that she is sending him down. Eddie arrives a minute later. Rose grudgingly gets up from behind her desk and picks up a couple of tongue depressors from the box on the filing cabinet. "Come on over here, young man. Let's have a look at you." She directs Eddie toward the window where the light is good. He glares at her and follows. "Stand still!" she snaps as he tries to pull away. Rose has to concentrate to separate his long hair with the tongue depressors so that she can get a good look at the hair closest to his scalp. When she finishes, she walks to the door of Marilyn's office. "Lil's right. He's loaded."

As always, Marilyn hates the news. It means that Eddie will have to be excluded from school. Often children have to wait for hours for someone to pick them up. Sometimes no one comes at all. But Eddie is an easy one. His mother is always home and will come for him without objecting; in fact, Tess never objects to anything. "OK, I'll call," Marilyn tells Rose.

Not more than 15 minutes later Nan comes in. "Marilyn, you got a minute? I need to have you listen while I call Mrs. Mather. I checked all the fifth-grade rooms for lice this morning. Then I checked all the 'sibs.' Lilly and Jasmine have it bad. The bugs are just jumping all over their heads. I've got to send them home. I hate to do this. They're only here half the time. I've talked and talked to Arlene about cleaning up the place, but she won't do it. She's going to be real mad when I call her, so I want you listening in case she calls your boss or something."

Marilyn pushes the phone across the desk. "Arlene? . . . This is Nan. Listen, I just checked Lilly's room and then I checked Jas . . .

Yeah. They've both got lice again this morning . . . Real bad. They've got to go home . . . No, Arlene. I don't think they got it from school. They were out Thursday and Friday of last week and yesterday too . . . Nah, it's only 10:00. They didn't get them since they got here this morning . . . I know you're trying, Arlene. I really do, but you gotta get the lice out of your house . . . You shampooed everybody? . . . Yeah, I know you did, but—Arlene—it's not enough to shampoo. You've gotta get them out of the house—clothes, rugs, furniture."

"Listen, do you have a washer and dryer?. . . They're broken. Have you got some garbage bags? . . . Good. Put all the clothes and toys and stuff in garbage bags and put them out in the garage for a couple of days. That'll kill the bugs. Can you do that? . . . OK. Good. Y'got an iron? . . . Does *it* work? Good . . . Iron the couch . . . Yeah, *iron* the couch. The heat'll kill 'em . . . Yeah, it really will. Will you do that, Arlene? . . . Y'got a blow dryer? . . . Blow dry the rug . . . Get the girls to do it for you. Just be sure that they go over every inch of the rug. OK? If you can get the lice out of the house, the girls won't keep getting them over and over. That's real important, Arlene. They're missing a lot of school. I'm worried about that . . . Yeah, I know you are too. You got enough of the shampoo left? . . . Good."

"Another thing. The kids have thick hair. It would help if it was shorter. You want to think about cutting it? . . . Yeah. I can't tell you how bad I feel. I don't think I would have called if I'd just found dead bugs. But I found the dark ones too. Arlene, can you get this all done today?. . .Yeah, it's a lot of work, but they need to get back in school just as fast as they can. They're missing too much. Will you send them back tomorrow? . . . Great! I'll look for them first thing . . . Yeah, I'll have to check them when they come back . . . I have to do that, Arlene . . . I'm not picking on them. They'll be clean, though, if you do all this stuff. They really will. OK, Arlene. Thanks a lot! Bye."

"Geez." Nan pushes her hand through the stubble on the top of her head. "I sure hope that does it. I don't know. Arlene usually doesn't follow through, but maybe she will this time. At least she didn't get *real* hostile. I just hope she doesn't keep them home for 2 weeks. Those kids are hardly ever here. Did'ya ever think how good our attendance would be without head lice? Catch you later." She waves and grins as she leaves to take care of Jasmine and Lilly. Marilyn smiles and turns back to yesterday's mail.

9

The next 2 weeks pass without any major disruptions or conflicts or surprises from out of nowhere, and Marilyn begins to breathe more easily. She feels as if they have all finally settled into the year. Still, she continues to worry about Star and Corine. She knows that Corine is complaining about Star and the bad boys in her class and about the fact that she has 30 students.

Right after lunch one afternoon, Nan comes in with Cory and closes the door behind her.

"Cory and I need to show you something," Nan says matter-of-factly. "Cory, show Ms. Wallace your arm."

On the soft, fair skin of his upper left arm is a small blue bruise. "Cory, how did you get that bruise?" Marilyn asks.

"Mrs. Conrad was mad at me."

"Mrs. Conrad made that bruise?"

"Yup. And this one too." He turns to show Marilyn a companion bruise on the back of his arm. She takes his arm in her hand and slowly rotates it back and forth. There they are—unmistakable shapes of a thumb and a finger.

"Tell me how this happened, Cory."

"Well, I was in the time-out corner. James yelled something at me, and I yelled back. She came over and grabbed my arm and told me that she'd teach me not to talk and that I would have to sit there all year 'til I learned my lesson."

Marilyn's impulse is to report the incident as child abuse, but she is afraid of the trouble that could cause.

For the rest of the day little else is on her mind. She tries to think of someone to call. Frank? No, she knows what he would say: "You think the parent will complain?"

"No. I don't really think so. She isn't very much involved with Cory. She probably won't notice or, if she does, won't care."

"Then leave it alone."

"This teacher *bruised* a student. I can't just let it go."

"Goddamn it, Marilyn. Leave that one alone! You want the union crawling all over you?"

No, she won't call Frank.

Pam? A 6-year-old girl in Pam's school was murdered over the weekend. The man living with her mother raped and strangled her. Marilyn called Pam first thing on Monday, and, when Pam called her back late that afternoon, her anger was immense. "We worked all last year and now this year to get her help. We knew what was going on. And she was so sick. Really messed up. We were finally getting somewhere. She was going to start day treatment next week, and Children's Services was ready to take her out of that home. And now she's dead. For *over a year* we've been trying to say that child was in danger. The newspapers are calling. They want to talk to me. You know, I'm just about to the point that I'm going to tell it like it is. I'm so sick of always covering up and excusing. Nobody gets protected in these bureaucracies except the bureaucrats."

No, Marilyn can't call Pam. A bruise is small potatoes next to a murder. Neither will she talk to Nan or Jane about it. As close as she is to them, she'll have to do this one alone.

She sleeps fitfully that night, but by morning she knows what she's going to do. She gets to school early and writes Corine a memo much more formal in tone than her usual notes:

To: Corine Conrad
Re: My Concern Over Your Treatment of a Child

I have had occasion to observe two bruises on Cory Mason's arm. When I interviewed him as to how he received these bruises, he indicated that you caused them. I would like to talk with you about this incident at 3:15 on Friday, October 17. Because the information which I gather during this meeting could lead to a reprimand, you may wish to bring a representative with you.

Please let me know in writing if this day and time are convenient for you.

Thank you.

Just before the meeting, Marilyn looks up to see the union rep sitting in the outer office. Her Italian leather briefcase sits in the chair beside her. Marilyn didn't know Pauline was coming, but she isn't surprised either. Pauline is a sleekly beautiful woman—tall with a runner's frame. Her softly draped grey gabardine dress gives a lovely silver cast to her well-cut, prematurely grey hair. A large antique cameo hangs from a heavy gold chain, and diamonds flutter on her fingers. In her quiet moments, Pauline's shoulders fall, her face softens, and she seems sad. In her public moments, she is alert, poised for the attack. Marilyn and Pauline are close in age and have faced each other more than once. There was a time when Marilyn hoped the two of them might find common ground. She thought she sensed that, in a different time and a different place, they might have enjoyed each other and so entertained the possibility that they could speak honestly. But those ideas have come to seem naive.

A few minutes later Corine comes into the outer office, and Marilyn goes to the door to usher them in. The three women position themselves—Marilyn behind her desk, Pauline and Corine in the side chairs. Pauline pushes her chair back just enough to make it clear that she is the outsider. She sits carefully and crosses her long legs, perfectly at home and perfectly confident. She takes her tortoise-shell glasses out of their needlepoint case, puts them on slowly, and peers at Marilyn over their rim. Then she takes a yellow legal pad and a Mont Blanc pen out of her briefcase. She opens the conversation with the usual small talk by asking Marilyn whether she's taken any interesting trips lately. Marilyn hasn't. She doesn't travel much. Then they settle down to the script for that afternoon.

Marilyn has the opening line. "I don't want to keep us here late on a Friday afternoon. Let me explain to you, Corine, what I observed with Cory and then you can respond." Corine says nothing. Marilyn goes on to describe her meeting with Cory quickly and matter-of-factly. She waits while Pauline finishes scribbling on her yellow tablet.

"Corine denies that she inflicted the bruises on Cory's arm," Pauline says without looking up from her writing. Then she nods at Corine to cue her line.

"I did take Cory by the arm. He was not paying attention to me, and so I took his arm to get his attention. But I did not take hold of him hard enough to bruise him." Her short speech has been carefully rehearsed.

Marilyn makes no attempt to disguise her skepticism. "How do you think he got the bruises, then?"

Pauline nods at Corine. "I have absolutely no idea," she answers blandly, ". . . unless he pinched himself."

"Why would he have done that?" Marilyn asks.

A nod from Pauline. "To get even with me. He's a vindictive child."

Marilyn pauses for a couple of seconds to let her anger ebb. She picks up the keys lying on her desk and puts them down again. Then, she begins to talk very slowly, very quietly. "Corine, I have interviewed Cory and, based on what he has told me and on what you have said, it is my opinion that you grabbed him hard enough to cause the bruises on his arm. Furthermore, I am convinced that it would have been physically impossible for Cory to inflict the bruises on himself. I direct you, in the future, not to touch Cory or any other child in such a way as to hurt him." Marilyn does not notice her own cold fluency.

"*I* never touch children." Corine's voice grows shrill and accusatory, and, for the first time since she has come into the room, she looks directly at Marilyn. She knows what Corine is getting at: Marilyn does touch children—all the time. Pauline looks back and forth between the two women, clearly interested in the electricity between them.

Corine goes on. "Besides, these couldn't have been very serious bruises. Cory's mother came in with him this morning, and she didn't say a word about those little marks. *I* had to bring the subject up. *She* wasn't upset. She understands completely that Cory must be disciplined." Marilyn feels Corine trying to turn the tables by insinuating that she, not Corine, is the emotional one. Marilyn's anger rushes back. It's the same dreadful mentality—if no one complains, nothing wrong happened. Marilyn keeps her thoughts to herself.

Pauline tries to get back to the script. "Are you going to put a letter in Corine's file?"

"Not this time. I will if there is another incident of this kind."

"Are you going to keep a record of this incident?"

"Yes. I will keep a copy of my memo to Corine in my correspondence file."

"Why would you do that if you don't intend to use it?"

"Because I keep a copy of all my correspondence as a routine practice."

"Why?"

"To create an accurate record of the matters I've dealt with."

"You have no reason to keep this memo if you have no intention of using it," Pauline repeats.

Marilyn is no longer interested in playing her part. "Look, Pauline, you and I know that I can put a letter in Corine's personnel file immediately if I choose to do that. If you give me a hard time about the memo, that's exactly what I'll do."

"If you do, we'll file a grievance."

"It is a grievance that I would welcome, but at this point, my interest is not in building a file on Corine. My interest is in having this sort of behavior stop. And as far as I am concerned, this meeting is over." And it is, for the time being at least; but Marilyn knows, from years of meetings like this one, that this is just the beginning.

She realizes that the safest thing to do is to let the matter drop, but all weekend long she returns to Corine and Cory. On Monday morning, she calls Cory's mother. "I understand that you talked with Mrs. Conrad about the bruises on Cory's arm."

"Yeah," the voice on the other end of the line says. Nothing more.

"I just wanted to let you know that I've talked with both Cory and Mrs. Conrad." Silence. Marilyn struggles to think of what to say next. "Are you feeling all right about everything?"

"Yeah. I figure Cory had it coming. He has a real mouth on him. I know I got worse when I was in school. Kids got to learn not to mouth off."

Corine is safe.

Marilyn is almost glad when Rose comes in to interrupt her thinking. "Emily Halloran's mother is out there wanting to see you. She's mad about something."

Marilyn brings the young woman in and invites her to sit down. "I know Emily pretty well, but I don't think I've ever met you. I didn't get your name."

"Patty." She pulls a paper out of the side pocket of her purse and brandishes it at Marilyn. "Look at this paper! Just look at this paper. You've got a teacher in this school who can't spell. Did you know that?"

"May I see?" Patty hands Marilyn a spelling test. She scans down the list of words. Two correctly spelled words are marked wrong and one incorrect word is marked right. She looks at Patty. "I see what you mean."

"I'm really upset about this. I was so upset that I took time off from work this morning so that I could come in and get Emily moved out of Mrs. Bannister's class."

"Before we do anything, I'd like to find out what this is all about. Maybe there's an explanation."

"What explanation could there be? That teacher can't spell. It's as plain as anything. And I can't have my daughter in a class with a teacher who can't spell. If you don't do something about it, I'm going to the school board. Spelling is important. I know. I make my living at it."

"What do you do?"

"I'm a legal assistant. I work downtown."

"So you're a good speller?"

"Yes. I am. I always have been. But I had to teach myself a lot of other things—punctuation, grammar, all of that. It's been really hard, but I have a good job now."

Marilyn looks at Patty as she listens to her. She is wearing a green suit with a white blouse and pumps. "I've made a life for Emily and me because I learned how to write. I can't let her have a teacher like that."

"We don't know that Mrs. Bannister corrected that spelling test. It might have been one of the other children. There might be an explanation." Patty looks doubtful. This is a new idea. "I don't want to put you off, especially when you took time off from work, but I think we owe it to Mrs. Bannister and to Emily to find out more about this. How does Emily feel about Mrs. Bannister?"

"She really likes her and the rest of the kids. I hate to move her because of that, but I can't let her spend a whole year with a teacher who can't spell. She doesn't know what's best for her. She's only 9."

"Do you think Emily is a good speller?"

"I thought she was. She got 100s all the time last year, and she likes spelling. But if she has a teacher like this, she'll go downhill really fast."

Good for you, Marilyn thinks, keep fighting for that little girl. Do everything you can to make sure that she gets what she needs.

She says, "I really understand your concern, Patty. If it were my little girl, I'd be worried, too, but let's get some more information. I'll talk to Mrs. Bannister and call you back this afternoon."

Marilyn knows that Marcia Bannister isn't a good speller, but she's also pretty sure that she's a good teacher. And she doesn't really think that Emily will be ruined by spending a year with a teacher who can't spell, but she also knows better than to try to explain that to Patty.

As she knew she would be, Marcia is upset by the news that Patty has come in. "I was tired, Marilyn, that's all. It was late, and I just couldn't concentrate."

Marilyn is sympathetic. She sees Marcia dragging out armloads of work every night and knows that she gets to it only after her three small children are in bed. "How's Emily doing?"

"Oh, I love her. She's one of my best leaders. She's a wonderful little girl. I'd just hate to lose her. But I guess if her mom insists, there's not much we can do."

"I'll call her mom, see if I can talk her out of it."

"Listen, Marilyn. I'm sorry about this. I'll try to be more careful."

When Marilyn calls Patty, she does the best she can at telling the truth without letting Patty know that Marcia really is a bad speller. At the end of her explanation, she says, "You haven't asked me, Patty, but I think you should leave Emily where she is. She's very happy in that class, and Mrs. Bannister is a good teacher. She is very fond of Emily. All of the other classes are so big, and Emily would have to get used to a whole new group. I think it would be hard on her."

"Yeah. I talked it over with a couple of the lawyers in my office, and they say the same thing. I just don't know what to do."

"Why don't you wait for another 3 weeks until parent conferences? Come in and meet Mrs. Bannister and see what you think. Then, if you're still worried, call me and we'll talk about it again."

Patty hesitates before she agrees. Marilyn knows how torn Patty must feel, but for now she has overpowered the woman with sympathy and persuasion.

One day just before Halloween, Jolene comes in to see Marilyn. She has been copying a flyer to send home advertising the PTA pumpkin-carving contest, but that is not what she wants to talk about. "Do you know Star Williams?"

Marilyn nods.

"It don't seem like she has anywhere to live. She's around the neighborhood a lot at night—lots of time with teenagers. The skateboard guys—you know, the ones that come up to school and hang out—they really like her. It's not good for her or for our girls. I'm afraid Stephanie will get ideas. Don't Star have nobody to take care of her?"

"She doesn't have much family. We're worried about her too, Jolene. I'll check into things and see if we can work something better out for her." Marilyn feels awkward and dishonest as she slips into these evasions.

"I really feel sorry for her. It's not right." Jolene shakes her head. "An awful lot of kids have it real hard—you know, mixed-up families, no place to live, short on food, hardly any clothes."

"I know, Jolene. I wish we could do more."

"It's never enough, is it?" Marilyn walks out of the office with Jolene. It's time for lunch duty.

Nan and Marilyn have their lunch after everyone is back in class. They catch up with each other and exchange information about lunch hour developments—who got into a fight, who didn't show up for duty, the noise in the cafeteria. Marilyn is still thinking about her conversation with Jolene. "Nan, do you know what's going on with Star?"

Nan shakes her head as she pours dressing on her salad. "Not much."

"Where are we with the custody situation?"

"Ahmm." Nan searches her memory. "That's right. Children's Services let her stay with Randy and Debbie."

"You sure?"

"Yup. I talked to the caseworker. There aren't any placements. Especially any good ones. You read the paper Saturday? They've just taken a bunch of kids out of another home. All kinds of abuses—dirt, rodents, tying up the kids, beating on them. Real bad stuff. That tells you how scarce foster homes are getting if they have to use people like that."

"Jolene came in to talk to me this morning. I guess Star's running with teenagers in the neighborhood. She thinks Star is sexually active and that she'll be a bad influence on Stephanie and the other girls."

"She's right about that. Star's real popular—just mysterious and mature enough to fascinate the other girls. I'll talk to her, see if she'll tell me anything about what's going on. I can try to talk to Children's Services."

" Let me know what you find out."

"Will do."

It's Monday of Thanksgiving week. As Marilyn drives to school in the dark, her mind is not on the day ahead but on everything she has to do to get ready. She cleaned and shopped on Saturday, but she still needs to pick up and cook the turkey tomorrow after work. For 3 years, she's been telling herself that she should have a potluck dinner. Then she gets to November and doesn't open the conversation with her grown children. All the women at the school have been doing the same thing over the weekend, cleaning and shopping, and the talk around the lunch tables will be about recipes and families. When she comes in from the parking lot, she sees Mr. Schneider working in his closet in the short hall between the back door and the cafeteria. "Hi, Mr. Schneider."

"Oh, hi, Marilyn. We're looking good." Mr. Schneider is surveying his inventory in preparation for putting food baskets together on Wednesday. His closet is nearly full. "Looks like we'll have enough for 20 baskets. Thriftway is giving us 10 hams, and the chickens from Food Mart can go to the smaller families. Dave's Bakery said they would donate bread and rolls—day-old, but that'll be fine. We'll buy turkeys with the money from the teachers.

"How many families on the list?"

"A lot. Twenty-seven the last time I looked. And I've got to find out about the Hansens."

"Oh, right. They were evicted last week. Do you know where they are?"

"No. Nan thought that the city was putting them up in a motel over on 128th but that they'd be moving in with friends today or tomorrow. Either way, they'll need food. I just don't want to run out. We never have, but it seems like there are more names this year."

Mr. Schneider has been getting names from Nan, Marilyn, and the teachers for a month. He meticulously checks and double-checks them to make sure there are no duplicates. That's not an easy job since children in a family often have several last names. Then he goes around to everyone to check one last time, just in case he's left someone out.

On Wednesday after lunch, he'll line up cardboard boxes along the stage and bring his class down to fill them. Florence stays late after her shift in the kitchen. Mr. Schneider and Florence show the children how to pack the boxes—heavy cans first, then the frozen turkey or chicken, bread and paper products on top. The children scoot from box to box checking to be sure that each one is fair, that there's something sweet in every box—a bag of marshmallows, a box of chocolate cookies, instant pudding or jello. By the time school's out, the boxes are full.

Chuck, who also stays after he's finished sweeping out the cafeteria, helps load the boxes into the back of Florence's pickup. Then Florence and Mr. Schneider take off to make their deliveries. At every stop, Florence jumps out of the pickup and climbs into its bed to push a box over to Mr. Schneider who carries it into a house or an apartment. As Mr. Schneider leaves, he says, "Happy Thanksgiving from Madison School!"

Marilyn has asked Mr. Schneider about a basket for Star and Debbie and Randy a couple of times. The problem is that no one has figured out for sure what Star does at night. She gives vague answers and insists that Randy and Debbie are still taking care of her.

Corine comes up to Marilyn at lunch. "I don't know what I'm going to do with Star. She'd sleep all morning if I'd let her. When I try to get her to finish her work, she's totally uncooperative. She snarls and snaps at me like an animal. Looks like one, too. Tells me to mind my own business and things like that. I'm not going to stand for this much longer. I don't have to put up with that kind of talk. That child's trouble."

"We're trying to find out what's going on with Randy and Debbie and, if that's totally fallen apart, to get a foster placement for her. But it's slow going, Corine."

"What's new?" Corine quips as she goes on down the hall. Marilyn sees her stop to talk to Estelle and Jane.

Jane comes toward Marilyn shaking her head. "Corine's upset."

"I know, but I don't care," Marilyn snaps. Jane looks hard at Marilyn and moves the conversation.

"Did you see the Thanksgiving bulletin board?"

"I haven't looked at it yet today. Why?" Marilyn is still short with worry.

"Let's go look," Jane says softly.

The board is right in the middle of the main hall. Lil Wagner's class puts it up every year. It features a fat turkey with feathers fanning out in autumn colors. Next to the turkey is an invitation to "Write what you are thankful for this Thanksgiving." Melanie Crawford wrote, "I'm thankful that we are all going to our grandma and grandpa's for Thanksgiving dinner." Leticia wrote, "I'm thankful for my teacher. She's niz." Every day more messages crowd onto the board as the children catch on to the idea."

Jane points to Star's message. "I'm thankful that I still have some family left." Jane's tears beat her to the end of the sentence.

Marilyn shakes her head, takes off her glasses, and rubs her eyes. "What family? Most nights Randy and Debbie don't even bother to pick her up." Marilyn hasn't told Jane that until now, and, as soon as she says the words, she's sorry.

"How's she living?" Jane asks, alarm spreading over her face.

"She says that she stays over with friends."

"What kind of friends?" Jane wants to know.

"She's evasive about that, but I've got an idea that she's with a bunch of teenage boys. I think she probably beds down with one of them."

"How could that be? Parents wouldn't let something like that go on." Jane knows how naive the question is, but she asks it anyway. "Can't we do anything?"

"I've got Children's Services working on it. I think they're about ready to take her into custody." Marilyn's answer is small consolation.

On the long Monday after Thanksgiving, the staff meeting breaks up late, and Marilyn is still in her office at 6:00 writing notes to put in teachers' boxes before she goes home—a note to Susan about observing her next week, another one to Grace to tell her that she'll be receiving a new student, a thank you to Mr. Schneider for the work he did on the food baskets. Gus has already made his rounds and locked the front doors. In the middle of a reminder to Rose, Marilyn is startled by the pounding on her window. She turns around in her chair to see Randy and Debbie. "We gotta talk to you," Debbie shouts through the closed window.

"I'll come around and open the door," Marilyn shouts back.

They come in and stand shivering in the vestibule. "Have you seen Star?" Marilyn shakes her head. "We've been looking for her all weekend. We can't find her nowhere. It's like she got swallowed up or something."

"Did Children's Services take her into custody? They were trying to get that worked out."

"Nah. We talked to that caseworker. She don't know where she is."

"Have you talked to the police?"

"We filed a missing person report on her."

"You don't have any idea where she might be?"

"The thing we're afraid of is she's run away with some older kids. She was hanging around with a lot of teenagers. They was bad news. She got real hostile with us when we tried to tell her she was too young for them kids. She kept saying one of them was her boyfriend."

They talk for a few more minutes without having anything to say. Marilyn pushes open the heavy front door to let Randy and Debbie out and watches them disappear in the dark. As she slowly pulls the door closed, she sees her reflection in the black glass. She looks tired and small and defeated.

The next day, Marilyn calls Children's Services and the School Police. Star is gone. And she's not back in a week or in a month. By spring Jane and Marilyn don't ask each other about her anymore. But in spacious moments, when she is planting flowers in her garden, or waiting for the water to boil for tea, or working at her desk late in the day, she sees Star walking along beside Jane, holding her hand, her curls blowing lightly in the breeze of a fall day. Marilyn doesn't tell anyone how Star haunts her, not even Jane.

III

Cody, Eli, and Jewel:
Between the Cracks

10

I went to see my uncle last night. At my grandma's." Marilyn is revising the art specialist's schedule for the third time since October and is so absorbed in frustration that she doesn't realize La Shanda is standing by the corner of her desk. Knowing she'll soon be in trouble, La Shanda has begun to explain without waiting for Marilyn to look up from the papers spread in front of her. She is glad of the interruption.

"La Shanda! Hi! I didn't see you."

"I went to see my uncle last night." La Shanda has fallen into the habit of going to her locker for her coat and coming down to visit Marilyn instead of going back into the classroom. Harriet has complained about this behavior several times: "If *she* gets to do it, all the kids will want to, and I'll never know where anyone is."

Knowing Harriet's sentiments, Marilyn usually tries to discourage La Shanda, but today something about the little girl peaks her curiosity. "I don't think you've told me about your uncle."

"His brain is hurt."

"What happened to his brain?"

"Somebody hit him on the head. With a baseball bat. He had to stay at the hospital for a long time, but he didn't die."

"The person must have hit him very hard."

La Shanda nods vigorously. "*Real* hard. So that his legs don't work no more. He sits in his wheelchair. Just watches the TV."

"Does he know you?" La Shanda nods. "Does he talk to you?" She smiles and nods again.

"Do you know why someone hit him?"

"I do. He had some cocaine what someone wanted, so they hit him. Hard. It was a big man what hit him. He shouldn't have been messin' with that cocaine."

"How old is your uncle?"

"Seventeen."

Marilyn puts her arm around La Shanda. "I'm sorry about your uncle." She lifts the little girl's face toward hers. "I hope you won't ever, ever fool around with that stuff. It's so bad. It makes your mind and your body sick."

"I won't. I already got too much bad goin' around in my body."

Marilyn pushes La Shanda to an arm's length. "What's going around in your body, La Shanda?"

"That sickle cell anemia. It's got ahold of me." It is hard for Marilyn to think of this beautiful child being so afflicted. She has no words.

Just then the bell rings. "I gotta get back down to Mrs. Fletcher. She be mad I left."

"I'll write a note and tell her we had something important to talk about." Both La Shanda and Marilyn relish the conspiracy. She scribbles the note to Harriet and starts to go out into the hall to direct traffic.

Already children are milling around in the office waiting to use the phone. Teachers are crowding in to take care of snatches of business and to check out. Suddenly two frightened boys come tearing in from outside. "Come quick! Come quick! A truck ran over Tino!"

"Shall I call 911?" Marilyn doesn't answer for a second. "Shall I call 911?" Rose repeats insistently.

"Yeah, call," Marilyn says over her shoulder as she pulls on her jacket and heads for the door. "Better be safe," she thinks.

She strides out into the rain that's been coming down all day—not the usual steady January rain, but a torrent to be measured in inches. It's the kind of day when parents sit double-parked, waiting for their children to run out and across the street. They scramble into the cars, vans, and pickups and bang the doors shut as their parents roar off.

Marilyn looks around, trying to sort out the confusion, and sees a huddle in the middle of the street. She breaks into a run. The circle gives way to let her in. We need 911 all right, she thinks, as she crouches beside a small boy sprawled on the wet pavement. The gash starts in the middle of his forehead and runs a jagged diagonal close to his eye and down his cheek. Marilyn feels steely and methodical as she looks at the blood welling up out of the cut. She can see bone and registers detached surprise that its white is of a different quality than the mottling of the exposed flesh.

A woman kneels beside the child sobbing prayers in another language. In a flash of recognition, Marilyn realizes that she has been holding her image since driving to school on opening day in September. She was the woman kneeling in the door of the shack. Tino is one of the new Romanian children. His mother begins to gather him in her arms. Almost instantly, Marge Friedman, who has just finished loading her Special Ed students on their bus, is on her knees at Tino's feet. Her arm is stretched out in front of her, hand up, palm flat forward signaling Tino's mother to stop. "No. Put him down. His head or back might be injured. We don't know. He must be still until the ambulance comes." In the panic of the moment, Marge's English is gibberish to Mrs. Gravescu, but she understands the gesture and the tone of Marge's voice perfectly.

Marilyn sees Joey and Sylvia among the bystanders. "Joey, go get Mr. Campbell! Tell him to bring blankets. Sylvia, go find Mrs. Reed. Nan. Any of the teachers. Tell them to come." The children start to run before the words are out of her mouth. Marilyn moves around to crouch beside Mrs. Gravescu. She tries to talk to her, but it's no good. Only Tino and Marge inhabit the mother's universe at this moment.

Marge keeps talking: "Look at me, Mrs. Gravescu. Leave Tino where he is." She stops trying to put her arms around her son. "That's good," Marge coaches. "Hold his hand." Marge takes Tino's hand to show the mother what she's saying. "He needs to know you're here. Talk to him." Not because she understands Marge, but because it is the natural thing to do, Mrs. Gravescu starts making soothing noises and singing softly and forlornly to Tino.

Tom comes running across the lawn, his arms full of blankets. He kneels to pack them around Tino, tucking them as tightly as he can without moving the boy. Then Tom presses clean, white towels over the gash and holds them there. The bleached white of the towels contrasts starkly with the grey of Tino's skin. Tino whimpers, then cries, and the crying begins to modulate to screams. That's not pain, Marilyn thinks. He's scared. She forces back a laugh of relief.

"Keep talking to him, Mrs. Gravescu. Talk to him," Marge coaches. The mother-talk calms both mother and child.

Marilyn stands up to see what is going on around her. For the first time she realizes how wet she is. Her light shoes are so soaked that she feels as if she's standing on the pavement in her bare feet. Her drenched jacket sticks to her back, and her dress clings to her legs. She can barely see through her glasses.

Christine and Rachel have come from somewhere, and Jane is crossing the street at a run. They begin to move among the children and parents, quietly talking to the children and telling them to leave, asking the parents to go on their way. Reluctantly the little crowd thins. Marilyn is grateful that the three women know what to do without being asked and wonders momentarily where Nan is.

As Marilyn takes in the scene, she notices a battered green pickup stopped in the middle of the street and a woman standing beside it. The woman seems familiar, but Marilyn doesn't quite know her. She is young, in her early 20s. Her bleached hair hangs around her face in thick, wet hanks, and her mascara makes rivulets down her cheeks. Marilyn walks over to her. "Was it your truck that hit him?" she asks gently, urgently.

The woman is sobbing too hard to talk, but she nods her head. Then she pulls herself together enough to ask, "Will he be all right?"

"I think so," Marilyn reassures. "Do you hear him crying? That's a good sign. He's conscious."

"I didn't mean to. I don't know where he came from. I was going real, real slow. I was barely moving. Do you think he'll be all right? Oh, God, I didn't mean to. Will he be all right?"

Marilyn sees the hysteria coming and puts her arm around the woman to help absorb it. She's tiny, she thinks. "Tell me your name."

"Lynette."

"Lynette, can you look at me?"

Lynette gives Marilyn a tentative glance. "That's good. Just keep looking at me. Now, I want you to breathe with me. We're going to take some long, slow breaths." At first Lynette doesn't respond, but then—little by little—her breathing slows and her crying subsides.

Minutes pass while the rain continues. Marilyn moves back and forth between Lynette and Tino. After a few more minutes, she hears the sirens, and suddenly a police car, a fire truck, and an ambulance fill the street. Marilyn stands close by while the paramedics load Tino into the ambulance. As it pulls away, a police officer comes up to her. "Are you the principal?" She nods. "Do you know who hit the boy?"

"I think the woman standing over there was driving the pickup."

"OK. I'll need to talk to her." The officer begins to move toward Lynette.

"Wait. She's upset. Let me tell her you want to talk to her. We should take her inside."

The officer agrees.

Marilyn walks back over to Lynette. "Let's go inside, Lynette. The police officer needs to talk to you. OK?"

"Can you stay with me?"

"Sure." For the first time, Marilyn notices Cody standing beside Lynette and realizes that she has seen Lynette with him often. "Oh, Cody! You've been here all the time."

He hurls himself against Marilyn, his wet, blond head burrowing into her stomach. She squats down beside him so that their eyes can meet. "I-is that o-other boy d-dead?"

"No, Cody. He's hurt, but he isn't dead. Didn't you hear him crying?" Cody nods. "So you know that he's alive, don't you?" Cody nods doubtfully. "They've taken him to the hospital so that they can help him."

"W-what's going to happen to M-mommy?"

"Nothing, Cody. The policeman just wants to talk to her to find out how Tino got hurt."

"W-will h-he t-take her to j-jail?"

"No, no, honey." Marilyn doesn't hear herself mimicking Cody's stutter. "No, no, not to jail. She's going to go home with you. She's going to be OK. And *you're* going to be OK. Let's all go inside and dry off and get warm."

When Marilyn walks in through the front doors with Cody and Lynette, the teachers are waiting in the vestibule to see if they can do anything more. Marge hands Marilyn a towel. "Pretty rough out there, huh?"

"Boy, that was a bad one," Marilyn confirms. "Thanks for your help. You were wonderful with Mrs. Gravescu." Marilyn takes off her glasses, and Marge holds them while she rubs her hair and face with the towel.

"Need anything more?" Marge wants to know.

"No, I think I can finish up. You take off—it's late."

Rachel and Jane have been helping to dry off Cody and Lynette. Marilyn thanks them too and brings Cody and Lynette into her office with the officer close behind. On her way past Rose's desk, she asks, "Did you call Renshaw's office with an accident report?"

"No," Rose says flatly, without looking up from the attendance report she has in front of her.

Marilyn's impatience flares, but she calms herself in the next second. "Well, better give them a call now. I would, but it's going to take me a while to finish up with the police officer." She feels the anger coming back. Why should she make excuses to Rose?

After a half an hour of questions, the officer is satisfied, but Marilyn isn't. She asks Lynette to stay for a while longer. "What are you going to do tonight?" she asks, hoping that her question doesn't make her sound like a busybody.

"Me and Cody'll just go on home." Cody gets out of the chair he has been sitting on and climbs into Lynette's lap. He has gotten much too large to sit easily, but Lynette scoots him close to her body and swings his legs around into a familiar position. Then she circles him with her arms and rocks back and forth as she talks around his head.

"Will anyone be there with you? You're still a little shaky."

"No. Just me and Cody. But we're good company for each other. Me and him have always been mostly on our own. We take care of each other. Don't we, buddy?" She rumples the little boy's wet hair and kisses him on the cheek. He snuggles closer.

"Don't you have a friend who could come over?" Lynette shakes her head. "Is your family close by?" Lynette gives Marilyn a puzzled look as if she doesn't quite understand why this woman wants to know, but she also seems to appreciate the interest.

"Naw. I ain't talked to them in a long time."

"How do you take care of yourself ?"

"You mean money? I'm back on food stamps and AFDC now. I was off for awhile. Got a job working for a cleaning service and I did real good 'til I broke some woman's little statue. She was mad, and my boss had to pay for it. Cost $300 and that got me fired. Then I thought I could do it on my own. You know. Get some houses. I figured I could make $50 a day easy. But it just didn't work out. My truck kept on breaking down, and, if I just missed one time, they'd get mad and fire me. Sometimes they didn't like the way I cleaned, and then they wouldn't pay me. Those women was mean. Some of 'em was just plain nasty. Treated me like dirt. It just wasn't worth the hassle, so I went back on welfare. We get by."

"Do you have something for dinner tonight?" Marilyn asks.

"Oh, yeah. We'll be fine."

"I-I can fix dinner for me and Mommy. I-I know how to make soup," Cody offers.

Lynette smiles and rubs her hand down his arm, taking his chubby one in hers. "Yeah. He does. If I'm too tired, he'll heat stuff up and make us sandwiches or something. And he talks my problems over with me. Me and him share everything."

Six is too young, Marilyn thinks, as she pulls open her top desk drawer and takes out one of her business cards. "Here, Lynette. I'm writing my home phone number on the back of the card. If you want to talk tonight, you call me. I'll be home all evening."

"Thanks." Lynette takes the card and holds it uneasily. Marilyn realizes that it is probably unimaginable for Lynette to call her.

"Do you have a phone?"

"Yeah. We just got it hooked back up. It was disconnected for awhile."

"Well, could I have your number? If I hear anything more about Tino tonight, I can give you a call."

"That'd be good." The anxiety that had seemed to leave Lynette for a few moments, returns in a rush. Cody looks at his mother as he feels her body tense. "I sure hope that kid's going to be OK. You think the policeman believed me that I wasn't speeding or nothin'?"

"I think so. The visibility was really bad, and Tino ran out in front of you. He wasn't looking. Try not to worry."

"OK," Lynette says, but there is neither feeling nor conviction in her voice. Cody climbs off her lap and takes her hand, "C-come on, M-mommy." Lynette gets up and follows his lead. Marilyn watches them as they walk out the door and down the long sidewalk toward their truck. She wonders who is the younger and what they are going home to.

At about 7:00 that evening, Marilyn gets through to the duty nurse at the hospital and finds out that Tino is resting comfortably. He is staying in the hospital overnight for observation. The nurse sounds easy and relaxed, as if there's nothing to worry about. Marilyn tries several times through the evening to call Lynette but gets no answer. Where could they be? Lynette had sounded so positive they were just going home to spend the evening alone together.

11

When Marilyn gets to school the next morning, Nan is sitting in the staff room nursing a cup of coffee. "How's Tino?" she asks. Marilyn tells Nan what little she knows. "Good." Then, without looking at Marilyn, she says, "Listen, I'm sorry I didn't go out there to help last night. I don't know, but I hate blood and accidents. I just can't go around things like that."

"That's OK. We had plenty of help." Marilyn knows that it was hard for Nan to tell her this, and she doesn't want to make either of them uncomfortable by making an issue of the confidence. "What do you know about Cody Butler and his mom?"

"That's the little guy with the stutter?"

Marilyn nods. "That's him. His mom was driving the truck that hit Tino."

"Geez. I'll bet that really upset Cody." Marilyn nods. "I don't know a lot. They're new, but I've been talking to Cody—don't have him in a group or anything—just getting to know him. I think he's really upset about his mom's boyfriends."

"Boyfriends?" Marilyn is surprised. "Lynette talked like they were alone."

"Naw. I don't think so. I think guys move in and out, probably don't stay long. You know. 'Easy come; easy go.'"

"Cody ever talk about his dad?"

"Not much. Calls him Pop. Mostly talks about waiting for him to come and him not showing up. Usual stuff. His mom's real clingy. Always sits with him for breakfast, walks him to his classroom, gives him long kisses when she leaves. Hands all over him."

"Hmm. That's interesting. I thought she held him last night because they were both upset from the accident. But they're like that all the time?" Nan nods. "Well, I'll see if they're in the cafeteria now. I want to tell Lynette about Tino."

"Catchya later." They smile at each other as Marilyn gets up slowly. Her legs ache this morning.

She scans the crowded cafeteria and finally sees Lynette and Cody snuggled up against the wall at the end of one of the long tables. "Hi, Lynette. How are you, Cody?" They look up in unison. "I tried to call you last night. I thought you'd like to know that Tino is going to be fine. He stayed in the hospital overnight, but he'll come home today."

"Oh, God, I'm glad to hear that. I've been so worried. You don't know what went though my head."

"I-is that b-boy going to d-die?" Cody puts words to Lynette's fears of the night.

"No, Cody. He'll be fine. He'll get well." Cody still looks worried. "Really, Cody. He's all right." Cody looks only slightly reassured. "Did you end up going somewhere last night, Lynette?" Marilyn asks.

Lynette looks embarrassed. "No. We was tired, so we unplugged the phone and went to bed."

Marilyn acknowledges that she had gone to bed early as well. Neither Lynette nor Cody seems to want to talk anymore, so Marilyn leaves them to each other and makes her way among the children out toward the front hall.

Rose approaches her. "You'd better come. There's a new boy registering." As soon as Marilyn steps into the office, she understands why Rose had wanted her. The boy standing on the waiting chairs sees her and jumps to a sitting position. He rolls onto the floor and scoots under the chairs, wriggling on his belly until he is stretched out flat between the legs of the chairs, his head hidden under the corner table. A woman in her late 50s is by the counter watching him. Marilyn looks at the boy and then at the woman.

"That's my grandson. He's living with me now. I need to register him for school," the woman says.

Marilyn decides that she'll ignore the boy for now. "Well, let me get some information from you. Would you like to come into my office for a couple of minutes?"

"Sure." The woman looks hesitantly at the boy who is still lying flat on his stomach under the chairs.

"What's your grandson's name?" Marilyn asks.

"Eli."

Marilyn walks over to the chairs and talks to their seats. "Eli. I've invited your grandmother to come in to my office to tell me about you. I'll bet that you would like to hear what I ask her, and I'll bet that you have some things to tell me too. When you stand up, you'll see an open door right in front of you, and you'll see two chairs where your grandmother and I will be sitting. I'll put another one beside your grandmother's for you to sit in. Please come in and join us when you are ready." Marilyn turns back to the woman, "Now, let's go into my office, Mrs. . . . ?"

"Mrs. Sims."

"Mrs. Sims. Glad to meet you," Marilyn says as she arranges the three chairs. They sit down, and Marilyn asks Mrs. Sims to tell her about Eli.

"Well, I don't know too much. His mother's been living in Kansas with the boy and her companion. I ain't seen him but a couple of times since he was born. His mother's moved around a lot."

"Is she your daughter?"

"Yes."

"So she and Eli are staying with you?"

"I guess they're living with me. Until they get settled anyway. She had to leave Kansas suddenly. She don't know what she's going to do now. So I don't know how long she'll be here, but I thought we'd better put the boy in school."

"Does Eli have any brothers or sisters?"

"Two half-sisters. They're way older than him. They'd be . . ." She thinks for a second. "Sixteen and seventeen now. They don't live with their mom no more, so they didn't come out."

Marilyn is relieved that she has only Eli to worry about. She can predict, based on the last 5 minutes, that Eli has already been in more schools than he can remember, that he won't be here long, and that, while he is here, it will be tough going. One of him is enough. "What grade is Eli in?"

"Second," I think. I got no records or anything on him. His mother might have something, but she don't have a lot of her belongings. She came in a hurry."

"Well, that's no problem. If you can just tell us what school Eli last attended, we'll send for his records."

"I'll have to ask . . ."

Just then Eli breaks into the room and knocks crazily into the empty chair. For the first time, Marilyn gets a clear look at him. He is about average height for a second grader but very underweight. His hands and arms and neck are brownish gray from a short lifetime of never being well washed. He has a small head and a broad forehead. His nose is wide and flat, and his grey eyes are set in a permanent squint.

"Hi, Eli. I'm glad to see that you've come in. I need to ask you some questions."

Eli squirms and turns, head down, away from Marilyn.

"Eli. Eli, look at me. Look at me," Marilyn says sternly.

Eli sits as he was for a moment, turns to give her a swift glance, and then turns away again.

"Eli. Your grandmother tells me that you're in second grade. Is that right?" He nods. "Eli, look at me and say 'yes'."

Eli gives her another quick look and a fast, high-pitched "yes."

She tries another question. "What was the name of your other school?"

"Mark Twain," Eli spits out in his little voice.

"Where is Mark Twain?"

Eli shrugs. This conversation has gone about as far as it can, and there's not much to do but to get on with things.

"Eli, your new teacher's name is Mrs. Fletcher. I'm going to introduce you to Nan. She's our counselor. Did you have a counselor at your old school?" Eli shrugs. "Well, Nan will talk to you for a little while and then take you to meet your new teacher and the children in your class. And, Eli, one thing more. Try to look at me when we talk to each other. That may be hard for you until we know each other better, so I'll remind you when you forget. OK?"

Eli looks quickly at Marilyn and then away. "OK." It takes Marilyn another few minutes to hand him off to Nan and to get assurances from Mrs. Sims that she will call later in the day to tell Rose where Mark Twain is. As she finishes up, Marilyn stops at Rose's desk to gather a handful of telephone messages. Rose says, "We still need to have a fire drill this month."

"Yeah. That's right. Well, it's not raining this morning and it's pretty warm."

"Jolene wants to see you. It's not PTA business this time. She's worried about Stephanie's grades in math. And Marge Friedman. She wants you to come down to her room to see something."

Marilyn mentally arranges her day. "OK. Give me a few minutes to call the hospital about Tino and return these calls. I'll catch up with Jolene and then see what Marge needs. Let's try for the fire drill around 11:00, just before lunch. Remind me if I get bogged down."

"Will do."

Tino is fine. The phone calls don't amount to much. It's Jolene's usual worry over Stephanie. She doesn't know her multiplication tables, and Jolene can't get her to practice them at night. Marilyn can tell, as soon as she walks in that Marge has been waiting for her. "I've just had it with Gus. He makes me so mad. The other night I caught him throwing away three pair of scissors. I asked him why he hadn't picked them up, and he said that he wasn't supposed to pick up things when he sweeps. It just takes too much time. Can you imagine that? Think what that costs the taxpayers just because Gus is too lazy to bend down and pick up a pencil or a pair of scissors."

Marilyn promises to talk with Gus. But Marge isn't through. "He's messing with my VCR, too. I set something to record, and then I come in and it's disconnected or set on another channel. Sometimes the cables are all screwed up."

"I'll talk to him, see what's going on. He shouldn't be doing that. He's got a TV in the boiler room." Marilyn turns to leave.

"Well, that's not the end of it. This is the weirdest part of all. When I came in this morning, I found this on my table." Marge hands Marilyn a polaroid snapshot of Gus. "What do you make of that?"

"I have no idea."

"Well, I do. I've been using the polaroid to take pictures of the kids for my 'I'm Special' bulletin board. I left the camera on the table last night. What I don't get is why Gus just left this here. If he wanted a picture so bad, why didn't he take it with him?"

"It's a mystery, Marge. I'll talk to Gus tonight. See if I can find out what's going on."

At lunch time, Grace Johnson stops Marilyn in the hall. "Will you talk to Cody? He's off the wall. I can't get him to do anything. When the fire alarm went off, he started screaming and running around the room like a maniac. You've never seen anything like it."

"Don't you think he's upset about the accident?"

"He hasn't said anything, but it sure could be."

Marilyn finds Cody in the lunchroom. "Cody, when you finish your lunch, how would you like to come and talk to me ?"

"C-can I c-come now?"

"You still have a lot of lunch left. Don't you want to finish it?"

Cody doesn't bother to answer her question. He untangles himself from the table, grabs the cellophane wrappers around his styrofoam tray, and piles them on top of his uneaten noodle casserole. She follows him over to the garbage cans in the middle of the cafeteria where he throws away the sticky glob.

Marilyn shepherds him through the congested cafeteria. Once in her office, she sits down in her desk chair, and he perches on one of the side chairs. She rolls her chair up close to his so that their knees are almost touching. She looks at him for a couple of seconds. Four of his front teeth are missing. She notices how his curly blond hair nearly covers his shoulders and spreads down his back. His bangs all but hide his wide, searching brown eyes. His chubby little hand never stops twisting the curl that falls on his right shoulder.

Marilyn and Cody make comforting small talk full of small lies for awhile.

"How are you, Cody?"

"F-fine."

"How did your morning go?"

"F-fine."

"Did you have fun with the kids and Miss Johnson?"

"Yup."

Marilyn notices that Cody is looking out into the outer office. "T-there's T-Tino's teacher."

"Yes, that's Mrs. Wagner. She's looking at her mail, and then she's going to go eat her lunch."

"C-could I talk to her?"

Marilyn goes out to where Lil Wagner is standing sorting through her box. "Lil, Cody . . . Do you know who Cody is? He's in Grace's room. He wants to talk to you for a minute." Lil is puzzled.

"I don't think I know him."

"No, you probably don't. His mother was driving the truck that hit Tino, and he's awfully upset about it. Somehow he's figured out that you're Tino's teacher. I think he wants you to reassure him."

Lil nods and goes in with Marilyn to talk to Cody. The two women sit down while Cody watches intently. Marilyn introduces them, and Lil says gently, "Hi, Cody. I'm glad to meet you."

Cody searches Lil with his eyes. Then he takes a deep breath. "I-I'm sorry my m-mommy hit him. S-She didn't m-mean to. S-She's sorry."

"Oh, honey. I *know* your mommy didn't mean to do it," Lil says. "I *know* that, Cody. Tino's going to be just fine. You know that, don't you?" Cody nods, but his eyes say something different. Lil and Marilyn look at each other across the top of his head.

After school that afternoon, Marilyn goes to find Gus. For all his outspoken awkwardness, Marilyn likes him, and she doesn't relish having to bring up Marge's complaints. "Gus, the teachers have expressed some concerns to me."

"Yeah? What'd I do?"

"Well, they say that you've been sweeping up scissors and things like that and just throwing them away." Marilyn hates her habit of generalizing complaints—talking in the plural "they" instead of just coming out and saying that it's Marge.

"Them's my orders."

"Your orders? Who said that?"

"Downtown. We got to keep to our schedule. If I bent down and picked up everything them teachers let the kids leave on the floor, it'd take me damn near twice as long to get through them rooms. We got told not to pick up that stuff."

Marilyn is pretty sure that Gus is telling it right. The policy makes her angry, but she holds her tongue. She'll call the head of the physical plant in the morning. "OK, Gus. I'll talk to the teachers, see if they'll get the kids to do a better job of picking up their stuff. I can understand your letting the crayons or maybe used-up pencils go, but, if you see scissors or unifix cubes, could you pick them up? And let me know if you have classrooms that are especially bad. I'll speak to the teachers."

"OK, boss. I'll do m'best."

"Thanks, Gus. I've got a couple of other things, too. Mrs. Friedman has noticed that her TV is being used at night. Do you know anything about that?"

"Yeah. I go in there sometimes for my dinner break. I don't bother nothin'. Just eat my dinner and watch 'Jeopardy.'"

"Lots of times she has the VCR set to record, and, if you change the channel or something, then she doesn't get her program. Don't you have a TV in the boiler room?"

"I do. It's pretty little and the color's bad, but I can just stay in there if that's what you want. I didn't mean to bother nothin'."

"I know you didn't, Gus, but I think it'd be better if you used the boiler room TV. If it's that bad, maybe we can see if the shop can fix it."

"Mebbe. You said you had something else you wanted to say?" Gus is very tired of this conversation.

"Mrs. Friedman noticed that you'd left a photo of yourself on her table. She thought maybe you'd used the polaroid to take it."

"That's right. I did." Marilyn looks puzzled. Gus pauses, trying to figure out how to explain. "Well, it's like this, Ms. Wallace. I been feeling really down lately, low down, you know. So's I just took that picture of myself to see if I looked as bad as I felt . . . And I did."

"I know. It's the hard time of year. Well, just don't leave the evidence around next time. And I'm sorry about how you feel. I hope things get better."

"Thanks, Ms. Wallace. Say, how's the kid that got run over?"

"He's going to be OK. It wasn't a serious injury."

"That's good."

It seems as if, wherever Marilyn turns for the next few weeks, Cody is there. He tackles her around the middle and hugs her until she pries his arms lose. Usually he wants to tell her something about Tino: "T-That boy came b-back to school today. He's m-mad at me."

"How do you know that he's mad at you, Cody? Did he talk to you?"

"N-no. B-but he's mad."

"No, Cody. He's not mad. He knows it wasn't your fault."

"Y-yeah but he t-thinks it's m-my m-mommy's fault. M-my mommy tried to g-go see him, and his m-mommy wouldn't let my mommy come in the house."

Marilyn thinks how much courage it must have taken for Lynette to try to make that visit. "You're worried about your mommy, aren't you, Cody?" Cody nods a long, sober yes.

"S-she might have to go away. I-I'd be by my ownself."

"Cody, your mommy isn't going to go away. She's going to stay right where she is—with you. You and your mommy are best friends, aren't you?"

"W-we help each other a very lot."

"How do you help your mommy, Cody?"

"I-I do work. I clean up the apartment. S-sometimes I fix dinner. I-I make her not be lonesome when her boyfriend goes away."

"How do you do that, Cody?"

"S-she tells me how bad she feels. A-and I tell her that it will be all right. T-that she can get another boyfriend. S-she says that I'm her best boyfriend."

"Do you like your mom's boyfriends, Cody?"

Cody shakes his head. "T-they don't take good care of Mommy, and they don't like me. I-I like it when they go away."

"Then what happens?"

"I-I can take care of Mommy again. I-I make her feel better. I can stop sleeping in the sleeping bag on the couch, and I can sleep right up close to her in the bed. I-I can be her boyfriend."

A chill passes through Marilyn. She will watch Cody carefully.

It's a Friday afternoon, and Marilyn is standing by the buses as they finish loading. She has gone out every day since the accident to direct traffic. Today it feels as if there's snow in the air. She waves to the children in the departing buses and starts back inside, cringing at a bumper sticker on a car that drives away with three children in it: "I haven't had sex for so long that I can't remember who gets tied up."

Cody and Lynette are walking across the street to their pickup, and Marilyn is relieved that they are far enough away to make it difficult to begin a conversation. She is cold and eager to get back inside. Sylvia comes running toward her. "That new kid picked up a needle in the park. He put it in his mouth. I saw him put it in his mouth!"

Marilyn glances in the direction of the park. Had it really happened? Were the kids making something out of nothing? Then she sees Nan running out to the park. Good. I'll let Nan have this one, she thinks. This has been a long week: Cody can't get enough attention; Mr. Schneider has kicked Nathan out of class at least once a day; Joey gave Nathan a bloody nose. Eli is tearing Harriet Fletcher's class apart. A little girl named Jewel is back after having been gone for a couple of months and is giving Corine a harder time than Star had. She has barely gotten inside when Nan comes in dragging a dirty, bawling, wriggling child by the wrist.

"We got some talking to do," Nan says grimly, as she pulls Eli around the counter and into Marilyn's office. Nan pushes Eli into one chair and pulls up another to sit just as close to him as she possibly can. She puts her face right up next to Eli's. "What were you doing in the park?"

"Taking a short cut," he bawls.

"Did you pick up a needle?" Eli shakes his head in a vigorous "no." "Did you pick up a needle?" Nan asks again, shouting this time.

Eli nods a reluctant "yes."

"OK. That's better." Nan sits back in her chair. A pause. Then, in a soft voice, "Eli, did you put the needle in your mouth?"

Eli shakes his head "no" again, slowly this time.

"Look at me, Eli. Did you put that needle in your mouth?"

"No." He shakes his head again.

Gus comes in with a little plastic bag in his hand. "There was needles out there, all right. Damn fool junkies. If it was up to me, I'd shoot 'em all."

"Thanks, Gus," Marilyn says, taking the bag with three needles inside it. Gus turns and leaves muttering to himself.

Nan starts in again. "Is this one of the needles, Eli?" Silence. "Is it?"

Eli nods. He doesn't know if it is or not. A needle is a needle. Nan knows that too, but she wants him to own what he has done, *really* own it. She is out to terrify him.

"Did you put that needle in your mouth, Eli?" Nothing. "Did you?" Still nothing. "Eli, *answer* me."

"Noooo!" Eli wails back. "No, no, I didn't. I picked it up and looked at it. Then I put it back."

"Look at me, Eli. Show me your mouth." Eli holds up his face. Nan puts her hand under his chin, squeezes it, and turns his face from side to side. "Open your mouth." She inspects his lips, gums, tongue, cheeks. The examination seems to go on for a long time, with only the sounds of Eli's sniffing to break the quiet.

"OK." Nan leans back. I don't see any broken skin anywhere. I think you're OK, but you were really stupid. Really, really stupid. Don't you ever pick up a needle again. You understand me?" Eli nods, eyes wide, mouth open. "Do you?"

"Yes," he whimpers.

"Why, Eli? Tell me why."

"Because the needle might be c-c-c'tmn . . ."

"That's right! Contaminated. That means it could still have some of the drug left on it."

"Yeah," Eli chimes in. "And it could have the AIDS on it."

"That's right, Eli. Y'got it. OK. Promise. Promise that you'll never pick up another needle. Never."

"I promise."

"Say it."

"I promise that I'll never . . ." He forgets the rest.

"Never pick up another needle," Nan coaches. "Say it after me. Never pick up another needle."

"Never pick up another needle," Eli recites, watching Nan carefully.

Nan relaxes. She feels as if Eli realizes he's taken a solemn oath.

"I'm going to call your grandma and tell her so she can watch you extra careful tonight just in case you start to feel funny. I'm going to tell her to talk to you too about what happened in the park. I don't want you going over there. Now, you head on home."

Eli doesn't object. He is still too surprised at all the trouble he's gotten into to say anything.

Marilyn and Nan talk about Eli for awhile after Nan gets off the phone. "I have a funny feeling that Eli and his mother aren't really living there any more."

"Where do you think they are?"

"I don't know, but Mother is never there. I've called, and I've gone over, and I've never seen her. I think she lives somewhere out of the neighborhood and brings Eli over every day. Or maybe she's split and left Eli with Grandma. Something strange is going on."

"Well, let's not worry about it tonight," Marilyn urges.

The office is suddenly quiet. The phone isn't ringing anymore, and the conversations in the outer office have stopped. Marilyn looks up at the clock—4:00. She has the feeling that she, Gus, and Rose are the only people left in the building. Rose is sitting with a ledger spread out in front of her. She looks tired. "Why don't you pack it up for the week? I can handle the phones for the last half hour," Marilyn offers.

"Thanks. Maybe I will. These numbers are all running together." In another 10 minutes, Rose has gone, and Marilyn has the office to herself. She looks at the pink slips on her desk—five or six of them—and glances at the clock. It's getting late to return calls. She arranges the slips for first thing Monday morning—Frank's message is on the top. Then, she reconsiders. She calls him and is glad to hear his secretary say that he is out for the rest of the day.

The African violets are in full bloom against the darkening January window. She dusts the sill, lifting each plant and rearranging three or four of them. Then she dusts the top of the bookcases and considers taking the old brass school bell into the workroom to polish but decides against it. She lifts all the folders and paraphernalia off her desk and sprays the glass, rubbing the smudges out. It is Marilyn's compulsion that keeps Gus from ever getting her office clean enough to suit her, and she understands as much.

She sets the folders back on the desk and starts going through the papers inside them. Gradually she picks up momentum, and her fatigue gives way to the pleasure of being able to work uninterrupted. If I keep at it, I can get these cleaned out, she thinks. She glances at the clock—almost 5:00. She has just emptied the second folder when she hears someone in the outer office. She looks up. It's the bus driver. His eyes meet hers. "Hi, Ms. Wallace. Just thought I'd drop off this referral on my way back to the barn."

"Let me guess. Jewel again?"

"Yup. I can't get her to do nothin'. She was standing up and yelling swear words at the kids behind her. I told her to sit down and she said . . . Well, I'd rather write it than say it, Ms. Wallace."

Marilyn reads the referral. The string of profanity and obscenity is familiar. "This is Jewel's third or fourth, isn't it Vearl?"

"It's number five, Ms. Wallace. She's had three of 'em in the last week. You know, I'm not supposed to be letting 'em ride after three."

This boxed-in feeling is all too familiar to Marilyn. The head of the Transportation Department, a man who—to her knowledge— has never worked in a school, has made a rule that a principal must suspend a student from the bus after three incident reports. It's not that Marilyn doesn't understand the general logic of the rule; it's that she knows if she tells Jewel that she can't ride the bus for a week, she will stop coming to school probably for the next month.

She knows, too, that Vearl wants Jewel off the bus. He can handle the language from a boy, but when a 9-year-old girl tells him that he can "take the whole goddamn school bus and shove it up his fucking ass," he wants something done. He's serious; otherwise he wouldn't have taken the time to drive all the way back to the school. "OK, Vearl. I'll talk to Jewel first thing on Monday morning."

"Thanks, Ms. Wallace. That girl is a wicked one. 'Bout the worst I ever seen."

"I know, Vearl. She's really difficult. You have a good weekend, now."

"You too, Ms. Wallace."

Marilyn walks back slowly back into her office and stands looking at the violets. She rubs one of the fleshy leaves between her fingers. I'm not getting anywhere, she thinks. I'm just going from one day to the next and getting farther and farther behind. Nothing changes—the teachers, the children, the parents, this tangle of a bureaucracy. It's all talk, the same jargon, the same platitudes, the same excuses, the same directives. If they'd all just stop talking and look, look at the children. No one sees the children, really sees them. She turns away from the window and begins pushing papers into their folders to take home with her for the weekend. "I've got to work harder," she says out loud to herself.

12

Marilyn goes down to Corine's room to get Jewel right after school starts on Monday. She brought herself in to register the first week in December. "My mom's sleeping. She said for me to bring the papers home. She'll sign them." Corine had lost Star the week before, and, since hers was the smallest fourth grade class, she got Jewel. Marilyn is next to positive that Corine would take Star back any day in exchange for Jewel.

Most of the classrooms are noisy this time of day with lunch counts, the Pledge of Allegiance, sharing time, feeding the animals. Corine's children already have their math workbooks out and are doing the first of six pages listed on the chalkboard. Corine sits behind her desk correcting papers, glancing up every few seconds.

Jewel sits alone at the same small desk directly in front of Corine's that had been assigned to Star. Her workbook is open, but she is not doing math. Instead, she is tearing a piece of paper into tiny bits that float down to join hundreds more which blanket the floor around her chair.

She gets up with interest and follows Marilyn out into the empty hall. Not only are Jewel's hands and face dirty this morning, she smells. Maybe they should give her a shower at school a couple of times a week, Marilyn thinks. She'll talk to Nan about it at lunch.

Jewel is dressed up today. Even though snow is predicted for late afternoon, she wears a sundress with a black knit stretch top and a gathered white skirt with floral scrawls in broad, black lines. Left alone, it would drag on the floor, but Jewel has pinned up the straps with safety pins that strain to hold the bunches of fabric. The skirt hits her just below the calf where it meets thick, black anklets rolled down to the tops of patent high heel shoes two sizes too big. "Do you like my outfit?" She doesn't wait for Marilyn to answer. "It's my mom's. It was too long, so I pinned it up. See?" She grabs one of the safety pins at her shoulder and twists it so that she can look at it.

Marilyn notices a fresh scar on Jewel's forehead. "What happened to your forehead?"

"I had to have twelve stitches. Seven on the inside and five on the outside. I really bled a lot."

"How did it happen?"

"I hate the hair dryer. My sister was holding me and blasting me. I tried to jerk away from her—she's such a bitch—and I banged my head on the counter, right on the corner. I didn't feel anything, but she started screaming and then I screamed too. My mother came in and she started screaming. We were all screaming."

"Those cuts in your head bleed a lot. They're pretty scary."

"My dad bled a lot more when he got shot."

"Do you want to talk about that, Jewel?" Jewel has already told Marilyn her story several times.

"When I was 6, I lived with my dad in this little house out in the country. He was a biker. Me and my little brother lived with him and his wife. He had three girlfriends. One of them got jealous, and she came right in the living room and shot my dad in the head."

"What were you doing?"

"I was standing next to him."

"And you saw your dad get shot?"

Jewel nods solemnly.

Jewel's details change. Sometimes her dad gets shot out in front of the trailer where the bikes were parked. Sometimes Jewel is an eyewitness, and sometimes she isn't, but one fact never changes: Jewel's father was killed while she was close by. The shooting was 3 years ago when Jewel was 6.

After that she came to live with her mother. In addition to her 13-year-old sister, she has two big brothers who slap her around. Her mother works off and on at convenience stores but usually gets fired because the children come to the store, argue, shove each other around, and steal cigarettes and beer. After the last time she got fired, she moved back to live with some friends in the Madison neighborhood. Marilyn caught a glimpse of her last week when she came in after Nan had threatened to call Children's Services if she didn't.

When Jewel first came back, Marilyn was glad to have her, thinking she might be safer than she had been at Jackson—Pam McBride's school. She had been wearing makeup and smoking openly there. She told Pam that she hoped one of the neighborhood pimps would notice her. Marilyn thinks that maybe she's given up on the makeup since she's moved because she knows there aren't many pimps in this part of town. She still wears her high-heeled shoes, though, and breathless fourth-grade girls have come running into the office twice within as many days to report a cigarette butt in the girls' bathroom.

"Jewel, I have five reports now about your behavior on the bus. You're standing up and using bad language, and you won't do what the bus driver asks you to." Jewel gives Marilyn a cold stare. "Isn't that right, Jewel?"

"I guess so."

"We've talked about this before. You know the rules. I'm going to take you off the bus for a week, and then you can have another chance, but if you screw up again, I'll take you off for another week."

Jewel shrugs.

"Now, how are you going to get to school for this week and next Monday?"

"I guess I won't. I'll just tell my mom, and she'll let me stay home. She won't care."

"But we'll care. Ms. Friedman, and Nan, and Mrs. Conrad, and me. We'll all care."

"Not Mrs. Conrad. She don't like me."

"I know where you live, Jewel. It's not that far, and you're in fourth grade. How about walking for just 1 week?"

"Nope. My mom won't let me. She's afraid I'll get raped."

"Well, I don't know what else to do, Jewel. I guess that I'll just have to come and get you and take you home. How do you think that would work?" Jewel is surprised. She hadn't anticipated the offer. "You meet me in the office right after school, and we'll just buzz on home. OK?"

"I guess that'd be all right. I guess I'll ask my mom if it'd be OK if I walked."

"Well, you and your mom talk it over, but don't worry about it. I can drive you, and if I can't, I think Nan or Mrs. Friedman would help out. Now, you'd better get back to your math. I'll tell Mrs. Conrad about the plan, and then I'll see you after school." For the moment, Marilyn has the upper hand.

When she gets back to the office, Rose reminds her that she is almost late for a meeting downtown. As much as Marilyn hates these meetings, she's glad for the 15 minutes of driving and the chance to be alone with her thoughts. Jewel. Eli. Cody. She's worried about all three of them, not to mention at least 20 other children whose stories she knows and many more whose stories she can only imagine. Driving along the Interstate toward the city's center, she forms a picture of herself. She is a slow-motion figure whose field of vision has no depth or clarity. She is lost in dense underbrush, and, the farther she goes, the more confused she becomes. She hears the children's voices but she cannot find them fast enough, and she is afraid. Slowly the soprano recorder dancing through a Vivaldi concerto on the radio catches her attention, and she begins to breathe more deeply and to relax a little. As she pulls into the big parking lot and gets out of the car, she doesn't feel the the muscles in her neck and shoulders tighten nor does she notice her mood turning cruel.

She comes into the meeting just as it is getting started and takes a seat beside Pam McBride. Even before the talking begins, Marilyn takes a dislike to the woman at the front of the room arranging her overhead transparencies. Marilyn recognizes her as from the breed of consultants who send out glossy brochures promising to fix schools in a 3-hour workshop. She sizes up the tall, rail-thin woman and puts her in her mid-40s. She is wearing a bright silk print in reds, greens, purples, and yellows. A pear-shaped diamond pendant draws attention to her bony neck.

The woman is warming up the cold crowd. She tells a story about her physician husband. All the women consultants tell amusing stories about their families, Marilyn thinks. Did it ever occur to her that some of us aren't married? That we don't have diamond pendants? The woman flips on the projector for the first overhead. The strong light beams up at her face. Marilyn scribbles a note to Pam. "Women over 40 should never get near an overhead. It gives away all their secrets." Pam grins and nods.

The woman starts her spiel. "We all know that the 'effective schools' research says that the principal is the instructional leader of the school. It's up to the principal to set clear goals, have a sense of mission. What we are here today for is . . ."

Not the "effective schools" stuff again, Marilyn thinks. What's this woman getting paid? A thousand dollars a day to tell me that I need clear goals? What I need are social workers and mental health therapists, health care, family literacy programs, community police.

Does she really think that I can fix my school if I just get organized? Marilyn scribbles another note to Pam. "Do you think she's ever been in a school like ours?"

Pam scribbles back, "Want me to offer her a slot doing lunch duty?" They put on polite, remote faces for the rest of the meeting. As they are breaking up, Pam asks about Jewel.

"She almost made me late for this meeting. She's a mess. I don't think she's as promiscuous as she was with you, but she's acting out all over the place. I don't know how much longer we can hold on to her."

"I know," Pam agrees. "She probably won't make it to middle school."

"Not if we keep thinking she won't, but I don't know what to do. God, I hate this feeling. Wouldn't you like to watch that woman have a conversation with Jewel?"

"I'd pay to see it."

Over the next few weeks, Eli and Jewel and, most especially, Cody are never off Marilyn's mind for long. When she walks into the cafeteria or on the playground, she looks for him. And, when she finds him, he has always found her first and is watching, waiting for the contact. They talk sometimes, but—more often—Cody just comes close, and she gives him a hug and a pat as she sends him on his way.

Not a day goes by without Grace Johnson's talking to Marilyn about him. It's as if Grace has decided that, no matter what else happens this year, something is going to be done for Cody. Marilyn doesn't know what to make of Grace. Although she's 50, she could be taken for 45 or for 58. She is big boned with graceful long legs and carries a little weight in her midsection. Her cropped brown hair always looks as if she's just gotten out of bed. Some days she wears a two-piece knit dress with ropes of necklaces and looks like a school teacher from the '50s. Other days she's in a velour top and polyester slacks that hit above her ankle bones. Then she might be from the '70s. She wants to leave Madison. "Twenty years is too long to stay anyplace. I know I should get out," she'll say. "I've tried, but I always bomb in the interviews. Principals don't want me. I guess because I don't talk about the newfangled stuff."

Marilyn wouldn't hire Grace if she were interviewing her. In the last staff meeting, when Marilyn said that instead of using a textbook, the new social studies curriculum would make heavy use of "hands-on" materials, Grace made a perfectly awful face, turned clear around in her chair, her back to Marilyn, and gave an exasperated sigh for all to hear. Parents complain that Miss Johnson tears up papers because the children haven't put their names on them. But parents also request her as a teacher. Often, when Marilyn walks down the hall, she hears Grace yelling at her first graders: "No, no, no. I've told you a thousand times to put your name *here*, not here. Can't you ever do what I tell you?" Marilyn shudders when she hears the shrill, impatient voice.

Yet when she goes into Grace's room, the children are happy. She observed last week while they were having their morning meeting. The children gathered themselves in a circle on the floor. Grace plopped down among them "criss-cross applesauce," her legs spread at an embarrassing angle. She scanned the children—one by one—then the entire group, nodding at their contributions, her mouth half open in concentration. They went through the morning routines of taking attendance and lunch count, doing the calendar, and observing the weather. The children knew exactly how to proceed and were pleased about their business for the day. Marilyn realized, watching Grace and her children, that they had reached an unspoken understanding that it was all right for her to yell at them because she loved them.

At least once a week, Grace sends a child to Marilyn to read a book. Yesterday Lacey came with hers. She is a delicate child with porcelain skin and forget-me-not blue eyes. As she dangled on the edge of the chair, reading carefully and seriously, Marilyn thought of Eppie in *Silas Marner.* With Grace's unflagging encouragement, Lacey wrote and illustrated her story, dedicated it, and thoughtfully composed the last page that tells about the author: "Lacey Sorenson is 6 years old. She lives with her father. She likes to read, watch TV, and ride her bike. She wants to be somebody's wife and a model when she grows up."

After Lacey finished writing her story, Grace took it home, made a cover, typed the text, and bound the pages into a book. Each of Grace's children will write several books before the year is out. As she listened to Lacey read, Marilyn had no doubt that this child would be—in fact already was—a reader and a writer because Miss Johnson had taught her much more than consonant sounds.

Grace wants as much for Cody as she does for Lacey or any of her children. Her years of teaching have convinced her that if he leaves first grade without reading, the chances are unbearably high that he will never be a good reader. "He's not getting any better. He's getting worse and worse," she tells Marilyn.

"I know. You'd better refer him to the Screening Committee. It's time for us to look at him."

This is the first of three conversations like this that Marilyn has within as many days. When she comes into the staff room for coffee the next morning, Harriet, Susan, and Melanie are eating their breakfast, one of Florence's best—french toast with plenty of butter and syrup and little link sausages. "Marilyn, we need to talk to you about something," Susan says. Marilyn knows the tone in Susan's voice well. She gets her coffee and goes over to sit down with the women.

Susan has been named spokeswoman. "Marilyn, do you realize what Harriet is having to put up with?" The question is rhetorical, so she goes right on talking. "That new boy is destroying her class-room. Did you know that?"

"I know Eli's got a ton of problems. Nan and I are spending a tremendous amount of time with him right now."

"Well, who's helping *Harriet,* is what I want to know? She can't be expected to teach 27 other kids and manage Eli at the same time."

Harriet joins in. "It's really getting bad, Marilyn. He spent most of the day yesterday under the table. I'm not kidding you. He crawls around on all fours. He babbles. I can't even get him to look at me."

"I can't get much eye contact from him either. Although I think he's getting a little better. Don't you?" Marilyn tries to nudge the talk toward the positive.

"Not much," Harriet says. "And he says weird things. I told him to do something yesterday, and do you know what he said? 'I'll cut out your stomach. No problem.' And, by the tone of his voice, he might as well have been saying, 'Have a nice day.'"

"Has his file come from Kansas yet?"

"No, but there won't be anything in it anyway."

"You know how that goes. They take everything that matters out of those files before they send them," Susan says.

Marilyn hates being ganged up on. The women are right, and she hates that as well. She throws out the only suggestion she has, knowing it offers only a long wait and very little possibility of any real help. "Well, let's do this, Harriet. Why don't you call Kansas and see if you can talk to his teacher there? Then do a referral to the Screening Committee. We should be able to look at him next week. In the meantime, do you think you can manage him in your classroom?"

"Oh, yeah. I can manage him. He's not too bad if I don't put any pressure on him. If I let him play with the blocks and things like that, he's fine by himself for hours."

"Well, why don't you just let him do that? It's probably what he needs right now," Marilyn snaps back much too quickly and sharply.

"You mean you want her to let him play and not *teach* him anything?" Susan asks with exaggerated incredulity.

"I guess I don't think he *can* do anything else right now. If he doesn't begin to feel comfortable and safe, he's not going to be able to learn no matter how hard Harriet works. I don't want to set her up for power struggles," Marilyn says, trying to pull back to safer ground.

"Well, that's not *my* idea of teaching. Is that what you'd want for your granddaughters, Marilyn? It's certainly not what I'd want for my Tyson," Susan says.

"It's not quite the same, Susan," Marilyn says to cut off the conversation. She resents having details from her private life brought into these arguments. It's for this reason that she tells the people at school as little as she possibly can about herself while still being polite. Knowing that she's been curt, she tries for another, more gracious ending, "Well, let's hang in there for a few more days until we can get some information and a game plan. OK?"

"Fine by me," Harriet says, the tone of her voice indicating that it's not fine at all and that she doesn't intend to let the matter drop.

Jewel will also come before the Screening Committee. Nan has tried to put her on a behavior contract, but it doesn't even come close to working. She has gone from tearing up paper to tearing up books. Marilyn notices that Corine has begun to call in sick at least one day a week. She doesn't smile or say good morning and sits alone at lunch. Because she has no grounds for demanding that Jewel be taken out of her class, she complains about small slights: The science teacher came late to her room, Rose didn't get a phone message to her quickly enough, someone parked in her space.

Marilyn goes to see Marge. "Do you think you could give Jewel a little time in your room? Corine's desperate."

"Sure thing. Tell you what, let me take her for a week—see if we can get her stabilized."

Marilyn checks with Marge off and on over the next few days.

"How's it going?"

"She's a hard one. She's fighting us. Calling the other kids names. They're really mad at her, but we'll make it. We'll hold on to her."

After 6 days, Marge stops Marilyn. "We've got to go to work on Jewel. She's as disturbed as I've seen, and I've seen a few. She bit me today."

"Marge!"

"Yup, she got me on my left breast. I've got a good-sized bruise and teeth marks."

"Geez. I'm sorry. Maybe Corine is up to taking her back."

"Not on your life. I'm not going to give up on that kid now. She's had a piece of my flesh. No. I've already told Jewel that she's mine; *I'll* tell Corine the same."

"That'd really help, Marge. But what about Special Ed? They're not going to let you keep a child in your room who isn't labeled."

"I'm not telling if you don't."

13

The Screening Committee meets on Wednesday mornings as close to 8:00 as the women can manage. Marilyn gets to school early on this particular Wednesday to be sure that she's ready for the meeting. Chuck is waiting for her. "We had a break-in last night. Nothing taken. Well, not much anyway. That I can see."

"What'd they do?"

"Broke into classrooms—got Nan's room, Wagner's, Friedman's, and Schneider's. Must of taken a baseball bat or something and knocked out windows. Went after the rooms on the courtyard, so no one could've seen them from the street. Things are a real mess—glass everywhere. I've got a crew coming from downtown. We should be about cleaned up by the time school starts."

"Any of the teachers here yet?"

"Yeah, Mrs. Wagner's down in her room, and I think Nan's around somewhere."

Marilyn walks quickly down to Lil's room. When she walks in, a blast of cold air from the broken windows hits her. From the middle of the room on, glass crunches with every step. The window sill is lined with end-to-end shoeboxes in which the children have been building their favorite scenes from Judy Blume's *Tales of a Fourth Grade Nothing*. Lil stands picking glass out of the boxes. "Hi, Lil."

"Why would someone do something like this? Look at the children's projects! They're ruined."

"Is there anything missing?" Marilyn asks.

"Not much. Chuck said that a work crew was coming out to clean up and board up the windows. You know it'll be months before they put in the glass. It's going to be so awful for the children. I just hate this, Marilyn. I hate it."

Marilyn feels the familiar helplessness. She wants the glass replaced *now*. Not weeks or months from now. She will see if she can light a fire under someone downtown, but she doesn't expect much to come of it.

"I guess I'll ask Tom if I can bring the children down to the gym until they get the room cleaned up," Lil says.

"Good idea. If you can, give me a list of anything that's missing. I'll get replacements for you right away."

"Thanks, Marilyn, but it's not the stuff that was stolen that matters. It's the way they ruined the room and the children's projects. They loved those projects so much. And you know what else? They won't feel as if the school's safe now."

Marilyn puts her arm around Lil. "Come down and get some coffee. You can't do much until the work crew finishes."

They walk back down the hall together, and Marilyn turns off to go into the Screening Committee meeting.

When Marilyn comes in to the room, several of the women are already there. Christine Bailey is putting out agendas and minutes. She's trying to be efficient so that the meeting won't get off to a slow start. Dolores Davis, the psychologist, and Connie Stanley, the social worker, are sitting with their toast and coffee, their hair still damp from morning showers. Diane Westover, the speech pathologist, comes in and sits down. These three work for Special Education and are each assigned to several schools. They are considered outsiders, and Marilyn and the teachers do not not quite trust them. Grace Johnson and Corine Conrad straggle in. Then Harriet Fletcher comes along. The women sit talking quietly or saying nothing at all, breaking off pieces of toast soaked with butter, sipping the weak, acrid coffee. The fluorescent lights accentuate fresh makeup that is strangely theatrical over their sleepy, still-private faces.

"Where are Nan and Marge?" Christine asks. "We need to get started. We have three big ones this morning."

As if on cue, they come in. "God, I'm so disgusted!" Nan says.

Everyone except for Marilyn looks at her in surprise. "Oh, they ripped off my room last night. Marge's too. They're both a mess— broken glass all over the place, muddy footprints. Looks like a herd of elephants have been in there."

"I saw Lil's room," Marilyn says. "It looks terrible, but she didn't have much stolen."

"I didn't either," says Marge. "But, hell, that's not the point. Those bastards violated *my* space. Who's going to reimburse me for that?"

"They got my answering machine," Nan laments. "The PTA bought me that machine. I need that machine."

"We can get you another answering machine, Nan," Marilyn offers.

"I know," Nan says. "But I want my old machine, and I want this *not* to have happened."

Christine can't let the grieving go on any longer. "I think we need to get started. We have a hard agenda this morning." Marilyn glances across the table at Nan. She looks tired.

Christine begins. "We have three new referrals—Jewel Chute, Eli Sims, and Cody Butler. I see that none of their parents are here, so we'll listen to what their classroom teachers have to say." Parents are always invited to this meeting. It's the law. The fact that they almost never come is a source of relief to the women. "Let's begin with Jewel."

It is Corine's turn, and she has rehearsed well. "Jewel is a willful, disobedient child who, in my opinion, should not be in a regular classroom. She has very low academic skills and no motivation whatsoever to learn."

Marge jumps in. "Jewel has been spending time in my classroom for the last couple of weeks, and I am pretty sure that she's bright—maybe very bright."

"That may be, but it's not going to do her any good with her attitude and behavior," Corine rejoins.

Marilyn begins to talk to get away from the discomfort of listening to Corine. "I am concerned about Jewel's behavior. It is far outside any kind of normal range. She's very aggressive, and I don't see her forming relationships either with adults or peers." She looks at Marge for reinforcement.

"None at all. She's feral—bites, scratches, spits, yowls, and howls."

"She's got a ton of history. You want to take time for the family background, Christine?" Nan asks wearily.

"Give us a quick sketch." Nan goes over the story of Jewel's seeing her father die, the changes in schools, her mother's life.

Dolores, the psychologist, enters the conversation for the first time. "This looks like a hard one to me. We're not going to be able to find her learning disabled with that history."

"Why in the world not?" Corine asks. "She's unmanageable. Can't do a thing. Nothing."

"Can't or won't?" Nan asks Corine, noticeably irritated now.

"How should I know? I'm too busy picking up the paper and books that she's tearing up to ask myself philosophical questions. I'm not going to have that child in my class."

"I understand that she's been with Marge for the last 2 weeks," Christine says, trying to diffuse the tension.

"That's right, and she can stay with me if that's what's best," Marge says.

"We can't leave her there indefinitely, Marge," Marilyn says. "She's an illegal guest, and your kids are all a lot younger than she is."

Marilyn is nervous because she doesn't want Dolores or Connie to report back to her supervisor that Marge is taking Jewel. Christine is nervous because the meeting is veering off. "OK. Let's get back to Dolores," Christine says. "Dolores, you're saying that you don't think she'll qualify for Special Education?"

"That's not *exactly* what I was saying. There might be a discrepancy between her ability and performance based on what Marge and Corine are saying, but based on Nan's description, it sounds as if the discrepancy is environmentally induced, not the result of a learning disability." Marilyn has heard this speech a hundred times.

"Who cares, Dolores? Who the fuck cares?" Nan is almost shouting. "The kid's not learning. She's a mess. I'll guarantee you that if she doesn't get help, she's going to be a hooker by the time she's 12."

"The feds care, that's who cares," Dolores shoots back.

"I'm tired of that crap. What does it matter *why* the kid's not learning? The point is that she needs help, and she needs it now or 2 years ago or 4 years ago." Marilyn wonders if she should stop Nan. But Nan is saying what Marilyn is afraid to say, so she lets it go.

Dolores takes a deep breath and tries a new tack. "Well, why don't we try for an SED label?"

"That's just great. You want to hang a 'severely emotionally disturbed' on the kid? You think that will help? That kid's not crazy; she's making a perfectly intelligent response to her perfectly insane environment," Nan says.

Marge comes to the rescue. "Yeah, but the point is that if going SED is the only way we can get her help, we'd better take a look at it. Right?"

"If she qualifies, she'll be eligible for a self-contained classroom and for psychological and social work support, won't she?" Marilyn asks Dolores, knowing the answer as well as Nan does but wanting Nan to hear it anyway.

"Oh, good. That's good." Nan mutters. "Don't you love it when a kid can *qualify* to be SED, like getting into Harvard or something?"

"Yes, that's probably the way it would go," Dolores says, "although she *could* continue with a placement in the regular classroom with support. It would all depend."

"So what do you want to do?" Christine asks, "Go for a full evaluation—psychological, academic, medical—and see what happens?" She gets nods all around the table. She checks off the boxes on the referral form and hands it off for everyone else to sign.

"What are we going to do about her in the meantime?" Corine asks, staring right at Marilyn.

She wants me to send her home or put her on half days. I can't do that to Jewel. She'll roam the streets, Marilyn thinks.

"She can stay with me. We've been doing a little better the last few days." Marge volunteers.

"I appreciate that, Marge, but what about having her half-time with you and half-time with Corine?" Marilyn asks.

"Nope. Not a good idea," Marge says. "Jewel needs to know where she is and who her teacher is. Let me have her for one more week, and then we'll talk about it."

Marilyn agrees, glad to have the decision postponed for a few days.

"Let's go on to Eli Sims," Christine says, eager to move the meeting along. "You all know or have heard about Eli. He transferred here from Kansas and is in Harriet's class now. Harriet, did you ever get ahold of his mother to tell her about this meeting?"

"Yes. Well, not exactly. I talked to Grandmother. She told me that she'd tell his mother."

"That's the best we're going to do," Nan says. "I've never seen or talked to Mom. Only Grandma."

"Me, too," Marilyn adds. The women look at Marilyn to see if they can go ahead with this kind of flimsy approval. "I think we'll be all right."

"Harriet, I believe you talked with his teacher in Kansas," Christine prompts.

"That's right. He wasn't there for long. He had the same problems that we see—almost no reading skills and all that hyperactivity. They were able to qualify him for Special Ed—not self-contained, just regular classroom with a lot of Resource Room support—an hour or so a day. I guess he really liked his Resource Room teacher—had lunch with her and that sort of thing. But his classroom teacher said that he was totally out of control in her room. He could only manage situations with a lot of structure and consistency. Transitions made him fall apart all over the place."

"Is his file here now?" Marge asks.

"It came last week. He qualifies for the Resource Room. We can start him in there right away," Christine says.

"You know, he's a funny-looking kid," Nan muses. "Did you ever look at him? His head's real small and his features are real flat."

"You aren't thinking he's fetal alcohol, are you?" Dolores Davis asks.

"I don't know. It's a possibility."

"Well, let's get that checked out. We have a pediatrician now who does those assessments." Dolores is trying to get back onto a better footing with Nan.

"Good, Dolores," Christine says. "Let's go for it."

"Well, that's fine, but that's not what worries me most," Harriet says. "He has a hard time keeping it together. I have to put him out in the hall a lot or send him down to the office to do his work." Harriet is taking a long time to get to the point. Marilyn shifts in her chair and starts playing with her keys to forestall her impatience.

Harriet pauses again. "There's more. He's always talking about violent sex. He told La Shanda the other day he'd rape her if she didn't give him the clay. He told another girl he'd bring his knife and slit her open from her nipples to her vagina. I could tell you more stuff like that, but you get the idea." She stops and sits back in her chair, looking around at the other women, glad to have this part over.

There is silence for a moment. They all look at each other.

Marilyn puts her keys down. "Thanks, Harriet. Will you start writing these things down when he says them? Give us the dates and times so that we can get an idea of the frequency and type of comments, and under what conditions he makes them. We'll see if we can establish any patterns."

Harriet nods. She is relieved.

"And, Nan, can you get Mom or Grandma in here ASAP?" Marilyn goes on. "We need to get going on this kid."

"I'll give it a huge try," Nan says. "I'll push counseling with them, but that's probably a long shot."

"Good," Marilyn says. "Now, what about assessment? We've got the Resource Room placement. We'll go for the FAS. Do we want to look at anything else?"

"He's not going to make it in the regular classroom. I can tell you that right now," Harriet says.

"If he's not FAS, he's probably SED," Christine says. "Dolores, do you think we should look at him for both?"

"Yeah, why not?" When the paper gets to Marilyn, she looks at it a long time before she signs.

By the time Marilyn finishes signing, Christine has already opened discussion on Cody. Grace Johnson spreads out Cody's "cum" folder in front of her as she begins to talk. Those folders are our scripture, Marilyn thinks. Then she begins trying to pay attention to what Grace is saying.

"Cody Butler is in first grade. He has not been retained. This is his first year with us." So far she is following protocol. Then she looks up from the cum folder. Her hands have been folded, but now she begins to move them, palms up, from center to side and back again. She senses the futility of the facts and launches out into the subjective territory of her own impressions.

"He looks like a girl. He has fine features and long hair. I don't think he used to realize it, but now he's gotten bitter. Momma won't cut his hair. I've asked her, but she won't. She loves it. I keep telling her that he wouldn't get the lice so bad if she cut his hair. I think she wants him to be a girl. What chance does he have if Momma feels that way?"

Marilyn wonders, What chance at what? Is Grace saying that she's afraid Cody will turn out to be gay? Is that what she wants us to fix?

Grace goes on, "He wasn't too bad in the fall, but since the accident, he's gone to pieces. He's forgotten everything. Maybe things are a little better at home now. I think she's kicked out the boyfriend. He wasn't doing Cody any good, I'll tell you that. He was hitting him an awful lot. Now he's suffering terribly from ear and bronchial infections. He's been to the emergency room twice. I don't know why she keeps bringing him to school."

Marilyn pieces these details together. Grace is saying the same thing that Nan was saying about boyfriends. When was the boyfriend there? Maybe before the accident—earlier in the fall. Or maybe one has been there recently for just a few weeks. Why is Grace talking about the bronchial infections? Is she saying that Lynette is neglecting Cody? Or that his hearing is being affected? Where is this going?

Then Christine interrupts Grace, "How is Cody's work?"

"His work? His work is just awful. He can't find a line. His letters are all over the place. If you sit with him, it gets a little better. But, his eyes go every which way. Momma's like that too. His math isn't much better. He can do the 'hiding assessment' to eight. I guess he knows his math facts to 12. His pictures are just scribbles. The least little movement throws him. If it's not straight on, he can't get it. He's a stutterer. It gets worse if he sees his pop. And, of course, it's been just awful since the accident."

Grace suddenly stops talking and looks around the room. The women sit silently, trying to make sense out of Grace's outpouring. Then Christine asks, "Well, what are you recommending, Grace? Do you want an academic and a psychological?"

"I don't know. You're the experts. Just whatever we need to do to get him some help."

"We'd better get a medical, too," Marilyn says, "to rule out those bronchial infections."

The women talk about Cody for a little while, but then Harriet points out that school starts in 5 minutes. "Who's going to talk to his mother about testing him?" Christine wants to know. Marilyn and Grace look at each other.

"I'll do it," Marilyn says. "I know Lynette pretty well." The women hurriedly agree to do all three assessments, sign the referral form, and begin to gather up papers and coffee cups. The meeting has dissolved.

14

The next morning, Marilyn finds Lynette sitting with Cody at breakfast as usual. She asks her to stop by the office after she drops Cody off in class.

"You knew we discussed Cody in the Screening Committee yesterday, didn't you, Lynette? I thought you might want to come."

"Miss Johnson told me I could come, but I thought you'd know what to do. Besides, I didn't have nowhere to leave Cody that early."

"Sure, I understand," Marilyn said. She could imagine how frightening it would have been for Lynette to come into that meeting and try to hold her own against the weight of all the jargon and information. "Well, Lynette, we've recommended several assessments for Cody." Marilyn wonders if Lynette knows what *assessment* means, but she doesn't want to patronize by asking or explaining. "We'd like to find out what's going on with his school work, have him get a physical, and then do a psychological."

"Psychological? What's that about?"

"We want to find out about his social adjustment and his learning."

"You mean how smart he is?" Marilyn nods. "Yeah. That's OK. I know he's smart. Then what about the *adjustment* part? You want to know about his family and stuff?"

"That's part of it, Lynette. And what it was like when you were pregnant. About his birth. Things like that. How he feels about himself now."

"Are they going to ask me a lot of questions?"

"Yes. I'm sure they will."

"You know, it's always been me and him. Just the two of us. I had it real bad when I was young." Lynette has begun to tell the story that she imagines she'll be asked to tell. "My dad kicked me out when I was real young—15. I thought I did, but I didn't know nothin'. I ended up on the streets real fast. Before I knew it, I was into drugs pretty bad. I lived like that for a year. Then I met Norman. He's Cody's dad. But he don't come around much.

"We had it nice for awhile. Just me and him. We lived in a little apartment. He didn't ask me to work or nothin'. I just stayed around the apartment, kept it picked up, cooked. You know. Norman didn't do drugs, so I didn't neither. Things was nice. Then I got pregnant. You wouldn't believe how happy I was. I could just imagine it—me and Norman and the baby. You know, it was funny, but I always thought I'd have a girl. I was going to call her Angel. I imagined all about her, how I'd take her to the store and all the old ladies would tell me how cute she was and stuff.

"I was going to tell Norman about the baby when he was feeling good and loving me. Then I got sick—real sick. I just barfed and barfed. One night I'd barfed for about the sixth time, and he started to yell at me, wanted to know what was wrong. I blurted it out—'I'm pregnant!' I was kind of screaming and crying. He just looked at me real slow, and then—'POW! POW!' He hit me hard, first on one cheek and then on the other. I about passed out. But at least I forgot for a minute how bad I felt.

"That was about the end of him and me. He wasn't even there when I started to have Cody. I had to go next door to get the old lady to help me. She was nice, called the hospital and stuff. I had such a bad labor. I didn't know anything could hurt like that did. I really, truly wanted to die.

"Then it was a big surprise that Cody was a boy. Cody. That was Norman's idea, so I thought, fine. Maybe if he gives him his name he'll like him. It didn't do no good though. Cody was an awful hard baby—had the colic. Just cried and cried. Stiffened up his little body and cried like he was pushing me and the whole world away from him. Well, Norman couldn't stand it. He just never came back to the apartment no more. I knew he'd gone for good when he took his hunting knife with the silver and turquoise handle. Then I knew it was just Cody and me."

"And you've been alone ever since?"

"Well, mostly. Sometimes I get a boyfriend, and he hangs around for awhile. But an awful lot of guys don't like kids. Or they're mean. Or they just want me to support them. It don't never seem to work out." Lynette pauses. "I suppose you think that's bad for Cody."

"I'm sure it's hard for both of you, Lynette."

"You think I'm doing all right by Cody? I'd die for him. I really would."

"I know how much you love him, Lynette. I know that you want what's best for him. Let's just see what these assessments tell us so that we can all work together for him."

"Sure. You bet," Lynette says, but Marilyn can sense the anxiety. Lynette is worried about the fate that she'll suffer at the hands of all these "good women" who are going to poke and pry into her life.

Late in the same morning, Nan comes in to tell Marilyn that she has talked to Eli's grandmother. "She was as evasive as hell. Sort of said that she'd come in to talk about Eli, but I don't think she means it. If she doesn't come by tomorrow, I'm going over there."

Friday morning Harriet brings a note down from Eli's grandmother to show Marilyn. "Please send Eli's things home with him. He goes to another school on Monday."

"What do you think?" Harriet asks.

Just then Nan walks in. Marilyn hands her the note. "I'm going over there. I want to talk to that woman face-to-face."

Nan is back in a few minutes. "Yup, they're pulling him out."

"What's going on?" Marilyn asks.

"The usual. We put the heat on, so she's going to put him in the school where his mom's living until they put the heat on."

"Did she say what school?"

"Yeah, Webster."

"OK. I'll call over there so they can be ready. At least they won't have to waste all the time we did."

Right after school is out, Marilyn is standing behind the counter negotiating with Stephanie about whether it's OK for her to call Jolene to pick her up. Stephanie's excuse is flimsy—"I got too much stuff to carry," she whines. Both Stephanie and Marilyn know, though, that Marilyn can't win on this one. Jolene wants Stephanie to have special privileges, and Marilyn doesn't want to alienate the PTA president, so she reluctantly gives in one more time. She can feel Rose's disapproval at her back as she pushes the phone across the counter for Stephanie to use. "Make it quick, honey. A lot of people want to use the phone right now." Stephanie nods in agreement as she dials her number.

Marilyn turns away from the phone and sees Eli standing at the end of the counter. He is holding a paper bag almost as big as he is. It is spilling over with art projects, his lunchbox, school supplies, math and spelling papers.

"I came to say good-by."

Marilyn leans across the counter and puts her hand over his small, dirty hand. "I heard that this was your last day, Eli. I'm sorry. We're going to miss you. A lot."

"I'm going to miss you."

"You'll like Webster School. I know some of the teachers there. They're nice."

"Nan and Mrs. Fletcher told me that, too. Everybody but me knows somebody there. But I don't think I'll like it anyway."

"Are you worried about what it will be like, Eli?"

Eli slowly wags his head up and down, looking Marilyn straight in the eye.

"Can you feel the worry in your stomach?" Marilyn asks.

Eli nods again.

"I know it's tough," Marilyn says.

"Could you come around here for a minute?" he asks.

"Sure," she says as she comes out the swinging door and around the corner of the counter.

Eli drops his paper bag, and its contents spill on the floor between them. He wades through the egg cartons, popsicle sticks, and papers to throw himself at Marilyn. "I'll *really* miss you!"

She holds him tightly for a couple of seconds. "I'll miss you too, Eli." She can make no promises or pledges; she can't even say that she'll always remember him. She knows how quickly the children's names and faces fade.

Harriet checks out a half an hour later. "Well, we really lucked out on Eli Sims. Whatever you and Nan did, thanks for getting him out of here. We can let Webster figure out to do with him—if he stays there long enough."

When the building falls quiet, Marilyn walks down to Jane's room. She talks about odds and ends for awhile and then stops. She sits turning her keys over in her hands. "What's the matter, Marilyn?" Jane asks.

"Oh, I don't know. Just thinking about Eli Sims. You know him?"

"That crazy little guy in Harriet's room?"

"That's the guy. Well, we lost him today. We had him all set up to get some help. Dolores was even willing to recommend that he get screening for FAS. As soon as his grandmother and mother got wind of what we were trying to do, they pulled him out. I hate it when we lose a child like that."

"You can't help it, Marilyn. You've got to stop carrying those kids around all the time."

Marilyn shrugs and gives Jane a lame smile. "Look who's talking."

"Before we do anything else, I want updates on Jewel and Cody. It's been a month now, and we still don't have anything on them." Marilyn has come into the Screening Committee meeting in a bad mood and, without having made a conscious decision, intends to run things. She moves her keys back and forth from one hand to the other. All the women sit looking at the papers in front of them, waiting to see what's next.

"Dolores, have your people finished testing Jewel?"

Dolores shuffles her papers trying to buy some time. "Well, let's see." She can't find the papers she needs, so she tries to explain. "You know this isn't my only school. I have three others. I'm trying to handle 15 kids right now. It's hard to remember where they all are with their testing."

Marilyn doesn't say anything. No smile, no forgiving nod. No one else talks either. Finally, Dolores comes up with the right piece of paper. "Here it is. We're all done with the psychological and the academic. We're waiting now for the medical."

"For the medical," Marilyn says. "OK, where are you with that? Has the appointment been made?" Dolores turns to Connie Stanley, the social worker, who is sitting beside her. "Can you fill us in on that, Connie?"

Connie moves uncomfortably in her chair. "Well, I've scheduled two or three appointments for her, but Mom never gets her there. "

"Have you tried taking the forms to her?" Marilyn is pushing hard now.

"No."

"Have you suggested that you will drive Jewel and her mother to the appointment?"

"No."

"Why not?"

"I've got as big a caseload as Dolores. I don't have . . ."

Marilyn runs over Dolores. "Well, you'd better find the time. That's the only way we're going to get results. You're spending more time making phone calls and rescheduling appointments than it would take you to pick up Jewel and take her to the doctor yourself."

"You know, I really don't feel comfortable going into that home alone. I've heard it's pretty awful. I guess they've got a pit bull." Connie says, showing just a tinge of anger.

Oh, boy, Marilyn thinks. Here we go. Now she's going to say that I'm endangering her. "Nan, can you go along with Connie to do this home visit?"

"Sure thing," Nan says.

Nan isn't afraid of anything. She'll shame Connie into making the visit. But now Marilyn is even angrier. Why should she have to use her own staff to help the Special Ed people get their work done? "I want to hear next week that Jewel has her medical and that we're ready to look at placement. Now, let's talk about Cody."

"Marilyn, you're not going to like this, but the last report we need on Cody is from the speech pathologist, and Diane's been out for a week with the flu. We can't go ahead without speech path on this one because his language is such a big question," Christine says as quietly and as carefully as she can.

Marilyn knows when she's been beaten. "OK. We'll start out with these two again next week, and by then I want something definite. Let's call it quits for this morning." She gets up and walks out of the room, leaving the the women to cluck.

The next meeting begins right on time. "Dolores, what's the latest on Jewel?" Christine asks.

Connie answers the question. "She's gone." All the women look at her.

"Yup. That's right," Nan says. "Connie and I went over to where they were living—just an old trailer parked in the mud— and it was empty. They're gone."

Marilyn had heard the news the Friday before. When Jewel was still absent on Monday, Marilyn called Pam McBride. "Pam, Jewel Chute hasn't shown up, has she?"

"Gosh, no, I don't think so. If she'd come back, I would have heard about it. Can I put you on hold for a minute?"

Pam came back on the line. "No. No one has seen her."

"Looks like they've picked up and moved. Listen, if she shows up, we've done all the screening on her for SED except for the medical. Let us know right away, and we can hand off the paperwork to your people. But it may be months before she shows up anywhere."

"That's right. We'll let you know if we see her. Are you going to let Children's Services know?"

"Will do, but they won't do anything until she's good and missing."

"I know."

"Well, hang in there. If you get Jewel back, you can send us one of your hard ones."

"It's a deal."

The women on the Screening Committee are discouraged. "I don't know what to do next," Connie says. "All that work for nothing."

"We've done all we can do for now," Marilyn says.

"Let's go on to Cody," Christine says. "Good to see you back, Diane. Are you feeling better?"

"Much better, thanks. Cody has a language deficiency all right. As you all know, his stuttering is severe and he's below normal in both receptive and expressive language. I'll be able to add him right away."

"How much service can you give him?" Marilyn asks.

"I can see him three times a week for 15 minutes."

"Do you think that will be enough?" Marge wants to know.

"No, but it's a start. I'm seeing 60 children right now. But we'll monitor him to see what happens and look at him again for academics next fall. He may be far enough behind by then to qualify for Resource Room support."

Marilyn feels the knot in her stomach tighten. Three months have passed; Cody has gotten worse and worse, and all that anyone can offer is 45 minutes of speech a week. She closes her eyes and tries to imagine the years ahead for Cody. This is malpractice, she thinks.

"Marilyn?" Christine is talking to her. "Marilyn, are we ready to move on? We have four more students to discuss this morning."

"Yes? Oh, . . . sure. Let's go on."

Christine starts in. Marilyn has lost interest in running the meeting. Eli's gone. Jewel's gone. Cody will probably be gone by next year. How can we hold them? How can we keep this from happening?

She has no answers.

IV
Amy:
Pain That
Never Goes Away

15

Where's my picture? I saw you take my picture. Put my picture up next. Pleease," Sylvia teases.

"I'm coming to yours. Just hang on while I finish putting up this one of Joey and Miss Hamilton." It's breakfast time, and Marilyn is stapling photos on the bulletin board just outside the cafeteria. Sylvia and five or six other children crowd around. Marilyn pumps the last staple into a picture of Joey giving Rachel Hamilton a bouquet of yellow daisies and purple statice after the Winter Program. Rachel's face is radiant from the pleasure of a good performance and the relief of having the weeks of planning and rehearsal over. Ten years from now, music programs will run together in her memory, but the thrill of this fine first one will always linger to remind her of why she loves to teach.

"Where shall we put this?" This shot is a close-up of Sylvia and her best friend. Sylvia points to an empty space on the bulletin board, and Marilyn positions the photo. She takes four or five rolls of film a month with her point-and-shoot camera and uses them all—good and bad. When she tried to do the same thing at Lincoln, children stole them, scratched out faces of classmates, and inked in moustaches. At Madison the children study the photos—carefully, thoughtfully, over and over.

Marge explained the contrast: "The pictures give the children memory. So little in their lives is commemorated—Christmases, birthdays, Sundays, paydays. These remembrances help them construct their past." The children often ask Marilyn to photograph them, and Marilyn learned always to say "yes" the day Cory tugged on her sleeve. "Please take my picture with my little sister. She's in first grade. Nobody ever took our picture before."

After she finishes putting up Sylvia's picture, she puts up one of Lacey and her father. Marilyn aimed her camera at them as they walked down the hall at the end of the program. They stopped and put on smiles for her. "Hi, Lacey. Is this your dad?" She nodded. "Hi.

I'm Marilyn, Lacey's principal. She brought in her book for me to read the other day. She's quite a fine little reader."

"Yeah. You bet. Seems like she takes to it." He hesitated, then risked a question: "Do you think she's doing all right in school?"

"Oh, very well."

"Well, I worry. It's just me and her, you know, so I worry that I don't do right by her. She has to be alone a lot. I work swing. I leave her dinner for her and tell her to be sure to read. Not just watch TV. She knows to lock the door and to leave the answering machine on."

"Her mother . . . ?" Marilyn started to ask.

"She left us when Lacey was a baby. She don't like kids. It's been 5 years now, so I guess she's gone. Sometimes I wish I could meet someone, but it just don't work out. I've got a lot to do, you know. And then I can't go out working the hours I do. The money. After I get through taking care of expenses and buying Lacey the clothes she needs, I'm about broke." Marilyn has often noticed Lacey's pretty dresses and coordinated knit pants and T-shirts. "Then I try to save some each month. Not much—$25. But I want Lacey to have a little college fund. As smart as she is, I figure she'll want to go to college."

As Marilyn finishes putting up the photo of Lacey and her dad, she thinks that she could use a school full of Mr. Sorensons.

The bell rings, and the children swarm out of the cafeteria. She stands among them, encouraging them down the long hall. Teacher after teacher turns into her classroom after the last child, pulling the door behind her with habitual precision. The hush that settles over the school belies the reality that more than 500 human beings are contained in its space. This is the time of day when Marilyn has a chance to gather her thoughts. She goes into the workroom, pours a cup of coffee, and then walks back into her office to finish the teacher observation schedule. Every year she vows both privately and publicly that she will get underway with observations by the middle of October, and every year it takes her until late winter to get started.

She is absorbed with writing in names and times on her calendar when Nan comes in and flops down. "We need to start doing head lice sweeps every week."

Marilyn puts her pencil down with a reluctant sigh. "You sure?"

"It's really getting bad; there are kids in every room just alive with them."

"Will it do any good to check?"

"Oh, sure. If the parents get the idea that we're checking, they'll clean up the kids—most of them will anyway."

"OK. How do you want to do it?"

"Let's do the checks on Tuesday mornings when the nurse is here. I can go through the rooms and send the suspicious ones down to her for a double check." The nurse's name is Irene, but she is here only once a week, and, since a different nurse is assigned to the school every year, no one is in the habit of calling her by her first name.

"I don't think the nurse likes to do head checks," Marilyn comments.

"Naw, she hates it, but that's what she gets paid to do."

"You know she'll only go through the motions. Parents are going to get mad when we exclude kids. It's just not that easy, Nan." The reality of the project is giving Marilyn second thoughts.

"It'll be worse if the lice get totally out of control. We just gotta do it, Marilyn."

She knows Nan is right, but she also feels her chances to get her observations done slipping away.

"We can give it a try." Marilyn picks up her calender, erases two observation times, and writes "head lice check" instead. "This is why I never write in ink."

"If you take kids home, be sure you put some paper over the headrest in your car. Better take along a can of spray, too."

Marilyn laughs. "I thought it was so cold in the car these days that they'd die. You're always telling the parents that hot and cold kills them."

Nan doesn't see anything funny. "I know, but you want to be careful anyway. I got them once, and it was awful."

By 9:30 Tuesday morning, Nan has worked through two class-rooms and has sent down enough children to take up all the waiting chairs. The nurse is checking children in the workroom as fast as she can. Marilyn signs exclusion letters. Rose calls parents of children who are "active" to explain. She is also trying to keep up with the attendance sheets that students are bringing in, get the lunch count to Florence, and distribute the morning mail.

Marilyn sees Rose is swamped, so she takes over the telephoning and tells Rose to wait on the mail. Even so, they can't keep up. Amy and Stuart and his two big brothers, as well as a couple children Marilyn doesn't know, are waiting to go home. Not having anything to do, they're getting bored and feeling humiliated and angry as people come in and out of the office and notice them sitting there. They start to horse around, and every once in awhile, Rose yells, "Hey! You kids settle down right now!" After the third time Rose tries to quiet them, Marilyn puts down the phone and goes out to size up the situation. "What do we have, Rose?"

"A mess. Amy's mother said she'd get here when she could; April doesn't have a phone, so someone will have to take her home." Marilyn knows that the "someone" is her. "Stuart's mother's got the phone unplugged again. She sleeps days."

"OK. I'll get going on them." Marilyn talks with the children for a little while, asks them how they're feeling about things and if they think their parents can get them treated today so they can come back tomorrow.

By 10:00 the situation is worse. Amy and Stuart and his brothers are still waiting, and Nan has sent down four more to be checked. Three other children have the flu. Great, Marilyn thinks. All we need is for someone to throw up in the middle of this. She establishes an emergency infirmary out in the hall, gets chairs for the children, and stations a wastebasket beside each of them. She figures that the sick children are feeling too miserable to run around or make much noise, so they can be safely relegated to the hall, but the head lice children had better stay in the office where Rose can keep her eye on them.

"Call down and tell Nan to stop checking for awhile. We've got to get some of these kids cleared out of here. She can start again in 20 minutes," Marilyn snaps at Rose as she comes back into the office.

"Will do," Rose says, glad for the chance to have a break.

Marilyn begins calling again. She has just picked up the phone when she hears Candy Jenkins in the outer office. "I want to see that principal *right* now! I've had it with you people. I've just had it!"

Marilyn puts down the phone, takes a deep breath, and goes out to the front desk. "Hi, Candy. Come on in. Let's talk."

"You're goddamn right we're gonna talk. What's the matter with you people? Why can't you keep this goddamn school clean?"

Marilyn sits down and motions for Candy to do the same. Candy doesn't like the idea, but she is tired and the chair looks good to her.

"I'm sorry, Candy. I know this is hard on you."

"It's not *us*. You know that, and I know that. Our house is clean," Candy insists.

"I know you really work at keeping the lice down. But Amy is still showing up with it. We've got to get her cleaned up, Candy. This is too hard on you and on her. I'm really worried. She's missing so much school."

"It's your fault. You keep sending her home. I just about died when you guys called this morning." Candy's voice ebbs, and her body sags.

"Are you having it rough, Candy?"

Candy invites back her anger. "Yeah, I'm having it *rough*. My old man's going down for the count."

"What do you mean?"

"What do you think I mean?" Candy snaps. "He's still using so he came up positive on his U.A. His parole officer is about ready to send him back, and I'm going to have this baby in a week."

Marilyn can't believe it. Candy barely looks pregnant—5 months at the most.

Marilyn shakes her head. "Wow. Well, look, Candy, you need to get this lice problem cleared up before your baby comes."

"Yeah, I know," Candy says, "but *how*? I don't have money for that medicine. Do you know how much that stuff costs? I've bagged up all the clothes and stuff in the house, but they come back. I don't know what I'm going to do."

Marilyn can't imagine what Candy will do either, and she hates herself as she blandly asks the impossible. If we really wanted to help, she thinks, we would have shampoo here and someone who could wash Amy's hair and give her a shower, too. We'd have someone who could help clean up the house. Instead, we put it all back on Candy.

She goes over, unlocks her closet, and fumbles around trying to get money out of her leather purse. Finally, she turns back to Candy and hands her a 20-dollar bill. "Here. This will at least get you some shampoo and rinse."

Candy doesn't like being on the receiving end of this handout, and she doesn't like having the responsibility for the lice thrust back on her through bumbling charity. But she's not about to walk away from 20 dollars. "I'll see what I can do, but you guys better do something about your problem, too." As Candy leaves the office, she nods to Amy, "Come on, babe. We gotta get you cleaned up."

Marilyn is glad to get back to dealing with the remaining children so that she can shake off Candy's unmistakable and well-founded disapproval. The five who are left are ones whose parents can't or won't pick them up. Marilyn doesn't have much choice. Either she lets them sit in the office for the rest of the day, or she starts taking them home. Her job is made a little easier because they all live in the same apartment complex. Even so, it takes quite awhile to rouse Stuart's mother. By the time Marilyn finishes her last trip, it is lunchtime. Richard, who is in Marge's class, is sitting at a little table in front of the office with a lunch in front of him.

"Principal, I think I'm about to throw up." Marilyn smiles at the little boy's impeccable syntax.

"That doesn't sound like much fun. Your stomach hurting?"

"Uh-huh. Teacher says I might got the flu."

"Do you feel like eating any of your lunch?"

"Nope. But Teacher says 'try.' It might make me feel better."

"Have you tried?"

"Nope. My stomach keeps on telling me not to."

"I think you're smart to listen to your stomach, Richard. What are we going to do about you?"

"I don't know. Nobody's at home. My grandma lives too far away. She'd have to come on a bus to get me, and she's old."

Richard has it right. Rose has talked to his mother.

Marilyn tries to figure out what to do with Richard. Marilyn checks and finds out that someone is already on the nurse's cot, so she goes into the staff room to find Marge.

"We can't get Richard home. If I can run down a mat and a blanket, can you bed him down in the back of your classroom?" Marilyn asks. Estelle, Harriet, and Corine are sitting at a nearby table, and Marilyn can feel their disapproval as she asks the question.

"Yeah," Marge says reluctantly, "I guess we can take him. Sure hope he isn't contagious."

"I don't know if he is or not, Marge, but by the way the kids are dropping today, I think everyone's contagious. Between lice and flu, we'll have half the school out by Friday."

Nan brings her salad over and sits down. "That's right, and we have Exclusion Day coming up on Thursday."

"Oh, you're *right*. I'd forgotten about that," Marilyn groans. "Why in the world did we decide to do a head lice sweep during the same week?"

"How many kids do you figure you'll exclude?" Marge asks.

"Probably 20 or so," Marilyn says. "It's a huge hassle. Some of the parents say the children have had their shots but that they can't find the records; some of them don't know whether the children have had the shots or not, especially if there's been a custody change. They don't know where to go to get the shots, and, of course, the nurse isn't here to answer any of their questions."

"We might as well close school Friday and give ourselves a 3-day weekend," Nan offers.

"Hey, gang! Nan's just made a motion. No school on Friday!" Marge shouts.

Mr. Schneider comes into the staff room amid all the "Hear! Hears!" Since he usually eats lunch in his room so as not to have to endure the women's gossip, the fun stops short while everyone watches to see what he wants. He walks up to Marilyn and drops something from his closed fist into her hand. "Nathan's sitting in the office. You can take it from here."

A ring with a small, light green stone set in thin gold filigree lies in Marilyn's palm. She turns it over. Its thread-like band is broken. She looks at Mr. Schneider, waiting to hear the story. "I took it away from Nathan. He was showing it to the girls like it was some big deal. I don't know where he got it, but I don't want him to have it. He's got the girls going so much I couldn't get any of them settled down to work on their presidents' reports. Some of them haven't done a solitary thing. This is their major grade for the quarter, and they don't even care." Mr. Schneider has been assigning the same reports for more than 30 years, first to eighth graders who might have been able to get something from them and now to fifth graders for whom they almost certainly have no point.

"Do you know whose ring it is?" she asks.

Mr. Schneider shakes his head. "Don't have any idea. That's your department."

Nathan is glaring at Rose who is doing her best to ignore him. When she sees Marilyn, Rose says loud enough for Nathan and everyone else in the office to hear, "Boy, does that kid have a mouth on him. If you ask me, he should be sent home."

Marilyn sits down beside Nathan. "Nathan, Mr. Schneider gave me a ring he said you were showing to the girls." Nathan stares straight ahead.

Marilyn looks at him for a moment or two, then asks, "Nathan, have you eaten yet?" He shakes his head. "Well, we need to talk about this ring, but I want you to eat first. OK?" Nathan nods. "I'll go into the cafeteria with you and tell Florence what the deal is. Then, I'm going to call your mom and ask her what she knows about the ring." Nathan gives her a sharp stare, and she knows she has the screws in good and tight.

"Mona? Mr. Schneider gave me a ring Nathan apparently brought to school—a gold ring with a green stone."

"My emerald. My emerald. Did that kid steal my emerald? I'll be right down. I'm coming down there and get that kid. Boy, when I'm done with him, he won't know what hit him."

"Mona. Mona, let's talk about . . . ," Marilyn urges to a dial tone.

When Mona comes through the front door, Marilyn is waiting for her. "Where is he? Where is that rotten kid? You know what? You know what?" Mona is dancing up and down on the balls of her feet, dragging her hands down from her cheekbones to her chin hard enough to leave long red marks. "He stole my diamond earrings, too. My diamond earrings! They were half a carat. I'm not kidding—*half a carat!*" Marilyn remembers the earrings. She's sure they're not diamonds.

Marilyn tries again. "Mona, come on in and sit down. Let's talk for a minute before . . . ," but Mona sees Nathan through the open cafeteria doors and heads toward him. She hauls him up from the table and pulls him across the cafeteria into the hall. Marilyn follows the pair, trying to calm Mona. The 200 children who are eating lunch have stopped talking.

Mona shoves Nathan across the hall, and Marilyn moves around them to lead the way into the office. Mona pushes Nathan into a chair. "Where are my diamond earrings?" Nathan looks directly at her, eyes narrowed and nostrils flared. He says nothing. "Where are they?" Mona demands. Marilyn is convinced that if she weren't standing there, Mona would be hitting Nathan. Mona looks around in her frustration, wildly searching for a threat big enough to force the truth. Then she finds her inspiration. "If you don't tell me where my diamond earrings are, I'll cut off your tail. You creep, I mean it."

Nathan reaches around to the curl of dark hair at the nape of his neck and fingers it protectively. He weighs the odds and decides to keep his silence; he is frightened but not ready to give in.

"Are you going to tell me?" Mona screams. Nathan does not answer. "Well, that does it. We're going home, and you'll be sorry!"

Marilyn tries to intercede. "Mona, let's have you and Nathan and Nan talk about this."

"No way. This kid has had enough talking."

"Mona, Mona, be careful . . ."

"Don't you lecture me. He's my kid. You know," Mona turns to Nathan, "I have a good mind to give you to the state, just give you away. That's what *they* want me to do. Is that what *you* want me to do?" Nathan watches his mother. "Well, come on. Get up. We're leaving," she says to him. To Marilyn, "Don't worry, I'm not going to hit him. I should beat the shit out of him, but I'm not. I'll get it out of him, though."

Marilyn watches them leave and then goes in to the staff room to eat her yogurt. When she gets back to her office, there is a phone message from Pam McBride. She's glad to return the call. "Hi, Pam. What's up?"

"I thought you'd like to know that Jewel showed up this morning."

"She did? Boy, am I glad she's surfaced. Where she's been?"

"Don't know. She just said, 'Helping my mom.'"

"How does she seem?"

"About the same. Maybe a little more ratty. She's still off the wall. Didn't you tell me that you'd done the screening on her?"

"You bet. She just needs a medical, and then she should be eligible for a self-contained classroom. You want me to have Dolores Davis, the psychologist, call you? She was managing the case."

"That would be great. She's only going to last in the regular classroom a few days."

"That's right," Marilyn agrees. "Pam? Are things crazy for you, or is it just me?"

"Oh, God, no. It's so crazy I can't even talk about it. I've got this mother coming into the school all the time. She's paranoid-schizo.

Threatens everyone. Walks right into the middle of the cafeteria full of kids. Starts yelling and screaming. She's the kind that would turn violent in nothing flat. Has a history of carrying a gun. I spend about all my time just trying to deal with her."

"Can't you get a restraining order?"

"We've got one, but she comes anyway. It's just that I never know what she'll do before the police get here. You know, I'm about to the point that I think we need security guards."

"I know. It's just that that would be so awful for the children."

"Sure it would. But so's this. Anyway, I haven't done a single observation yet this year."

"Me, either," Marilyn confesses. "It's making me sick. I'm all tied up in knots. I can't get any of my work done—no observations, no curriculum, nothing we're supposed to be doing. This 'instructional leader' stuff is just so much garbage." They talk a little longer and agree to get together soon without setting a date.

Marilyn hangs up and sits thinking about Jewel. This is not going to work. She'll disappear.

After school, Nan comes in to talk for awhile. "Do your feet hurt?" Marilyn asks.

"You said it! And I want a cigarette worse than usual." Nan has been trying to quit smoking for the last couple of months. "I know it was a hard day, Marilyn, but I think we did a pretty good job, considering. We can do the lice gig better next week if we pace ourselves."

"Yeah, that will help a lot. You're really sure that we have to do it every week?" Marilyn would still like to find a way out if she could.

"It won't be so bad after today. The parents will get the message that we mean business. In a funny way, they'll appreciate it." Marilyn looks doubtful.

"Really. It'll get better," Nan says, watching Marilyn carefully. She's afraid that Marilyn is going to veto the whole scheme if they have another day like this one.

16

Marilyn gets to work early the next morning determined to finish the observation schedule and catch up on some other work before the day gets underway. She has been at her desk nearly an hour when Florence comes in with a cup of coffee and some cinnamon toast. "Here you go, boss. You didn't come in to get any breakfast, and I thought you might be hungry."

"Thanks, Florence."

"Say, would you do me a favor? Could you talk to Nathan? He's giving me tickets that don't have our numbers on them. He must've stole them from a middle school kid or something."

"I'll try, Florence, but it may take me a couple of days to get to it. Right now I'm dealing with him on something else, and he's pretty upset. I don't think I'll get anywhere with the lunch tickets until I work through the other problem."

"OK, boss, you know what's best. But I don't think kids should go around stealing." Marilyn winces at insinuations that because she doesn't act swiftly and surely, she condones every sort of petty offense.

Rose settles at her desk. Teachers are beginning to check in, and the phone has begun to ring. A child is crying in the outer office. The crying turns into sobs, and then a long wail. Marilyn finishes a note to Susan confirming an observation for 9:30 and goes out to see what the crying is about.

Amy is standing by the window, and Rose is beside her holding a tongue depressor in each hand. When Amy sees Marilyn, she begins to cry harder.

"She's still got nits. Not many, but they're sure there—down along her neck. I just told her that she needs to go back home so that Candy can comb them out for her," Rose explains.

Marilyn gets the picture. "It's OK, sweetie. You and your mom have done a good job of getting rid of the live bugs, but you still have some of the little nits. Do you know why you have to get them out, too?" Amy is crying too hard to answer. "They'll turn into live bugs, and then you'll be right back where you started. You can come back tomorrow." Amy's crying has not slowed. "Amy, what is it? What's wrong, honey?" Amy's sobs subside into long shudders.

"Nan was going to take me shopping today," she wails, and her sobbing begins all over.

The pieces fall into place. Every month the Fire Department buys new clothes for one child, and today Amy was going to get to go shopping with Nan to pick out an outfit. To Amy's way of thinking, if she doesn't go today, she will lose her chance. Even Rose understands how much the shopping trip matters. "They really aren't too bad," she intercedes.

"Come on, Amy, let me take a look." Marilyn puts her arm around Amy's shoulder and steers her toward the workroom. "Put your head down, honey." Marilyn parts Amy's shining hair and begins to look for nits. "You and your mom really worked hard on your hair, didn't you?" Amy nods. "Your hair looks just beautiful."

Marilyn strips off the nits one by one. Amy stands perfectly still. The silence grows between them. The phone rings, and Marilyn hears Rose say, "She can't come to the phone right now. She's with a child. Can she call you back?"

Finally, Marilyn says, "Rose was right. I think we can let you stay." She goes on working while Amy submits to her small ordeal. Then, very softly, Amy says, "I love you."

"I love you, too, Amy," Marilyn says.

They begin to talk a little. "How did Eddie do in class yesterday?" Marilyn asks.

"OK. He didn't get mad very much."

"I wonder why Eddie gets so mad."

"I don't know," Amy muses. "I guess it's because the kids make fun of him. They make fun of me, too. They call me 'scabie legs.' But I don't have scabies. I'm allergic to flea bites."

"Do you have a cat?"

"Uh-huh."

"I have a cat, too. Do you like cats?"

"A lot. I don't care if the fleas bite me, but I wish I wasn't allergic. My legs look so bad."

Marilyn finishes up. "There you go!"

As Marilyn follows Amy out of the workroom, Rose says, "Mona and Nathan are here to see you," and leans her head toward the waiting chairs. Marilyn stares in shock. Nathan is completely bald. Mona has exacted her punishment by shaving his head. Marilyn has no words, but she doesn't need them. Mona sees her, stands up, jerks Nathan to a standing position, and strides into Marilyn's office.

"He won't tell me what he did with my diamond earrings. I cut off his tail, and he still wouldn't tell me. So I shaved his head. And he still won't talk. But I didn't hit him. Isn't that right?" Nathan looks at her with narrowed eyes. "*Tell* the principal. Tell her I didn't hit you!"

Without taking his eyes off Mona, Nathan gives the smallest shake of his head. Marilyn wonders if shaving a child's head constitutes abuse. No, probably not. Not physical abuse, anyway. Emotional? Very likely, but it would take more evidence than she sees today to establish it. "Do you and Nathan have an appointment with your counselor this week?"

"Yeah. Tomorrow. I don't know if I can make it, though. I might be busy."

"You make it, Mona," Marilyn says in a steely monotone. Mona looks at Marilyn sharply, feeling the surprise of the other woman's anger.

"Yeah, OK. We'll go."

Marilyn pushes her point. "I'm going to call Children's Services tomorrow just to be sure you showed up." Then she eases up. "I'll take Nathan down to Mr. Schneider, Mona. You can go on home."

Mona is relieved to feel the tension pass. "OK. That'd be fine. You let me know if you find out anything about my diamond earrings, though."

"I will," Marilyn says as Mona leaves.

Marilyn turns to Nathan. "How do you feel about going to class today?"

"They're going to laugh at me."

"Would you like to wear a cap?" Marilyn offers.

"That'd be OK."

Marilyn rummages around in her closet until she finds an old Oakland As cap that she took away from a fifth grader last year. He didn't come back to claim it, and she forgot to return it. "Here, you can borrow this cap. Do you like the As?" Nathan shrugs. He isn't a sports fan, but he seems glad enough to put on the cap.

"Let's take a detour through the workroom. There's a mirror in there. You can see how you look."

He looks in the mirror for a long time. On the way down to class, Marilyn asks about the earrings, but Nathan intends to guard this secret. She wonders how many other secrets he holds and how much bigger they will grow as he gets older.

Half an hour later, Marilyn stops at Rose's desk. "I'll be observing in Susan's room until 10:00, maybe 10:15." Marilyn goes into the first-grade classroom quietly and takes a child's chair toward the back of the room. The children sit cross-legged in rows of semicircles around Susan, who is sitting in a teacher's chair pointing to letters on a large chart beside her. She glances up at Marilyn but gives no other sign of acknowledgment. "This is a *c* day." Susan's voice is tense, loud, and pitched at midrange for endurance. She points to *c* on the chart and calls out, "All right, everybody, say with me, c-c-c." She makes a rapid panting sound from the back of her throat. She's working on hard *c* at the moment.

The children chorus "c-c-c" with Susan.

"Again!" Susan orders, "This time alone."

"C-c-c," the children repeat in ragged unison.

"Again!"

"C-c-c."

"Good. Now, let's say these words." She points to *can* and pronounces each of its sounds with long, exaggerated emphasis. "C - a - n. Say *c - a - n* with me."

The children repeat the word, then they say it alone, just as before.

"All right, class, let's put *can* in a sentence. Would you like to do that?"

The children give her a practiced "yes."

She points to *can*. "The girl *can* ride a bike. All right, class, let's all say this sentence together." The children say, "The girl *can* ride a bike" with Susan and then repeat the sentence by themselves. Susan has finished with *can*. She moves on to *cat, car,* and *cake.* Her voice gets louder and higher and more tense. She doesn't smile at the children; she doesn't look at them.

Marilyn thinks, why didn't she use *caw*? Caw. Caw. Listen to the teacher caw. Marilyn scribbles on her yellow tablet, taking a rough verbatim of the lesson. As she goes along, she makes hard, fast arrows in the margin to remind herself of questions that she wants to ask Susan later. Why don't you look at the children? Why don't you ask them to help think of words? Why do you only have them work in unison? Why don't you ask them to say the words to each other, to whisper and then shout them, to volunteer them? You don't know who's getting them and who's not. Why don't you use the children's names in the sentences instead of saying "the girl"? Why don't you let *them* think of the sentences? Let them into the lesson, Susan, let them in.

But Marilyn will not ask these questions or say any of these things in their follow-up conference. Instead, she will compliment Susan on putting the words into the context of sentences for the children, and she might, very tentatively, ask, "What would it be like if you asked the children to think of some of the sentences using their own words?" She can predict what Susan will say, "Oh, that would take too long. I wouldn't get through my lesson if I waited for them to come up with sentences."

And Susan does indeed have a long lesson. After hard *c*, she takes up a digraph and introduces *chair, chew,* and *check.* As Susan takes the children through their paces on *check,* Danny waves his hand wildly. Susan ignores him. He can't be brushed off. "Mrs. Parrish. Mrs. Parrish!"

"What is it, Danny? What do you want?"

"Mrs. Parrish, how about the *c* at the back of that word? What kind of sound does it make?"

"We're not talking about the ends of words today, Danny. You know that."

Marilyn makes two angry arrows in her margin. Susan is now ready to take up *c*s with the *s* sound—*circle, cent, city.* Marilyn makes another arrow. Why did Susan sandwich in a digraph? Then she scribbles through her arrow. Why raise a point like this one when there are so many other more serious problems with the lesson?

To get away from the misery *c,* Marilyn begins to look around the room. The bulletin boards are filled with large, plastic-coated pictures—one of laughing children hanging out of an old-fashioned school house with a huge bell, another one of a kitten, a puppy, and a bunny sitting up and listening to a goose in a bonnet reading, a cutout of a birthday cake with the months and the children's birthdays listed underneath. Marilyn glances around at the children. One of the little girls is wearing a crown made out of yellow construction paper. That's nice, she thinks. Susan celebrates their birthdays. She jots herself a note to remember to mention that to Susan. She also writes, "There is no student work displayed in the classroom."

Just then the phone on the wall by the door rings. Susan gets up to answer it and hands it toward Marilyn. It's Rose. "Jolene wants to talk to you."

"Tell her that I'll be down in 5 minutes. OK?" Marilyn says as softly as she can.

She sits back down, but her concentration is broken. Susan has finished her lesson and is giving instructions to the children. "Your math packets are on your desk. I want you to get up and go quietly and quickly to your seats. No talking, no pushing, no shoving. Start working on your packets. I'll be around to check on you."

This is what Susan means when she says she's individualized her program, Marilyn thinks. She has copied drill sheets and stapled them together. The tubs of brightly colored math manipulatives sit unused on their shelves.

As she walks back to her office, she thinks about Susan's lesson. Why is it that Susan and so many others think that phonics is reading? she wonders. Marilyn has watched the Susans teaching strictly phonics for 20 years and more. She has watched children learning to read in kindergarten and first grade. And trying again in second grade. She has watched them still trying in fourth and fifth grades, only now it's remedial reading; she has watched them still trying in high school, only now nearly all the students who haven't learned to read have left, and no one knows where they are.

Marilyn has noticed that many children who don't learn to read eventually do learn phonics. They learn to sound out words laborious syllable by laborious syllable. In fact, they become much better at phonics than their classmates who are good readers. But these children do not find their language, do not learn to love it or to make it their own.

They aren't connected, Marilyn thinks. She means more than making connections between print on a page and the words the print represents and the meanings the words carry. No one has shown them that. Of all its uses, the first and most fundamental use of language and of reading is to connect one human being with another one. Susan's lesson didn't connect; it isolated and tyrannized. It destroyed meaning and feeling.

But Marilyn already knows that she will not try to say any of this when she meets with Susan for her observation conference. She remembers all too well what happened at Lincoln School. It was just this sort of lesson that she began to criticize. She began to ask about the logic of teaching a letter a week and whether it made more sense to teach phonics as sounds appeared naturally in the stories the children were reading. She urged teachers to rely as much on the questions the children asked as on the information they wanted to present. She praised classrooms that were crammed with children's own art and projects and let the pretty rooms that the teachers decorated by themselves after school pass without comment. And the teachers' anger grew until, at last, they told the parents that Marilyn was requiring them to give up their time-proven approaches and that, as a result, whole classes of children were not learning to read. They told the parents that, unless Marilyn left, *they* would leave and that then there would be no hope for the children's ever learning their sounds.

Marilyn will never forget the night that she tried to suggest that the children didn't need more drill and practice; that, instead, they needed to be held while they talked and were talked to, held while they read and while they listened. If children formed bonds with adults who loved them and who cared about reading, and if they experienced environments rich in language, Marilyn suggested, almost all of them would learn to read and write, and they would seem to learn without effort. Only a few would need strenuous intervention.

Marilyn can still see the young, intelligent mother. She was thin with blond curls, small features and wide-set, clear blue eyes—a beautiful young woman with three beautiful blond sons. When Marilyn finished talking about her dream of beginning with 5-year-olds who didn't seem ready to read, by holding them and rocking them and reading to them, the young mother leaned across the table, her neck mottled, her voice shaking. "You're telling us that we're not good parents. You're trying to do our job. It's not your job to do that; it's *your* job to teach students to read."

After a year of trying to hold her own against the teachers' union and the beautiful young mother, she realized that, except for Jane and three or four other teachers, she was standing alone. She had thought that her supervisors were behind her, but she was wrong. They had made a pact with the teachers and the parents to send her away. Just before Christmas, the superintendent—whose pragmatism stretched to the sinister—forced her into her assignment at Madison on 2-days' notice. The price she paid for trying to stand her ground was to be exiled. The reality that she had been convicted of a crime came clear in their final conversation before the hasty transfer, when the superintendent said, "You go out there for 3 or 4 years and see if you can get along with people. Then we'll see if we can give you something better." And, like a small child hearing her father's voice, she acquiesced.

Marilyn learned something once and for all that Christmas. She learned that being a "good principal" means never making anyone angry. It has nothing to do with believing in something and standing by it. And she learned—with absolute clarity—that she would never be a "good principal."

By the time Marilyn walks in the office door, her frustration has robbed her of her usual studied detachment. "Rose. Can you come into my office for a minute?"

"I thought I've told you not to interrupt me while I'm doing an observation." Marilyn's voice is shaking.

"I know. But Jolene said it was important."

"Too important to wait 5 minutes?"

Rose looks at Marilyn. "No, probably not. But you say that you always want to know when the PTA wants to talk to you."

"Yes, but not always immediately, and not when I'm observing. Listen, Rose, that time has to be protected. It's hard enough on a teacher to have me observing but even worse for me to be called out."

"I won't do it again."

"I appreciate that. Well, where is Jolene?"

"She isn't *here*. She called on the phone."

"OK. I'll get her at home."

Rose gets up and goes back to her work, and Marilyn dials Jolene's number. The line is busy. She is just picking up the phone again when Amy bursts in the door. She is radiant in her new clothes—a white sweatshirt with a band of fluorescent pink and green teddy bears all around the yoke, stone-washed jeans, and work-out shoes with pink and green shoelaces that match the teddy bears.

"You look wonderful, Amy. Just beautiful!"

"I got some new underwear, too, and some extra pairs," Amy volunteers.

"Good for you. I'm so glad you came in to show me your clothes. I was wondering what you'd choose."

"I wasn't," Amy laughs. "Well, I'm going to class now. The kids won't believe it."

Marilyn dials Jolene again. This time there is no answer. She goes out to Rose's desk and, wanting to make amends, asks Rose as politely as she can, "Would you mind trying Jolene every few minutes? First her line was busy, and then I didn't get an answer."

Rose is still miffed. She nods, but doesn't say anything. "Thanks. I really appreciate it," Marilyn says, but she stops short of an apology.

Late that afternoon, Marilyn remembers that she still hasn't talked to Jolene. "Rose, did you ever get ahold of Jolene?"

"Yes." Rose answers flatly. "She said she didn't need to talk to you after all."

"Well, what was going on?" Marilyn asks.

"She saw a strange car cruising the neighborhood, and it scared her. She wanted your permission to send out a flyer telling all the parents to be on the lookout. Wanted to get it done before a.m. kindergarten let out."

Marilyn waits for Rose to finish the story, but Rose is not in a generous mood. "So, what happened?" Marilyn finally asks.

"I don't know. I guess she called the the School Police."

Jolene tells Marilyn about a suspicious car every few weeks and asks to send home warnings. She usually dodges the request by volunteering to check with the School Police and give the car and driver's description. So far, nothing has ever come of one of these reports; but every time Marilyn evades one of Jolene's requests, she feels uneasy. She doesn't want to alarm other parents, but there's always the outside chance that Jolene's fears are real.

"Thanks, Rose. I'll double-check with Jolene just to be sure she's satisfied."

Driving home that night, she remembers all the loose ends that she left behind. She didn't talk with Nathan about the lunch tickets. She forgot to ask Mr. Schneider to be on the lookout for the earrings. She didn't get back to Marge to see how the afternoon went with Richard. She didn't really know what was going on with Jolene. Tomorrow is Exclusion Day, so she won't have time then, either. She'll only add more.

Amy is one of the first children who has to go home. As Marilyn looks at Amy sitting forlornly with her new clothes on, she wants nothing so much as to tell the child that this is a mistake and to send her back to her classroom. But she knows that Rose would complain to the nurse, and the nurse would complain to her supervisor, and the supervisor would complain to Jack Renshaw. Within 24 hours, she would get a call from Jack asking for an explanation. She would have none that would fit within Jack's orderly, legalistic framework. Reluctantly, Marilyn goes over to talk to Amy.

"Amy, I can drive you home. If your mom takes you to the clinic this morning, you could be back at school by lunch time, and all the kids could still see your new clothes. Your mom hasn't had her baby yet, has she?"

Amy shakes her head. "Can you take me to the clinic? You could bring me right back faster than my mom could."

"Your mom has to take you for your shots, honey. I don't have permission to get shots for you."

"You could get it. My mom wouldn't care."

"I know she wouldn't, but this time, I need to take you home. I'll explain things to your mom."

Amy gives Marilyn a worried look. "I don't think you can come in. They're probably still asleep."

Marilyn doesn't want to embarrass Amy. "OK. We'll see."

Amy doesn't talk during the short drive to her house except to say, "You have a really nice car." Marilyn's old Honda might as well be a new BMW as far as Amy is concerned. Candy and George's apartment is in a square old two-story house on the busy street that Marilyn drives every day on her way to work. Delivery trucks back in and out of the adjacent driveway from early in the morning to late in the afternoon.

Amy's house was maroon 20 years ago, but most of the paint is worn off now. Someone has stapled plastic over the windows as a meager protection against the winter. The stubble of the front yard hints that grass once grew there. A lanky forsythia bush by the front steps and an old lilac off to the side of the house promise welcome color all through the spring.

Marilyn reaches over and unfastens Amy's seat belt. Amy opens the car door, scrambles out, and runs up onto the porch before

Marilyn can get out on her side of the car. "You need to be careful," Amy warns. "Watch out for the holes. George is going to put some boards over them."

"I'm OK. I see them."

Amy stops at the door. "You better wait here."

She waits while Amy opens the door a crack and squeezes through. Marilyn stands on the porch for 5 minutes or so, and then Amy reappears, opening the door wide this time. All that Marilyn can sense is cold, dark space that smells like a squalid cave.

By now Amy has had time to rehearse her script to herself and to assume her cheerful character. "It's OK. They'll take me right over to the clinic as soon as they get up," she says as she waves and closes the door. She is brittle and distant now, not at all the child who begged Marilyn to take her to get her shots.

Nan is standing behind the counter, going through the list of excluded children. Marilyn picks up a handful of papers that have accumulated in the wire basket and, as she comes through the swinging door, says, "Come in here, Nan. I want to see you for a minute." Nan walks ahead of Marilyn into her office, and Marilyn slams the door behind them. "Goddamn it, Nan. This is so incredibly stupid. I hate it. I just had to take Amy home. She begged me to take her to get her shots. She knows Candy will take days to get those shots. Leave it to the children. They know what to do. We need to set up a clinic here for the day. We could give the children their shots and have them back in school by 10:00. We wouldn't have all this confusion. The children wouldn't have the misery of being sent home. Why can't we ever do anything right?"

"You really want me to take the rest of the day answering that question?" Nan asks with a grin. "I know. It's awful. But you just have to do what you can, little by little."

Marilyn breathes deeply. "Yeah, I know. Well, let's get back to it. Thanks."

Nan opens the door to leave. "Want me to leave the door closed for awhile?"

"No. That's fine. I'm OK." As Marilyn sorts through the papers in her hand, she comes across a sealed envelope with the name "Dr. Wallace" printed in irregular capitals. She does not immediately recognize the handwriting. She picks up the small, carved letter opener that Jane gave her 10 years ago, runs it along the top of the envelope, and pulls out a piece of loose-leaf notebook paper:

Marilyn Wallace

It is my fault that Rose interrupted you this morning. I was very upset about what I had observed last night.

I wanted to know what to do in time to catch the kindergarten class, in case a flyer would be needed to be made and sent out.

My concern was for those kindergardeners who walk by themselves.

I will not disturb you or the secretary anymore.

I don't know how to get things taken care of policywise, so it's none of my business to be wanting to send a flyer home that may cause undue concern for our parents.

The School Police and district officer will be dealing with my suspicions for last night's incident.

I wish there was a handbook that told us how to deal with situations like this. I guess I should just look the other way, call the School Police, and hope nothing will happen to any of our children.

Please don't be mad at Rose. I won't be in the office disturbing you all while you're working.

Mrs. Jolene Ferguson

I should have gotten to Jolene yesterday, Marilyn thinks. She goes to the door. "Rose. Can you come in here for a minute?" She hands Rose Jolene's letter. "Why don't you read this?" Rose slowly reads the letter and then looks up. She is frightened.

"Rose, did you say something to Jolene about my having spoken to you when you called down to Susan's room?" Marilyn asks.

"Yes, I did mention it to her. I wanted her to understand what happens when she puts pressure on me like that."

"I see," Marilyn says, too angry to trust herself to say anything more. She pauses and then goes on. "Well, Rose, I can understand your not liking to be caught in the middle like that, but when I clarify procedures or make requests, I expect you not to discuss our conversation with parents. Is that clear?"

"Whatever you say," Rose says tersely, but she will continue to say whatever she pleases to Susan and Melanie, to Jolene, and to God knows who else. Why would she give up her most paralyzing weapon?

"Well, I'll talk to Jolene and try to straighten things out, and thanks for doing your part not to let something like this happen again." Marilyn tries to bring a civilized close to the conversation.

When school dismisses that afternoon, Marilyn makes sure that she is out in the hall. She spots Jolene waiting outside of Stephanie's classroom. "Hi, Jolene. I got your note, and I wonder if we could talk for just a minute?"

"I don't know. I'm pretty busy. I've got my Camp Fire Girls right now. I'm just waiting for Stephanie so's she can help get things ready."

"I'll only take 5 minutes. I promise. We can just duck into the library to talk."

Jolene and Marilyn sit down across from each other at one of the library tables. "Look, Jolene, I'm really sorry about the misunderstanding yesterday. I don't want you to feel that you can't get in touch with me whenever you need to. I tried to get ahold of you, but first your line was busy, and then you weren't home. I didn't mean to put you off."

"Oh, yeah. I understand. I guess I got too excited. I usually do."

"Don't feel that way, Jolene. I think it's important that we always check out anything suspicious that's going on around the neighborhood."

"That's all I was trying to do," Jolene says, looking at Marilyn for the first time since the beginning of their conversation.

"I know, and I'll keep trying to help. And I'll always get back to you just as soon as I can. Your suggestion about a handbook is a good one, too. Maybe we can get together and decide what to include in something like that," Marilyn says.

"Oh, I don't know. Maybe a handbook isn't such a good idea. You know, people probably wouldn't read it."

Marilyn agrees. The system's propensity toward handbooks for every topic imaginable doesn't have anything at all to do with communication. It has to do with putting words on paper as a poor substitute for making connections of feeling and caring with parents and children. Jolene is asking for a handbook only because she feels as if Marilyn doesn't care and because the system has trained her to think that a handbook is a legitimate response to a problem.

"I think you're right, Jolene. Let's just try to keep in touch and deal with these problems as they come along. Please come to see me if something's wrong. Or call. It really helps."

Jolene finally smiles. They get up from the table, and Marilyn gives Jolene a grateful hug.

In the confusion of the day, Marilyn has forgotten about Amy. It's not until she is driving home that she realizes she doesn't know whether Amy made it back to school or not.

17

Marilyn doesn't notice when Amy comes back to school, doesn't happen to see her in the cafeteria, and hasn't had any reason to go into Lil's room. Even so, she's vaguely worried, and her thoughts turn toward the little girl whenever her preoccupation with the moment eases—but never at times when she could ask Nan or Lil about her or go find her herself on the playground or in the cafeteria.

Just after school starts one morning the following week, Grace Johnson calls Marilyn. "Can you come down to my room and talk to Lynette? Cody's momma. I looked for Nan, but she had to take her car in to the garage. I think Lynette better talk to someone right away."

Lynette looks very small sitting in the rocking chair in the story corner. The children are hanging up their jackets and getting settled. Cody is following the routine with everyone else, but his eyes never leave his mother. Marilyn goes over to Lynette. "Hi, Lynette."

Lynette begins to cry softly. "I think I need help. I'm scared of my boyfriend."

"Come on. Let's go somewhere where we can talk." Marilyn says.

They walk back to Marilyn's office without saying much. When Lynette looks as if she's more comfortable, Marilyn begins to probe. "I didn't know that you had a new boyfriend, Lynette."

"Well, he's not that new. I've known him for awhile. He moved in last month—pretty soon after that accident." Marilyn nods and waits for Lynette to continue. "At first things was good. You know, he liked Cody and stuff. But then he started getting ugly. He would smack Cody real hard."

"And you, too?" Marilyn asks. "Does he hit you?"

"He hits both of us, but that's not what scares me." Lynette stops talking.

"What scares you, Lynette?" Marilyn waits.

"He's got a gun. He waves it around a lot. He says he's going to kill me and Cody. I think he means it. He tells everybody he's going to kill us. I asked and begged him to leave, but he won't go. I'd leave, but he'd find us wherever we went. And, besides, I don't have no money." Lynette is crying again, the kind of crying a woman does after she has already cried for more hours than she can remember.

"You need help, Lynette." Marilyn says softly.

"I don't know if there is any help. I don't know what I can do. I don't have nowhere to go."

"Do you know about women's shelters?"

"I heard about them places, but I don't know where they are or anything. I don't know how I'd get there anyways. He's got the truck, and he's driving around in it with his gun."

"I'll give you the number of the shelter," Marilyn says, hoping that she isn't pushing Lynette too fast. "You can call and explain what's happening. They'll give you good advice. If you decide to go there for a few days, they'll come and pick you up." Lynette listens intently to Marilyn.

"That'd be good. But I don't have no phone. He took it with him when he left so I wouldn't call no one."

"You can use my phone. I'll leave you alone a little while, and you can call them right now."

Lynette hesitantly agrees. When Marilyn comes back a few minutes later, Lynette is off the phone. "Did you talk to them?" Marilyn asks.

"Yes. They asked me a lot of questions. They said I should come there to stay, that he sounds dangerous. You was right. They'll come to get me and Cody."

"Good. I thought they would. Are you going to go?"

"I don't know. I told them I'd have to think about it. They said I should call them back and talk to them no matter what I decided."

"That's a good idea. Why don't you come and have lunch with Cody and call them then?"

"Yeah, I could do that. OK."

"I really think you should take their advice, Lynette. They know what they're doing. It's a good place. You and Cody need to be safe." Marilyn stops short. She is pushing too hard. She lightens. "Well, listen, you think things over. It's up to you. But either way, come back at lunchtime. It's a good lunch today—wiener wraps," she says as she walks with Lynette out into the outer office.

"You better take a look at Amy," Rose says grimly. The little girl sits with her head down, her hair falling all around her face. Her hands hide what her hair doesn't. Marilyn gathers herself for what she knows is ahead.

"Hi, Amy." she says quietly. Amy doesn't say anything. "Will you look at me?" No response. "Amy?" Still nothing. Marilyn looks across the counter at Rose. She returns the look and shakes her head. The phone rings, and she reaches to answer it.

As Marilyn bends toward the little girl, a shudder ripples through her body. She feels her abdomen tighten and, from far back in her past, the familiar impulse to become absolutely still. She closes her eyes for a couple of seconds. Then she draws a breath and stands up and puts one of her hands on each of the little girl's shoulders. She holds her voice steady. "Come on, Amy. I need to have you come into my office so you can show me." Amy drops her hands but keeps her head bent.

Marilyn puts her arm around Amy, walks her slowly into her office, and guides her into a chair. She keeps her head down and puts her hands back up over her face. The girl and the woman sit without moving, without talking for what seems like a long time.

The office begins to feel more and more strange. Marilyn's memory is trying to leave this room and this time, while her rational voice struggles to keep her in the here and now. The morning sun beats through the windows, threatening to burn the leaves on the violets, exposing everything—the dust on the bookcases, the smudges on the glass desktop. Marilyn gets up and lowers the shades a little. She looks at Amy sitting in the chair. These chairs are all wrong, she thinks.

"Amy, show me your face," she says quietly, insistently. Amy sits as still as before, and Marilyn mirrors her stillness. She wants to go with Amy to her quiet place. Their breathing falls into an identical rhythm. It slows. And slows even more. Marilyn knows how Amy's eyes feel closed tightly behind her hands. All she can see is the pink of her skin; all she can feel is the warmth and the light of the sun. She wants it to be dark. She wants to sleep.

Marilyn jerks her head. She can't go with Amy. She has to pull Amy back into the light. "Amy?" Marilyn reaches out and puts one of her hands around each small wrist and gently lowers Amy's hands to her lap. "Amy, will you let me see your face?" Marilyn cups Amy's chin in her hand and slowly raises it. She doesn't resist.

Marilyn sees her eyes before she really takes in the bruise—those beautiful brown eyes that had danced just a few days before when she had come running in to show her new clothes to Marilyn. Today, they are all pain. No fear. No anger. Only pain.

Marilyn scans Amy's face. The reddish blue bruise begins at the corner of her eye and sprawls across the whole left side of her face. Her mouth is swollen and a bit of dried blood edges along her upper lip. It was a broadside slap with an open palm.

"How did it happen, Amy?"

"I—I fell down the steps," Amy says with no trace of feeling in her voice.

"How did it *really* happen, Amy?"

Amy puts her head down again and starts to put her hands up to her face.

"Amy, please stay here," Marilyn pleads. Amy looks at Marilyn and nods. "Who hit you?"

"George," Amy says in a near whisper. Then, in a flood, "Please don't tell. Please. He didn't mean to. He's sorry. He won't do it again. Honest. He won't. I'll be good. I promise."

"Amy, you *are* good. You haven't done anything wrong." Marilyn can hardly stand to hear her own words. "It's not OK for George to do that to you, Amy. You have a right to be safe. Do you understand, honey?"

Amy understands; both Marilyn and Amy understand. They understand that this truth is not strong enough to protect her.

"I'm going to have someone talk with you, Amy."

"The policeman?"

Marilyn nods.

"Does he have to? Couldn't we just skip it this time? He's probably busy."

"No, honey. We can't skip it. It's the law. I'll call Nan, and you can go help her out until the police officer comes. Would that be OK?"

Amy nods. What else can she do? Marilyn looks at her, so small in the big office chair. Suddenly the woman opens her arms and gathers Amy into her lap, rocking her back and forth. For a few moments, Amy is safe in the way that only love can make a child safe. Marilyn is also breaking the rules, ruining a possible investigation, invalidating later testimony, compromising herself professionally. Reluctantly, she moves Amy off her lap and stands with her arm around the little girl while she dials Nan.

Nan comes in a minute later. She takes one look and closes the door behind her.

"George hit Amy this morning," Marilyn explains. "I've told her that we'll need to report it to the police. Do you think Amy could wait in your room until the officer gets here?"

"Sure thing, Amy. I could use your help right now. The kindergarten kids are coming in to play with the puppets. They'd really like it if you'd play with them. Would you do that?"

Amy nods. As she leaves, Nan looks back over her shoulder at Marilyn and shakes her head. "What are we going to do?"

"I don't know. Can the officer use your room when he gets here?"

"Sure. That'll be fine. I need to get into some classrooms pretty soon anyway."

Marilyn picks up the phone. "This is Marilyn Wallace at Madison School." Her voice is cold and official. "I am requesting an officer to come out to investigate a suspected child-abuse incident . . . Yes, the child is in school now . . . Yes . . . School is out at 3:00 . . . Someone can come out before then? . . . Good . . . OK, thanks."

Marilyn puts down the phone and sits with her head in her hands for a couple of seconds; then she gets up and goes out to Rose. "I'm going to close my door for awhile. I need to get caught up with some of this work."

She goes back in to her desk and arranges her phone messages in a neat stack, putting the message from Jack Renshaw on top. She pulls over the manila folder marked "Important" and flips through the memos and announcements. None of them makes any sense. She writes a note to Susan scheduling an observation conference for tomorrow. She has no stomach for talking to Susan today. She forces herself to put the call in to Jack.

"Top of the morning, Marilyn."

"How're things?" Marilyn asks dully, doing her best to take up the customary small talk while she waits to find out what he wants.

"Couldn't be better. Let's see—I know I have something here to talk to you about. Oh, yes. Here it is. Ahm, I got a call from a parent of yours, a Jolene Ferguson. Does that name ring a bell?

"Yes, she's my PTA president. She was upset with me, but I think we have things worked out."

"OK. Good. She says you refused to let her send home a notice to parents about a potential threat in the neighborhood."

"Well, not exactly. She did have a concern about a suspicious looking car, and she and I had a hard time getting together to discuss the situation. As she explained it to me, she decided to handle it another way." Marilyn knows better than to try to give Jack all the details or to talk about her own disappointment that Jolene has made this call.

"She also says that you don't want her to disturb you or to be around the school," Frank adds.

For a moment, Marilyn can think of nothing to say. "That's not true, Jack. She was hurt because of something Rose said to her, that's all. I've talked with both Rose and Jolene since. I'm sure everything is OK now, but I'll talk to her again just to be sure."

"OK. You do that. You fix it, Marilyn. I don't want any more calls like this. Keep those parents in line. You know how to do that, so do it."

Marilyn paces around her office for a couple of minutes, but she can't get back on track, so she calls Pam McBride. Pam isn't there. She isn't sure what she wanted to talk with Pam about anyway. She tries to go back to her paperwork.

Despite her efforts to distract herself, Marilyn slips back to a nameless night when she was 4. It seems as if it has been dark for a long time, but it is not dinnertime yet. She is in the kitchen, and her mother is patting out biscuit dough. "I want to make biscuits, too. My dolls are hungry. Alice is hungry. She wants some biscuits," Marilyn nags.

"No, I don't want another mess to clean up. Alice will just have to go hungry," her mother says absentmindedly.

"I wish I had another mother. I wish my mother would let her little girl make biscuits."

Suddenly her mother is paying full attention. "Go to your room. Your father will take care of you when he gets home."

Marilyn sits on the edge of her bed, hugging Alice and looking around the room. She is searching for a new hiding place even though she has long ago tried out all the possible choices. She can scramble under the bed, crouch in the corner between the dresser and the wall, or hide in the closet.

Tonight she chooses the closet. She opens the door, pushes the shoes and toys around to make enough room to sit down, and scoots far back against the wall beneath the clothes. She tries out the spot, and it seems good. Then she crawls forward on all fours to pull the door closed in front of her. She settles into her nest, holding Alice close. In the quiet and the dark, Marilyn imagines that no one can ever find her. She grows very, very still. She feels safe and, after awhile, begins to drop off to sleep.

The sound of the car in the driveway rouses her. Everything downstairs is absolutely quiet, but she knows what is happening. Her mother is telling her father what she said. What *did* she say? She can't remember. Then she hears him coming, his feet hitting every stair hard enough to make the coins jingle in his pockets.

He yanks open the bedroom door. There is a pause; then he yanks open the closet door. Marilyn feels the utter uselessness of her hiding scheme as the light from the bedroom fills the closet. Her last resort is to make herself so still that she will be invisible. But he sees her anyway. He pushes aside the clothes, grabs her by the arm, and pulls her out into the room. He throws her on the floor. She lies there, not moving. His face is red; the veins on his forehead and neck make pulsing purple ropes.

With one hand, he pulls her to her feet, and, with the other one, he reaches for the toy whip that he had bought for her at the circus the week before. He begins to hit her—her legs, her bottom, her back. She screams, and screams again. The little whip breaks in two. The biting lashes change into slow, solid hits, first from his hand and then from his fist. He lets go of her small wrist. The little girl slides to the floor, hot, dry, too exhausted to cry.

A slow, convulsing shudder makes its way up from Marilyn's abdomen to her chest. It dies away, and another one follows. And then another one. She shakes her head, trying to chase the memory back to its hiding place.

The static of a two-way radio in the outer office jars her fully into the present. She opens her door to see a police officer standing at the front counter. He has gone a little to fat, making his uniform all the more prominent for the tight fit. His revolver is strapped to his right leg, and he shoves down his radio antenna as he clips it back onto his belt. He pulls out his note pad and writes something, then absentmindedly reaches down to adjust his crotch before he goes on to his next piece of business for the day. Marilyn watches from the other side of the counter.

"You called in a child abuse report?"

"Yes. We've reported on this child three times already this year. Do you think you can do anything this time?"

"Don't know, ma'am, we'll have to see what we've got. Are there marks?"

"You can see the palm print on her cheek."

"Will it show up in a picture?"

"I think so."

"Good. That'll help. Where is she?"

"With the counselor. I'd like to have one of us sit in on the interview," Marilyn says.

"I'm sorry," he says with a tinge of sympathy in his voice. "We can't do that. It's so easy to screw up these cases. Sorry," he says again.

Even now, George has more protection than Amy. Marilyn knows how hard it will be for her to sit in a room alone with this matter-of-fact, well-intentioned guy.

The officer comes back 15 minutes later. "Thanks," he says.

"Did you get anything?"

"Nope, not much. The bruise turned out good in the Polaroid this time, so we've got that. But she wouldn't say anything. Didn't give me anything to go on."

"But she told me that George hit her," Marilyn insists.

"Who's George?" the officer asks.

"Her mom's boyfriend."

"Yeah? Well, she didn't say anything like that to me. She just kept saying that she didn't know how she got the bruise."

"She's afraid of you," Marilyn says to him softly. And to herself she says, She's as afraid of you as she is of George.

The officer stands looking at Marilyn. "Well, what are you going to do?" she asks.

"I'll drive by her house and see if anyone's there. If not, I'll leave a note for them to call me."

Marilyn knows what that will be about. George and Candy will get another warning and be encouraged to enroll in a parenting class.

This incident will be added to Amy's file at Children's Services, and Marilyn will send Amy home to George and Candy at the end of the day.

She gives it one more try. "Look, this isn't the first time on Amy. We're seeing bruises every few weeks now. Things are falling apart in that family. Her mother's going to have a baby any day, there's drug use. You should see the house—lice-infested, filthy. I don't think there's heat. It's really awful." Marilyn realizes the futility of what she's saying, so she stops talking.

"Sorry. I know how you feel," the officer says, "but we've got a lot worse. Maybe we can take her in next time."

"Maybe next time will be too late," Marilyn spits back.

"Don't tell *me* about it. I don't make the rules. Look, I don't like this detail anymore than you do." He shoves his notebook in his shirt pocket and turns to leave.

She hears voices in the hall and realizes that the children are starting to come into the cafeteria for lunch. She remembers Lynette and goes over to the cafeteria to see if she is there. Sure enough. She is sitting with Cody at a big, empty table. "Hi, you two."

They smile. "Hi," Lynette says. "Florence let us get our trays first. You were right. It is a good lunch."

"Sure is," Marilyn says. "We all eat hot lunch on wiener-wrap days." Marilyn waits for Lynette to say something, but she doesn't. "Do you want to call the shelter, Lynette?"

She looks at Marilyn. "Naw. I don't think so. He was back at the apartment when I got home, and he was real nice. Said he was sorry and all. I don't think he's gonna try nothin'. Things are OK between me and him now. We made it all up. Look, I'm sorry I bothered you this morning."

Marilyn tries not to let her worry show. "That's OK, Lynette. Listen, you keep that number handy. OK?"

"Sure thing," Lynette says.

The cafeteria is filling up fast now. Marilyn sees Nathan at a table across the room. He is still wearing the As cap. As Mr. Schneider crosses the cafeteria on his way to the staff room to pick up his lunch, Marilyn catches his eye, and he comes over to her. "Hi, how did Nathan's morning go?"

"He was pretty quiet."

"Did the other children give him a bad time?" Marilyn asks.

"Not that I noticed," Mr. Schneider says, "but they didn't have much of a chance to. I had them reading encyclopedias all morning and making note cards."

"Well, we'll see how he gets through lunch. Tom will keep an eye on him on the playground. You haven't picked up any clues about the earrings, have you?"

"No, haven't heard anything. Who knows where they are?" Mr. Schneider turns his palms up in a gesture of helplessness as he and Marilyn separate.

When school is out, Marilyn watches Amy walk down the sidewalk. She is wearing her old brown fake-fur coat with no buttons. As she crosses the street, Marilyn loses her in the press of children.

The next morning, Marilyn is waiting at the front door when Amy comes in. "Hi, Amy. Come talk to me for a minute."

Amy willingly walks beside Marilyn. Her bruise has darkened to bluish purple. "How did it go last night, Amy?"

"OK," Amy says brightly.

"Did George give you any trouble?"

"No, he was nice." Amy falls silent.

Marilyn hesitates. "Amy? Are you sure everything's all right?"

"Yup. Real sure. Know what? Mom and George say I can name the baby whatever I want. Bye, Ms. Wallace. I got to get to my class now."

As Amy walks off down the hall, Marilyn knows with dead certainty that the little girl won't be talking to her much longer. At least not about anything that matters.

V

Eddie:
Against All Odds

18

Eddie's going to kill somebody. We'll wake up and find him in the headlines. Some guy with a grudge will come back to school and shoot teachers, administrators, janitors. You'll read about *us* in the headlines." Leaving the weight of her prediction to settle over the three other women at the table, Estelle turns her attention to her small, polished apple. She painstakingly cuts eight sections, sets the sharp paring knife with a yellowed-ivory handle back on the rim of her china plate, and begins to nibble at one of the sections.

Melanie, who was Eddie's teacher in kindergarten, lets out a long sigh. "I know it. You're right. I just hope I'm out of here by then."

"Why doesn't somebody do something before it's too late?" asks Susan, who had him in first grade. She doesn't expect an answer.

Even though Lil hasn't finished her lunch, she pushes her chair away from the table. "I've got to get some stuff together for this afternoon." The other three women barely notice her leaving.

Estelle was Eddie's second-grade teacher last year, and Marilyn knew from the start that it was a bad match. After a couple of months, she suggested moving Eddie to another room. "Not on your life," Estelle said, her gun-metal grey eyes sparked with determination. "I'm not going to wish that boy on someone else. Besides, he'll get the idea he won." So Marilyn left her alone.

Or at least she tried to act as if she were leaving Estelle alone. The truth is that Marilyn turns the scraps of detail she has gathered about Estelle over and over in her imagination as she tries to tease a life out of them. Estelle came to teach second grade in Room 108 when Madison School opened in 1953. From all signs, it has changed little from that first year when she was 23 and a beginning teacher. Whenever Marilyn walks in, the children stop their work and chorus, "Good morning, *Dr.* Wallace," while Estelle nods and mouths the sing-song with them. She is the only teacher in the school who refers to Marilyn as "Dr."

Marilyn can't keep herself from gazing at Estelle's rules. Rules for periods jostle against rules for hanging up your coat. There are rules for apostrophes, rules for getting a drink, rules about proper nouns and nouns of address, rules for sharpening pencils, rules for heading papers, rules for going to the bathroom, rules for greetings on friendly letters, rules for asking for help. It must have taken Estelle several summers to print them all in two-inch letters on butcher paper that has now faded to a nameless shade. Over the course of 30 years, the roving crew of painters has come to Room 108 three times, and Gus likes to describe how each time Estelle complained bitterly about the work of taking down her rules and putting them back up again.

Standing among her second graders, Estelle seems delicate, even frail. Every year by April or May, two or three of them are as tall as she is and several outweigh her. Marilyn knows never to schedule a meeting with Estelle after school on Wednesdays. This is the afternoon she goes to the beauty shop to have her blond hair lightened, curled, and sprayed to last the week.

Once, when Marilyn asked Estelle what she was going to do for spring break, she said, "Mother and I are going shopping for a pattern and material for my Easter dress. It'll probably take us all week to make it." Marilyn guesses that Estelle has never owned a dress her mother didn't sew.

Estelle talks about Buffy, her 13-year-old toy poodle, and her doll collection almost every day around the lunch table. Buffy has a bad heart, so she carries her around the house and spends most evenings rocking her. "Mother has given me a doll for every Christmas and birthday since I was 2. I still have all of them. Now she mostly finds old dolls for me. We just don't like the new ones; even the facsimiles aren't that good. We'd rather rescue the old girls. I finally got so many that we had to move them across the hall into their own room."

Marilyn imagines that Estelle's bedroom has changed no more over time than Room 108. She has a notion of that second-floor back bedroom where Estelle sleeps in a small four-poster bed. Estelle's mother mends the priscilla curtains each spring as the sun breaks more of their spidery threads. The dressing table has a pink chintz skirt and a mirror top covered with bottles whose perfume has been left to evaporate.

Marilyn thinks of Estelle in that imaginary bedroom and watches her cross the hall where she moves from doll to doll, arranging a bonnet, straightening a stocking, retying a shoelace. She often remarks that each of her dolls still has the shoes, socks, and ribbons she wore the day Estelle opened the box and lifted her out of the tissue paper.

Estelle wistfully tells the other teachers that once the little girls in her class were as pretty as her dolls. "But they've changed. They used to come on the first day in their new dresses, their lunch boxes filled with tuna fish sandwiches and homemade oatmeal cookies. You see the way they are now. They're all on free lunch. If they do bring something from home, it's junk food. And even on the first day, their clothes are dirty—old torn T-shirts, girls in shorts and jeans. They look like they just got out of bed. Their hair stands up every which way. They need haircuts. They're always scratching their heads. I just want to scream when they do that. I know they're probably crawling with lice. I always tell my beauty operator to look my scalp over really well. You never know."

Estelle complains to Marilyn at every opportunity about the children's parents: "They don't care anymore. They just don't care." She wrote nearly every day last year to Tess, Eddie's mother. "Eddie struck another child today without provocation. Please speak to him about his behavior." . . . "Eddie refused to do his penmanship today. Please see to it that he finishes his assignment tonight before he plays or watches television." . . . "Eddie was kicking other children on the playground today. I recommend that he spend the evening in his room."

Tess did not answer the notes; she did not phone; she did not come in for conferences even when Estelle threatened, without Marilyn's knowing, to retain Eddie for his bad behavior. Estelle was not surprised that Tess didn't come. She taught Tess in second grade and remembers her as a passive, uncooperative child who never smiled and rarely spoke. She didn't like Tess then, and she likes Eddie even less now. "The apple doesn't fall far from the tree, you know."

For the most part, Eddie and Estelle's days together last year were miserable. But "art afternoons" were different. Marilyn observed in Room 108 on one of those afternoons. When Estelle came around behind Eddie to lower a large piece art paper over his head and spread it in front of him, he became a different boy.

He smoothed the grainy, not-quite-white sheet with slow, sweeping strokes. Then he reached under his table for the precious black and neon green mechanical pencil and the box of 36 crayons that Frances, his grandmother, had given him for his birthday. He arranged them thoughtfully and then began to fill the paper with astronomers. He gave nearly half the paper to a telescope and scaffolding that his tiny scientists scaled to look through their scope. Two of them perched on a high platform straining to see "farther out than Pluto." "There are new planets out there. Lots of them," Eddie told Angie.

"That's stupid," Angie replied. "The real astronomers already found everything."

"Have not," Eddie hissed in a voice just soft enough to escape Estelle's notice.

"Have, too," Angie taunted.

Eddie's face reddened, but he let her remark go. A girl wasn't going to spoil his art afternoon. He went back to drawing his planets—an orange one, a green one, one covered with water, one with ice, one peopled with monsters, and another one with "genius men who watch us all the time."

Estelle didn't pay much attention to Eddie's drawings. She preferred the drawings of flowers and princesses with triangle torsos that she could count on from the girls. Still, she liked art afternoons with Eddie. "The only way I can keep that child under control is to let him draw."

On Valentine's Day, Estelle set all the children to drawing so that she could get ready for the class party. She arranged sugar cookies on paper plates, filled small cups with heart-shaped candies, poured strawberry Kool-Aid. Once she had counted on room mothers to bring cookies and punch, but these days she buys the party food herself.

Eddie worked intently on his picture, creating his own underwater world. "That's not a Valentine picture," Angie declared. "That's a stupid picture."

Eddie's lines got harder and darker. His arm began to move across the paper in large scrawls. "It's *really* stupid," Angie hissed.

"Shut *up!*" Eddie hissed back. He clenched his pencil in his fist and drew a tearing arc across the page.

Angie changed the subject. "I'll bet you didn't give anyone any Valentines. You're too poor." Eddie's right arm shot out and hit Angie across the mouth. Before she had time to duck, he was on his feet swinging his arms and kicking at her. He missed more often than not, but he still landed blows. He worked quickly and quietly, his face growing more and more red. The children's code is to fight in silence so that the teachers don't discover them before someone wins. But Angie quickly had enough. She gave a yelp.

"Eddie, stop that!" Estelle shouted as she moved into the middle of the foray. By now Eddie had lost any sense of where he was or what he was doing. Estelle took a random kick in the shin. She jumped back with a surprised cry and moved to the phone to call the office. Angie scrambled away from Eddie, and Eddie stood in the middle of the room, eyes flashing, legs spread, fists clenched at his side, poised to take on anyone who came near.

"Estelle wants you. Eddie's lost it again," Rose relayed to Marilyn. When she walked into Room 108, Eddie still had everyone at bay. "He hurt me. He just out-and-out kicked me." Estelle's whimper turned into a demand. "I won't tolerate that. He's out of control. I want him out of here. *Now!*"

Marilyn knew this would not be an easy request. "OK. I'll try." She moved as close to Eddie as she could without coming into his range. "Hey, buddy. We need to talk. Want to come down to the office with me?"

Eddie gave her a fiery look and lunged toward her, spitting. He would hit her if she came any closer. Estelle watched carefully. Situations such as this reinforced her conviction that a woman should not be a principal. She wanted a strong man who would pick Eddie up and carry him out of the room.

"Eddie, I'm not going to force you to come, but I need you to leave the room. I'll go back to my office. If you don't come in 5 minutes, I'll ask Mr. Campbell to help you leave." Marilyn paused. "OK, Eddie?" His face didn't change, but he didn't spit or lunge.

Dismay and scorn shaped Estelle's face as she watched Marilyn leave. She walked down the hall without looking around to see if Eddie were following and went back to her desk. Three minutes passed. Then 5. No Eddie. She got up and started back down to Room 108. He was sitting in a chair by the front doors. As soon as he saw her coming, he turned around with his arm on the back of the chair and put his head down so that he couldn't see her.

"Thanks for coming, Eddie. I feel like you're safe now. I'll wait for you in my office. When you're ready, you can come in and we'll talk." No move, no sign from Eddie. She offered a bribe. "If we can talk, maybe we can work it out so that you can go back for the party." Eddie wasn't interested. Every 15 minutes or so, she went back out to check on him. He sat just as she had left him, carefully keeping his eyes hidden to avoid giving her any sign that he was listening to what she was saying. An hour passed.

Gradually it became clear that there would be no party for Eddie. The big chocolate chip cookie Florence had brought into Marilyn after lunch was still sitting on her desk. She went out to him again. "I'll go down and get your Valentines and your jacket. I'm sorry you missed the party. There's a cookie on my desk. Would you like to come in to get it before you go home?"

Estelle gathered up Eddie's things and handed them to Marilyn without saying anything. Marilyn was in no mood to talk either. Eddie watched her come down the hall, but she ignored him and went back into her office. A few minutes later, she looked up as she finished a folder and pushed it toward the front of her desk. Eddie was standing there—smiling. "I came to get the cookie." Marilyn pointed to it without saying anything.

"Maybe it's poison," he said.

"I don't think so. But, if you want, I'll take the first bite. If I don't die, I think you'll be OK," Marilyn said, taking up Eddie's game.

He pushed the cookie toward her, and she broke off a piece and ate it. As she chewed, she grabbed her throat and pretended to choke. Eddie laughed and picked up the rest of the cookie.

"Whew! I'm glad that you're back, Eddie. Sometimes I don't know where you go. You don't seem like Eddie. I guess an alien invades your body."

"How'd y'know?" he giggled.

"Just a wild guess." She tried to get serious. "I wish we could figure out how to keep you with us, Eddie. I'm afraid you'll hurt someone. Hurt yourself."

"It's Angie's fault. She made me mad."

"You did the hitting and the kicking, Eddie. If someone says something you don't like, it's not OK to hit and kick." Marilyn fell into script instead of asking him to explain why he thought it was Angie's fault. It was late in the day, and she had lost her patience for drawing him out.

"It is too," he said. Even on the good days, when Marilyn took the time to do it right, she could never get him to the point he could tell her—even with his eyes—that he had played some part in what had happened.

Eddie usually had a few quiet weeks after an outburst. These intervals were a large part of why the women on the Screening Committee never did more than talk about him and hadn't recommended anything further. It always seemed as if he were getting better when he was in a good period; then he seemed so "normal," better than "normal," even.

One afternoon a week or so after the missed Valentine's Day party, he bounded into Marilyn's office.

"Guess what? I got a new black kitten. He crawled under my covers and slept by me all night, so I'm going to name him "Sleepy.""

Another day he worked a whole afternoon on his "Career Day" poster of a space station. "This is where I'm going to work," he told Marilyn as she admired it. "Me and Sleepy. See, this is where he's going to sleep," Eddie said, pointing to a cone with a large hole in its face sitting on a small platform high up on one of the station's walls. "He can climb up where nobody will bother him and watch the astronauts. Or he can take a nap. I could go up there too and sleep with him if I wanted to. It's big enough."

19

Last year, the peace between Estelle and Eddie held until the Wednesday before spring break. Around 2:00 that afternoon, Rose came in to Marilyn's office looking puzzled. "Gus's out there. Says Estelle called him to come and carry Eddie out of her room."

"What?"

"That's right. Gus is supposed to go get Eddie."

Gus appeared in the doorway behind Rose. "What's up, Gus?" Marilyn asked.

"Dunno. She just called and told me to get Eddie. Where d'ya want me to put him?"

Marilyn's jaw clenched. *She'll take any man in sight before she'll ask for me. She doesn't want me going down there and coaxing Eddie. She wants action.* "I'll go down and see what's going on. I'll come get you if we need you," she said, trying not to let Gus see how angry she was.

"S'up to you. Don't matter to me either way." The tone of his voice, however, made it clear that Gus would have enjoyed the importance the request gave him.

The atmosphere in Room 108 was thick with suspense. The children—Eddie included—were going through the motions of working at their desks while Estelle stood by the door waiting for Gus. An anxious shadow crossed her face when she saw Marilyn. In the moment it took her to suck in her breath, she decided to stand her ground. "He won't do what I tell him to. He just won't. He has to learn that he can't defy me. I want Gus to remove him right now."

"What is it you want him to do?" Marilyn asked, her voice hard and formal. The women's eyes met.

"I want him to do *what* I tell him to *when* I tell him to. It's that simple." Estelle's rouged cheeks stood out in china doll contrast to the whiteness of her anger. Her voice climbed to a thin shrill. Every ridge and groove of her white knuckles found definition as her grip tightened on the teaching manual she was using to shield herself.

Marilyn walked over to Eddie. His face was red, and every muscle in his body constricted. She sat down beside him. "Eddie?" He did not speak to her or look at her. "Eddie, let's get you out of here for a little while." He ignored the offer.

Marilyn realized that Estelle was standing right beside them. She knew Estelle would be angry with the tone she was taking with Eddie. "I'm going to get Gus," Estelle said.

Marilyn wheeled around in the little primary chair. "Let's talk in the hall."

"I cannot leave my class, *Dr.* Wallace," Estelle replied quietly.

Marilyn tightened her grip on her keys. "Please walk over to the door with me, Miss Douglas," she said in a voice just beyond a whisper. It wasn't so much that she was afraid of being overheard as she was afraid that anger would claim her voice. Estelle knew a directive when she heard one.

"Estelle, I'm not going to have a custodian carry a child from a classroom. I *will* see that Eddie is removed, though."

"How? What are you going to do?"

"I'll go down and cover Tom's P.E. class and have him come. I think he'll go with Tom."

"What do you want me to do in the meantime?" Estelle wanted Marilyn to be the one to give the directions so that she could hold her responsible.

Marilyn walked back over to Eddie. "Eddie, I'm going to go get Mr. Campbell. He'll come and take you down to the gym. He'll come in a couple of minutes. You hang on; keep up the good job." Eddie shot Marilyn a quick glance that she took to mean agreement. "I think he'll be OK for now," Marilyn said to Estelle as she left the room.

"He'd better be," Estelle said under her breath.

Marilyn pulled open the heavy gym door and stepped into the rush and tumble of balls and children. She accepted long ago that Tom was a "throw out the ball" man, but she wishes that he spent more time on fitness and less on competition. She also knows that he may have the right idea. Competitive sports count in this neighborhood. A good pitching arm can keep a youngster in school.

Because Marilyn is uncomfortable in the gym, she doesn't go there often, so Tom was surprised to see her come in that day. He walked over to meet her and waited.

"Can you go down to Estelle's room and get Eddie?" she asked. "I'll cover for you here."

"Sure. What do you want me to do with him?"

"Just bring him back down here."

In only 2 or 3 minutes, Tom was back with Eddie. The boy looked very, very small standing in the doorway beside the man. "He came under his own power. Did a good job," Tom said. Tom's size must be reassuring to Eddie, Marilyn thought. He knows he has to do what Tom says and that if he doesn't, Tom is strong enough to pick him up and make him do something. That's always less clear with me. I just don't have the same kind of physical reality for him.

"You want me to put him in my office for a while?" Marilyn nodded. Tom guided Eddie toward the little room and invited him to sit on the oak teacher's chair. Marilyn followed and took another chair along the wall. Just as he had done on Valentine's Day, Eddie sat hunched and twisted to avoid contact with Marilyn. She tried talking once or twice and then waited.

Eddie had more staying power than she did. Marilyn picked up a soft black ball beside her chair and held it, turning it around in her hands. Then she tossed it toward Eddie. It bounced off his shoulder and back toward her. She tossed it again. Same thing. She tossed it again. This time Eddie used his shoulder to push it back toward her. The next time Marilyn tossed the ball, Eddie opened his body and caught it. He held it, looking straight at Marilyn. His face was without expression. Then he threw it. Marilyn caught it and threw it back. He returned the toss so hard that it bounced off the the wall behind her and across the room into Tom's bathroom. As Marilyn retrieved it, she noticed that Tom's class was breaking up.

She carried the ball out into the gym. "Mr. Campbell, would you mind if Eddie and I came out and threw the ball around?"

"No problem. I don't have a class next period." Eddie darted out of the office without looking at her and stationed himself in the middle of the gym floor. Marilyn took a place along the sideline and tossed the ball to Eddie.

Time after time, Eddie hurled the ball at Marilyn. Usually she couldn't catch it, either because he had thrown it too hard or because she was no good at catching and throwing, so she ended up scrambling after the ball. As she got more and more tired and winded, Eddie laughed harder and harder. Every time he hit her or she missed the ball, he threw back his head and shrieked with pleasure.

Finally, Marilyn sat down on the floor. "I'm too tired, Eddie. I can't keep up. You're better than I am."

"Yeah, I know," Eddie acknowledged. "OK. You can quit now." He leaned over and extended his hand to help pull her up.

"Thanks."

"That's OK."

"Eddie, school's almost out. How about I walk you home and we talk to your mom?" Marilyn asked.

"If you want to. You can see Sleepy if he's not asleep. Which he might be," Eddie offered.

"I'd like that a lot. I really like kittens. I want to adopt every one I see."

"Why don't you do it, then? You could have a house with a thousand kittens in it—the old principal with a thousand kittens."

"You could draw me a picture of that," Marilyn suggested.

"Yup."

Eddie and Marilyn laughed together.

They walked out into the cool sunshine. Marilyn remembers how the neighborhood looked hopeful that afternoon with the grass greening from the winter, patches of daffodils along fences, bright forsythia and flowering quince sprawling in corners of yards, and the occasional surprise of a fragrant daphne bush. The scene with Estelle seemed much less ominous now that Marilyn was out of the school. "You really going to walk all the way home with me?" Eddie asked.

"Sure," Marilyn said. "Think your mom will be home?"

"Yeah. She's always home. With the baby." Marilyn had seen Tess at school with Ricky two or three times. He was 8 months old, a chubby placid baby. Already it was clear that he wasn't at all like Eddie. Marilyn and Nan had talked about Eddie and Ricky just a few days ago.

"I think Eddie's real mad about the baby," Nan surmised. "He doesn't know who his dad is, and he wonders who Ricky's is. I talked to him about it awhile back. Tess hasn't told him that for sure Mitch is the baby's dad, and Eddie hasn't asked."

"How does Eddie like Mitch?"

"He likes him OK. They do things together when Mitch is around, but he's a hauler, so he's gone an awful lot. Tess and Mitch are talking about getting married during spring break, and that's next week. Of course, they haven't said a thing to Eddie. That's really crummy. He doesn't have a clue about what's going on except that Frances is looking for a place to live. That's got to be upsetting him. Frances has always lived with them. It's her house. She's really the one who's raised Eddie."

Nan settled back in her chair. "We go way back with Frances and Tess. They've always lived around here. Some of the teachers remember Tess from when she went to Madison. Estelle. Christine Bailey. She still talks about Tess, says she never knew a student so withdrawn. I think she's still worried about her. And you know Christine. She doesn't exactly get wrapped up in her students."

"I started counseling around here about the time Tess was deciding to drop out. I used to go after her to try to get her back to school. She only went one more year off and on after she left eighth grade. Got pregnant the summer she was 15. That was a funny deal too. Frances said she didn't ever bring boys around the house. And she never talked about anyone. If she had a boyfriend Frances sure didn't know about it. I think she just met up with someone—in the park or in the stands at the field. Could have been that she was raped. I guess Frances didn't even catch on that Tess was pregnant until she was nearly 7 months along. Tess didn't catch on either. You know, Tess isn't dumb or anything. She reads. She's smart, but she just didn't have a clue about her own body."

"Tess and Eddie kept on living with Frances. I'd go by sometimes to see if I could get her back to school. No dice. That was something to see. Tess and Frances trying to raise a baby. I watched Tess one time trying to give him his bottle. He'd push that nipple back out of his mouth with his tongue and just squall bloody murder. Turned away and screamed so hard that even the back of his head was bright red under that blond baby hair of his. Tess tried a couple of more times and then just put him back in the plastic clothes basket they'd fixed for him and started watching the TV. I sat there trying to talk to her, feeling like a total fool."

"After awhile, Frances got up and got him. She knew what she was doing, so Eddie settled down and took his bottle. As soon as he finished, Frances put him back in the basket, got a beer, and went back to the TV. I'll bet you my last dollar that no one ever held Eddie just to be holding him or took him out for a walk or talked to him. Let alone read to him. What's kind of funny now, though, is that I think Frances likes Eddie. At least she gives him things and stuff. I think she's the best thing Eddie's got going for him, and now she's moving."

When they got to the little green house, Eddie pushed open the front door and Marilyn followed close behind. Marilyn still remembers the bare, neat living room. Tess was watching TV. Ricky was on the floor in front of the vinyl couch, rolling around with his half-empty bottle.

"Hi, Tess," Marilyn said as she stepped inside.

"Hi. Eddie get in trouble or something?"

"Yeah, he did," Marilyn said.

"Humm," Tess muttered as she halfway went back to her program.

"He wouldn't do what Miss Douglas asked him to do."

"Yeah?"

Eddie was down on all fours playing with Sleepy, who was definitely not sleepy at the moment. He was a wild thing—as thin and skitterish as Eddie. Eddie didn't seem to be paying any attention to the women, but he was listening to them with every fiber.

Marilyn began to probe. "Anything special going on that could be upsetting him, Tess? He's been getting pretty uncooperative at school."

"Umm. Don't think so. Well, you know he don't get along too good with Miss Douglas." Tess stopped talking long enough to watch the closing scene on her "soap." Marilyn waited. "Well, I don't know. Could be too that my mom moved out last week. Maybe he doesn't like that."

"Could be," Marilyn agreed. "That would be a big change."

"Yeah."

"Mitch and Eddie getting along OK?"

"Yeah. Mitch takes Eddie places," Tess volunteered.

"Good." Marilyn changed the subject. "You still taking Eddie to his art therapy?"

Tess nodded. "Yeah."

"How did it go yesterday?"

"Yesterday?" Tess looked confused.

"Doesn't he have his appointments on Wednesday afternoon?" Marilyn knew the answer.

"Yeah. He does," Tess said, still confused, "but we didn't go yesterday."

"But it was Wednesday yesterday," Marilyn said. "Today is Thursday."

"Is it? I guess I got mixed up. I guess we forgot it yesterday," Tess said.

That's it, Marilyn thought. That's why Eddie's so angry today. Nan had worked weeks to get Eddie established with a good therapist at the "Y," but it was almost impossible to get Tess to take him for his sessions. They had missed so many appointments that the therapist was threatening to cut him off. She had a long waiting list. "Tess, you really need to go. Every week. Mindy will have to give Eddie's time to someone else if you don't get there. He really likes to go. He needs the counseling," Marilyn urged.

"Yeah. He likes Mindy. It's good for him—getting to draw and all that. I guess I had a hard time remembering with Mom moving and all the other stuff that's going on." Tess gave her excuses.

"I know it's hard," Marilyn agreed. "Does Eddie remind you about his appointments?"

Eddie was still chasing the kitten around the sleeping baby. He didn't look at Marilyn and Tess, but he nodded his head vigorously.

"I don't know," Tess said. "I guess he does. Sometimes."

"Maybe you could listen for when he reminds you? He can keep track. He knows he goes on Wednesdays. Could you do that, Tess? Would you let Eddie help? This is really important to him."

Eddie got up off the floor and came to stand beside the couch, and Marilyn turned her attention to him. "How about it, Eddie? Will you help your mom remember that you go to art therapy on Wednesday?"

"Yeah. I'll do that. I'll tell her," he promised.

"Is that a deal, Tess?" Marilyn asked.

Tess was watching the TV again. "What? Oh, sure. That'll be fine."

"Great!" Marilyn said without meaning it. "Thanks a lot, Tess. There won't be a session next week because it's spring break, but you'll be sure to go the Wednesday after that?"

"Yup, for sure," Tess repeated as she sank back into her soap opera.

As Marilyn walked back to school, she wondered how much Tess had really agreed to. She went down to Room 108. Estelle was setting her room to rights, bustling and humming as she worked, barely acknowledging that Marilyn was there.

Marilyn tried to explain why she had asked Tom instead of Gus to remove Eddie. "Oh, I *understand*. I completely understand, *Dr. Wallace*." Marilyn felt the contempt in Estelle's emphasis. "I just want to get Eddie the help he needs," Estelle said through her clenched smile.

"Yes, so do I, Estelle. Will you refer him to the Screening Committee? It's time that we got an assessment on him."

Estelle looked directly at Marilyn. "No, I think *you* should do it. I'm fed up with that committee. It takes too long. Nothing ever gets done."

"Principals don't usually make the initial referrals; they usually come from the child's teacher."

"Are you *telling* me to do it?"

Marilyn dodged. "No, I'll do it."

When Marilyn stopped Christine in the hall to ask her to add Eddie's name to the Screening Committee agenda for the first week after break, Christine looked worried. "The agenda's awfully long, Marilyn. We have 12 names already. And we've talked about Eddie so many times before. Is there something new on him that I don't know about?"

"His outbursts are accelerating; he's having a lot of trouble maintaining in Estelle's room. We'd better start the wheels moving for a placement," Marilyn said, feeling defeated.

20

The meeting started late. "I think we're all here now," Christine said. "Let's get started. We have a lot of names this morning. I'd like to begin with Eddie Harris. Marilyn has asked that we add him for discussion." All the women sitting around the three tables arranged in a U were wearing jeans and bright blue Madison School sweatshirts for School Spirit Day. Christine didn't take time to comment on the look. "Is Estelle coming?"

"I can give you the information you need," Marilyn said. Everyone knew where Estelle stood.

Christine nodded. "What about Tess? Is she coming?" Christine went through the formality of asking.

"She has a baby at home," Marilyn said.

"Do you have the paperwork on him?" Christine asked.

"No," Marilyn said. "I just want the committee's opinion about whether to initiate a referral." Marilyn had backed down from her position of 2 weeks ago. The more she thought about Eddie, the more confused she felt.

Nan was impatient. "Well, what are you looking at, Marilyn? You know he's bright. Gifted, I'll bet, so you wouldn't be going for Learning Disabled, would you?"

"No, I don't think so. He couldn't possibly qualify as 2 years below grade level in anything. I think we'd need to start with a psychological."

"God, Marilyn, I just can't see sticking him with an SED label," Nan said, shaking her head. "That's all we do anymore."

"No, I can't either, Nan. But his outbursts are getting more and more violent. He's just about impossible to control."

"Well, you'd be too. Tess doesn't pay any attention at all to him—ever. His anger might be the healthiest thing he has going right now."

"Maybe so. But it's not healthy for the school."

"You don't label kids because they're toxic in the school, Marilyn," Nan said, her frustration unmistakable.

"Of course not, but . . . " Marilyn and Nan were on the edge of an argument.

"Look," Marge interrupted, "we've been arguing about Eddie in this committee for 4 years—ever since he was in kindergarten. We all know he's getting worse. He's going to be a real mess next year—when he's in third grade and even more aggressive. The question isn't whether or not he needs help; it's whether we can get the right thing for him. I agree with Nan. I don't want to see him SED either. It's not right to label these kids. Some of them are already going to follow me to my grave. I don't want to do that to Eddie, too. I really like that kid." Marge, usually as tough as they come, was on the verge of crying.

Christine spoke up. "I've known Tess since she was a student here. Pathetic girl—passive, introverted. She just doesn't have what it takes to be a parent for Eddie." She cut herself off and turned to Dolores Davis, the psychologist. "Look, Dolores. This child is urgent. Is there any way that we could get a good psychiatric workup on him without referring him?"

"Through Special Ed, you mean?" Dolores asked.

Christine nodded.

"No way. Special Ed isn't going to pay for that kind of thing with a kid like this. Do it for him, and you'd literally have to do it for a thousand others. Isn't there any way his mother could pay?"

"Are you kidding?" Nan broke in. "Tess doesn't have anything— no job, no insurance, no energy, no motivation, nothing. She's not going to do a thing for Eddie. She doesn't know what's going on."

"Is she unfit?" Dolores asked.

Nan dismissed the question. "The house is clean. She gets Eddie to school. She drinks a lot of beer, but she's not into the heavy stuff."

"So, the bottom line is that Children's Services isn't involved, and there's no reason to think they should be, so we aren't going to get any psychiatric work funded through them." Christine brought the meeting back on track.

"That's right," Marilyn agreed reluctantly.

"OK. Anybody have any ideas?" Christine wanted to move along.

Nobody said anything for a few seconds. Then Nan spoke up. "Well, I'll keep after Tess to take him to his art therapy. If I get another practicum student next year, she can do a little one-on-one with him. If Tess actually got married last week, maybe Mitch'll have some insurance." Her voice trailed off. "I don't know. Honest to God, I don't know."

"And can we be really careful about who he gets for a teacher next year, Marilyn?" Marge asked.

Marilyn moved uneasily in her chair. She had already begun to worry about it. The way the enrollment was distributed, one of the sections would be a third- and fourth-grade split class. She would have to ask Lil to take the split; Corine could never handle it. How could she ask Lil both to take a split class and Eddie?

Christine was talking. "Let's put Eddie on the update list. We'll look at him again in the fall and see how he's doing. For now, we'll just keep monitoring. "Is that OK with everyone?"

It wasn't OK with anyone, but no one had a better idea, and Christine was determined to keep the meeting moving. "All right. Let's go on to Clayton. Who has anything on Clayton? Is he still into thinking that he's a wolf and a cat?"

"Yeah, all the time," Marge replied. "He's big into guns, too. Says he's already got one out in Gresham that he goes to visit." Marge talked on, but Marilyn had stopped listening. She was thinking about Eddie and Clayton. They'd already lost Clayton. Maybe, if they had been able to do something for Eddie this morning, he wouldn't be as sick as Clayton in a couple more years.

Estelle sat alone in the staff room. She was wearing a robin's-egg-blue dress with pearl buttons down the front, long sleeves, and white linen cuffs trimmed with lace tatting. Estelle does not join in on Spirit Days. As she watched Marilyn sit down at the table, the disapproval of a principal's wearing a sweatshirt and jeans was palpable. "We talked about Eddie in the Screening Committee this morning," Marilyn said.

"Yes?" Estelle laid her fork on the edge of her plate, folded her hands in her lap, and waited for Marilyn to continue.

"We don't have enough to recommend him for screening."

"You don't have *enough*? It's not *enough* that he refuses to do what I ask, that he strikes other children, that he kicks *and* bruises me, that he's uncontrollable?"

Marilyn looked down at her keys and turned them over in her hand. "I know, Estelle. I know, but the guidelines are very specific. We can't show that he's learning disabled, and we can't show that his emotional problems are interfering with his learning. You've always said that his work is excellent and that he's very bright."

"Yes, he *is* bright, and yes, his emotional problems *are* interfering with his learning. He'd be off the charts if he didn't have so many problems. And he's not even a particularly good student. I can't get him to do any writing; he absolutely refuses to copy anything off the blackboard. He only does what he wants to and that's mostly art and math."

"Well, even so," Marilyn said, "he isn't performing two years below grade level. He's not at first grade in any of his work, is he?"

Estelle shook her head, picked up her fork and began to eat the thinly sliced chicken breast. Then she hesitated and put her fork back on her plate and looked straight at Marilyn. "It doesn't matter to me; I can get through the next 3 months with him. But it will matter to whoever gets him next year, and it will matter when he kills someone someday. I don't think you understand how crazy that boy is, Marilyn. You haven't seen the look he gets when he's like that. Nothing gets through to him. Nothing. He doesn't even hear my directions."

"I'm sorry, Estelle," Marilyn said without really knowing what she was sorry about. That Eddie was so disturbed? That she hadn't pushed for screening? That Estelle was so upset?

"Me, too," Estelle said.

Marilyn got up and went out into the cafeteria to see how lunch was going. It was raining a little, but not enough for the children to stay inside. Just then Rose came rushing toward her.

"We need your help with Eddie." He was in the middle of the front hall—a silent confusion of flailing arms and legs. Children and teachers stood watching just outside his range.

"Get Nan!" Marilyn said to Rose as she moved toward Eddie.

"Eddie. Eddie." He didn't hear her. She watched for perhaps half a minute, waiting for a change. He stopped for a moment. Marilyn moved in behind him, put her arms around in front of him, and circled each one of his wrists with one of her hands. Eddie jerked and lunged, almost pulling her off her feet.

He kicked backwards toward her legs. She took a couple of hard hits. "OK, buddy. OK. I know you're angry. I'm going to take you into the office. I want to get you out of the hall." Her voice was low and smooth. Eddie lunged and twisted again. Marilyn began to back toward the office while she tried to sidestep his kicks. Slowly she eased him through the door.

Nan came. "What can I do?"

"Move those chairs. I'm going to take him down," Marilyn said. She was breathing hard.

"OK, Eddie. We're going to sit down. Marilyn squatted, pulling Eddie with her, then sat down, still pulling Eddie. He struggled, jerking from side to side. Marilyn spread her legs and watched his intently. His right leg shot out. She matched it with her right leg, circled it around his, and brought it to the floor. Eddie lunged and pulled harder. He bobbed his head down toward her arm, teeth bared, looking for a place to sink a bite. He had forgotten his left leg for the moment. Marilyn quickly hooked her left leg around his.

"It's OK, Eddie. I've got you. You're going to be all right. It's too hard to sit like this, so I'm going to scoot back toward the wall, and then we can have a little quiet time to talk. There. That's better. Are you OK?"

"What do you need?" Nan asked

"What do you think, Eddie? You're awfully hot. How about a cold washcloth for your face? Nan, do you think you could wash Eddie's face off for him?"

"Sure, I'll get a washcloth." In a few moments Nan was back. "Here you go, Eddie, this'll make you feel better." She reached toward him. He snarled and threw his head back against Marilyn's chest.

"Come on, Eddie, you'll feel better," Nan said softly. She reached toward his face again, and this time he stayed still. She gently bathed his hot, red face. "Good. That's good, Eddie. You're doing just fine. Just fine," she said.

He lunged again to show that he was still in the fight. "How about some water? I'll bet you're thirsty," Nan said. Rose handed Nan a cup of water. She offered it to Eddie.

He took a mouthful and spit it out. "Yuk. It's hot!" he exclaimed.

"I got it out of the faucet," Rose said.

"Did you hear what Rose said, Eddie? It isn't ice-cold, but it will still help you not be thirsty. Try just a little bit more." Eddie refused.

"I think Eddie and I can manage for awhile, Nan," Marilyn said. "Why don't you go see how the other kids are doing? You can check on us later. We're not going anywhere."

"Sure thing," Nan said, as she got up. "I'll be back in to see how you guys are doing in just a little bit." The office was usually crowded with children and teachers during lunch, but right now, except for Rose, Eddie and Marilyn were alone.

They continued on in their strange embrace. Then Marilyn slowly let go of one of his wrists. He socked her hard on the thigh. She took hold of his wrist again. "I guess you want me to hold you for awhile longer. I can hold you for a long time. For as long as you need me to. But I don't like holding you this tight. It hurts you, and I'm getting tired. If you can relax, I can let you go, but I'll still hold you. In an easy way. OK? Relax, Eddie, just relax. Can you feel me breathe? Here I go, I'm breathing. In . . . Out . . . In . . . Out . . . Feel how slowly I'm breathing? . . . Can you breathe with me? In . . . Out . . ."

Eddie began to match Marilyn's breathing. They sat for 5 minutes or so. "Good, Eddie. Good." The easing was barely perceptible at first, but gradually he grew limp. "Ah, I feel you letting your muscles rest. That's so much better, Eddie. I'm going to take my fingers off your wrists now, but I'll keep my hands close to yours. OK?" Marilyn eased her grip, and Eddie let his hands fall. Marilyn put her hands gently on top of his. "Good, Eddie."

They sat a few more minutes. "Would you like me to let go of your legs?" Marilyn asked. Eddie nodded. She unwound her legs, and they both shifted a little. He didn't want to get very far away. Nan came back in.

"How you two doing?" she asked.

"Fine, I think," Marilyn said. "We're both a lot more relaxed. I've been wondering if Eddie would like a *really* cold soda out of the machine."

"Eddie, what kind of soda would you like?" Nan asked.

"Dr. Pepper."

"You got it. Let's go get it, and then you can come down to my room with me. You might want to draw. Maybe take a nap. What do you think?"

Eddie scrambled to his feet and Marilyn after him. Nan put her arm around his shoulder and walked him out of the office.

"You all right?" Rose asked from across her desk.

"Yeah. I'm OK, but I think I'll be sore in the morning."

"He's a strong little devil," Rose sympathized.

"Yeah, especially with all that adrenalin shooting around in his system," Marilyn agreed.

"Did you get lunch?" Rose asked.

"No, I guess I didn't. Does Florence have everything put away?"

"Probably, but I'll go see."

"That would be great. I'll just sit in my office for a little while."

A few minutes later, Florence came in with a slightly shriveled hot dog and a mound of potato salad. "Rose says you had a rough go of it with Eddie. I'm real sorry, but I put away most of the food. I found this for you though."

"Oh, thanks, Florence. That potato salad'll hit the spot." Marilyn realized that she was very hungry.

"I know it's none of my business, boss, but why do you let kids pull stuff like that? If you ask me, someone should just beat that Eddie's butt. Do that a couple of times, and you wouldn't have no more trouble with him."

"I wish it were that simple." Marilyn smiled and shook her head.

"I know, boss. Just thought I'd get my two cents in," Florence said on her way out.

Rose came to the door. "You want me to hold your calls for a little while?"

"Thanks, Rose. Give me 15 minutes, will you?"

"Will do."

Marilyn sat eating, glad to be alone. I shouldn't have done that, she thought. I shouldn't have held him like that. Maybe I should just have cleared the area and let him punch it out with himself. Maybe he *is* SED. No. He seems so normal most of the time. If he just had another teacher. I don't think he'd be so bad with someone else. Lil could probably work with him. God knows, she'd try.

At the end of the day, Nan poked her head in. Marilyn was glad to see her. "Nan, what got Eddie started? Do you know?"

"He doesn't have any resistance right now. He's upset about Tess and Mitch going off and getting married. They never did tell him anything. Just left and came back married. And then Jeremy wasn't going to give him an inch." Marilyn looked puzzled. "You know Jeremy. He's the kid with the gravelly voice in Eddie's class." Marilyn nodded in recognition. "Well, usually all the kids are pretty good at ignoring Eddie, but this time Jeremy gave it right back to him, and Eddie went crazy."

"I guess."

"Come to find out, Jeremy's had a tough week last week, too. His dad moved out, and then his hamster died. He asked Eddie to move over at the lunch table so that he could sit by his buddy. Eddie wouldn't do it, and Jeremy tried to push him. Eddie started hitting him, and he slugged him back. Marge was on duty. She came over and told them to leave the lunchroom. They went out into the front hall and started fighting all over again. I guess when you came, somebody had already pulled Jeremy off, but nobody could do anything with Eddie. Except you," Nan added.

"Oh, I don't know, Nan," Marilyn said. "It didn't feel right, taking him down like that."

"You had to do it. He would have hurt someone. Besides, he needed to be held."

"How'd he do for the rest of the afternoon?"

"Good. Almost like nothing had happened. I had him draw for awhile. He drew a family of cats—black kittens and a black mother cat. He spent a lot of time on them. The mother cat didn't have any eyes. What do you make of that?" Nan asked.

"Looks pretty straightforward to me. Tess doesn't see him."

"That's right," Nan said. "That's what this is all about. Being invisible can make you crazy."

21

Despite everyone's predictions and Estelle's pronouncements, Eddie is doing better, not worse, this year with Lil Wagner as his teacher. Lil is 35, tall and shy, her short hair touched with early grey. She carries her weight easily and wears dark cotton pants, hand-knit sweaters, and earrings in intense blues, purples, and reds that hint at her love of art. She walks along the halls with her head bent and is quiet in meetings, but when she looks up to smile, her hazel eyes twinkle with humor.

Lil feels fortunate to be teaching and among the children. For 8 years she patiently made her way toward a degree while she worked for an insurance company. Then, after 2 years of substitute teaching, Marilyn hired her. The other teachers still don't feel as if they know her very well. "Lil keeps to herself," they say, but they like her. Marilyn does too, and, beyond that, respects her huge appetite for learning. She was the first to sign up for a summer class in the new art curriculum. Last winter she took one class in language development and another one in how to deal with drug-affected families. Whenever Marilyn mentions a book or article, Lil either nods knowingly or writes down the title and author.

Even though Marilyn has known Lil for 3 years, she has collected only a handful of details about her life. She is married; she and her husband are restoring an old house; they have no children, but they do have a golden retriever puppy. Marilyn wishes that she knew more, but she also appreciates Lil for not letting her life spill over into school. Despite her reticence, Marilyn senses Lil's support and doesn't want to take advantage of it, so it wasn't easy for her to ask Lil to take Eddie and a split class.

All through September Marilyn watches Lil and Eddie for signs of trouble. When Lil walks down the hall with her class, Eddie is at the end of the line—a few feet behind the next child. He sits by himself at lunch and stands alone by the corner of the building when the children are outside. He does not join in games, and he does not have friends. Warm or cold, inside or out, he wears his black jacket.

If it had been another child, Marilyn would have tried to talk him out of wearing it in class, but she decides to let Lil and Eddie negotiate the jacket between themselves.

Mr. Schneider notices Marilyn's leniency and doesn't like it. "That Eddie Harris kid—the one Estelle had all the trouble with— he's always got his jacket on. It's not a good example. The other boys will see him wearing it and get ideas."

"I think it'll be all right, Harry. Eddie's a loner. The boys aren't going to follow his lead. It would be different if Joey took to wearing a jacket. Then we'd see 10 boys wearing one the next day."

"Well, I don't know. I hate to get something like that started," Mr. Schneider says ominously.

After a month of watching, Marilyn sees Eddie in the cafeteria one morning. He has taken his scrambled eggs and toast over to the apron of the stage and is using it as a table.

"Looks like a good breakfast this morning." Marilyn starts out on neutral ground.

"It's OK," Eddie says, taking fast, big bites of the light yellow eggs streaked with white.

"How's it going with Mrs. Wagner, Eddie?"

"OK."

"Do you like her?"

Eddie takes a bite of toast and looks out toward the tables full of children eating breakfast. He nods his head ever so slightly.

"Good," Marilyn says. "I think Mrs. Wagner likes you too. Is Mitch home now?"

Eddie shakes his head. "Nope. Went to Texas. Won't be back for 2 weeks."

"Do you miss him?"

He shrugs.

Marilyn goes down to Lil's room after school. Lil is standing on one of the children's tables with a handful of clothespins in one hand and five or six pictures under her arm. She has strung wires across the room to use as picture lines for the children's work.

"I'll hand them up," Marilyn says.

"Thanks. The kids and I painted our self-portraits yesterday. We're going to write about ourselves tomorrow. We're trying to think of all the ways we can to tell about ourselves."

Marilyn hands up five or six pictures to Lil, then comes to one that stops her.

Lil looks at Marilyn, pauses, steps off the table onto one of the little chairs, and then to the floor. She takes one side of the picture, and the two of them stand looking at it. "Eddie."

Almost the entire field is smeared with red. In the bottom right-hand quadrant, a delicately detailed figure stands with legs spread. The figure wears a black jacket. His black hair hides his forehead and accentuates piercing eyes that stare out from the surrounding red. He has no mouth. His left hand falls straight down at his side. His right hand is raised at a right angle and holds a sword with drops of red dripping from its point. At his feet lies a tiny, but identical, figure surrounded by a pool of red. A small trickle connects this pool with the red of the background.

"Has he told you anything about this?" Marilyn asks.

"Not a thing. In a way, I don't think there's anything that he needs to tell me."

Marilyn sits down at the table, and Lil sits down across from her.

"How's he doing? "Marilyn asks.

"Well, I think he's trying very, very hard."

"At his work, you mean?"

"Yes. And at everything else, too. It's complicated. I don't think I can explain very well. But it's like he's trying to protect us. He does everything he can to put himself in a safety zone. He wants to sit at a single desk. Everybody else is at six-place tables. He never goes up to sharpen his pencil when someone is at the pencil sharpener. He walks behind everyone else in line."

"I know. I've watched him doing that. So, what's this all about?"

"He's trying to avoid any kind of contact that would set him off. He doesn't want to let his temper get the best of him. He really doesn't."

"Does he have any friends at all?"

Lil shakes her head. "No, I don't think so. No friends, although the children do respect him in a funny kind of way."

"What do you mean?"

"Well, it's a mixture of respect and fear, I guess. They respect how smart he is in math—he's the best in the class, better than any of the fourth graders. It's just amazing how quickly he comes up with solutions. And his drawing. His pictures fascinate all of us. I just wish they weren't so grisly."

"I didn't see any of that violence in his drawings last year, although we should probably check with Estelle to see what she picked up on. What about the fear?" Marilyn asks, not wanting to let this part of Lil's analysis get lost.

"They've all seen his outbursts. They're afraid they'll set him off, so they avoid him as much as he avoids them. It's just awful—how alone he is. I can't imagine how that must feel."

"But do you know how much you help him just by trying to imagine, Lil? I think it must make a tremendous difference to him."

"You know, I like him. I really do. I think the children do, too. If one of them starts to tease him or something, I can count on someone else telling the child not to bug him. It's more than fear. They sense how lonely and different he feels, too. Children are amazing—how sensitive they can be to each other. It's different with . . ." Lil's voice trails off.

"Adults?" Lil nods. "I know. We ask the children to do all the things that we aren't willing to do—share, compromise, listen." Marilyn can't explain further. "So you think that Eddie can maintain in the classroom?" she asks, drawing an inference that is perhaps too hopeful.

Lil hesitates. "I think so. It's not that he doesn't have problems. He has some major ones. He's really different, and sometimes I think he's just a time bomb, but . . . we're doing all right."

"Well, keep me posted, will you? If you start to see any changes, even little ones, let me know. If we need to, we'll bring him up again in Screening Committee. We're still carrying him on our review list."

"OK, will do."

"Do you have any contact with Tess?"

"His mom? No, I haven't seen her. I've written her a couple of notes, but she hasn't answered. I'm not pressing anything."

"That's about right. If it gets to the point, though, that you feel as if you have to talk with Tess, let me know. I've gotten to know her a little bit." Marilyn gets up. She stands there for a moment or two. "Thanks for being Eddie's teacher, Lil."

Lil smiles and waves Marilyn off as she climbs back up on the table. "No thanks needed. I like him."

Marilyn doesn't see much of Eddie all through October and November. When she does see him, he is willing to look at her and to give short answers to her questions. She is reassured.

It is the first week in December, a day too cold and wet for the children to go outside for noon recess. Some of them are watching a video in Marge Friedman's room, some are in the library, some in the computer room, and too many in the gym with Tom. As usual on "inside" days, Marilyn makes her rounds. She is coming back toward the office from the library when she sees Tom swing out of the gym door ahead of her. He is taking long strides, faster and more deliberate than his usual leisurely gait. But that does not take Marilyn's notice in the same way that something else does. Tom is carrying Eddie across his shoulder. Eddie is pounding Tom's back with his fists, but Tom is holding his legs high and tight so that he can't kick. Marilyn runs to catch up.

"He and Joey got into it. Joey went down to the office on his own, but Eddie's just tearing the place apart. I decided to show him who's boss," Tom says tersely. Marilyn feels a rush of sympathy for Eddie but has no suggestion for what Tom might have done differently. She hurries along beside them. Tom deposits Eddie in Marilyn's office. "He's all yours. I'm going to get some lunch."

Eddie stays in his chair. It looks as if he's not going to kick and hit. Marilyn looks out into the outer office and sees Joey sitting in one of the waiting chairs. "Listen, buddy. You stay put here while I go talk to Joey."

Joey sits slumped in his chair, staring straight ahead, his lapis eyes expressionless. "What happened, Joey?"

"Nothing."

"Oh, come on, Joey. *Something* happened. You're here and Eddie's in my office. Mr. Campbell doesn't bring guys down to the office for nothing."

"Well, this time he did," Joey says, still staring straight ahead. Marilyn waits. Joey stares. She is about to start pressing again when he blurts out, "All I was doing was walking around that kid and watching him. That's all. He jumped me, and I defended myself. I can do that. My dad says it's the law that you can defend yourself. Mr. Campbell didn't believe me. He didn't give me a chance to explain. That kid's weird."

"Why were you walking around him and watching him, Joey?"

"I told you. He's weird. I wanted to see what he would do. But I wasn't bothering him."

"Well, he thought you were bothering him."

"Can't he take a joke or nothin'?"

"Who said anything about a joke? You were harassing Eddie. That isn't funny, Joey."

"Well, I thought it was funny."

This is not going to be a day for negotiation. "Joey, I want you to stay away from Eddie."

"Why? It's a free country. I can walk by anybody I want to, and I can look at anybody I want to."

"Not at school, you can't, not when it bothers someone. It's an invasion of their privacy when you follow kids around and stare at them. It makes them feel creepy."

"He is a creep, a little creep."

"OK, Joey. I think you need a little time to cool off. You're not ready to solve any problems right now. I want you just to sit here until the bell rings. Then you go on back to class. I'll talk to Nan about what's going on with you guys, and she'll talk to you this afternoon. How does that sound?"

"Whatever," Joey says, still looking straight ahead.

Marilyn glances at the clock. Five minutes until the bell rings. She goes back to Eddie. He's sitting in mirror posture to Joey— slumped in his chair glaring straight ahead, still angry. "Joey was stalking you, wasn't he?" she asks. Eddie nods. "I guess that made you really angry, so you tackled him. And then you guys started throwing punches?" Eddie nods again. "Joey's not feeling like talking right now. He's still pretty mad. When the bell rings, he's going back to class.

"I'm going to explain what happened to Nan and ask her to talk to you this afternoon. Would that be all right with you?" Eddie shakes his head. "No?" Marilyn tries to clarify what Eddie means. "You won't talk to Joey?" Eddie shakes his head vigorously this time. Marilyn is not surprised. "That would be hard, wouldn't it? I don't know how we're going to get this worked out, Eddie. I'll talk it over with Nan and see if she has any good ideas. Will you talk to Nan this afternoon?" Eddie nods his head. "OK. That's enough for me." Marilyn hears the bell ring. "It's time to go to class. I'll walk down with you and explain to Mrs. Wagner what happened." The real reason Marilyn's walking Eddie to class is that she doesn't want Eddie and Joey to run into each other in the hall.

As Nan and Marilyn get out their lunches a few minutes later, she gives Nan her assignment.

"I don't know, Marilyn," Nan says. "This is going to be a hard one. Neither one of those boys has any problem-solving skills. Joey's just a mess right now. His mother out-and-out told him last week she doesn't want him. She's not coming back. Joey's real upset about it, and it's hard for him because his dad wants him to help so much with the little kids."

"I could tell he was having a hard time. I couldn't get through to him at all."

"I'll talk to those guys separately. See if I can get them to agree to leave each other alone. Joey could pulverize Eddie, and he knows it—that's why he's picking on him. He's looking for a target. And the trouble is that Eddie will rise to the occasion. If we don't watch it, they'll be on each other before the week is out."

"You know, it's funny, Nan. But nobody's ever beaten up Eddie. I don't think anyone's even so much as thrown a punch at him," Marilyn muses.

"You're right. I'd never thought about that. Wonder what it is about him."

"Well, we'd better not bank on it this time," Marilyn says. "Joey is in a nasty mood."

"Right. I'll get to them as soon as I finish here. I'd like—just once—not to have to mop up after lunch."

The next morning Marilyn goes into the cafeteria to get a piece of toast. "You seen Eddie this morning?" Florence asks as she spreads soft butter on the warm toast.

"No. Where is he?"

"Over on the stairs going up on the stage. Kinda hunched up. I wouldn'ta seen him except I almost tripped over him when I had to go up there to make an announcement on the mike."

Eddie's left eye is swollen shut. There's a long scrape down his nose and the side of his face. "What happened, Eddie?" He doesn't answer. "Did you have a run-in with Joey?" Still no answer. Eddie's not going to talk about it.

Out in the front hall, Marilyn encounters a cluster of excited boys. "Ms. Wallace! Did you see Eddie?"

"I sure did. Do you guys know what happened?"

"Yeah, we were tailing them. Joey said he was gonna beat up Eddie after school, so we watched to see what was gonna happen. Joey hid out in them big bushes across the street. Then, when Eddie came, he took out after him. Eddie's real fast. He ran hard all the way to the store. Then Joey caught up with him, just jumped on his back like he was a gorilla or something. Eddie was so mad. He fought an' kicked; his face was all red. Those big old veins on his head stood out like they was gonna pop.

"Then Joey pushed Eddie up against that cement wall back behind the store. He punched him hard right smack in the eye. Then he grabbed his hair and turned his cheek up against the wall and rubbed it. He was yellin' at Eddie: 'Don't mess with me, faggot. Don't never look at me again. You'll be dead meat. You hear me? Dead meat.' That's what he said, Ms. Wallace. He said those words.

"Eddie didn't say nothin'. He kinda leaned against the wall like he was out of it. Joey went into the store. We tried to talk to Eddie to see how bad he was hurt, but he just walked off. Wouldn't talk to no one. Pretty soon Joey came out with a Big Gulp. He looked around and said, 'Where's that little faggot? Where'd he go?'

"We said, 'You'd better be careful, Joey. You'll be in big trouble.' But Joey said no he wouldn't, that he was off school property and that there wasn't nothin' anybody could do about it, not even you, Ms. Wallace. Is that right, Ms. Wallace?"

22

The weeks pass without Marilyn's noticing Eddie much. He's seldom in trouble, and Lil seems less worried about him. Then she suddenly starts to hear about him again. In the space of 10 days, he fights with someone in the lunchroom, hits someone on the playground, pushes someone down when Rachel is bringing the class back to Lil's room from music, and hits three other children during an assembly. "We've got to do something about Eddie," Nan says as she signs in on a Friday morning. "I thought about him half the night. Everybody's complaining about him—Tom, Marge, Christine, Rachel. Estelle, too, but she doesn't count. She's picking up on what everyone else is saying."

"What about Lil? What's Lil saying?" Marilyn asks.

"Don't know. Haven't heard anything from her. She just puts up with it, I guess."

"Well, do you want to put him on a behavior plan?" Marilyn asks.

"No. No, I don't want to do that. I'll bet I've tried eight or nine plans with him since he was in first grade. He won't buy in. You know that, Marilyn," Nan says with an impatient edge.

"Screening Committee, then?" Marilyn makes the next obvious suggestion.

"Yeah. I guess so. I don't think it'll do much good. What we need is . . . " Nan doesn't finish her sentence.

"Tell you what. I'll talk to Lil, see how she feels about things. Then we'll go from there," Marilyn says.

"Sounds good to me. Catchya later," Nan says as she heads down to the boiler room for her morning cigarette.

Marilyn is still standing at the counter as Grace Johnson signs in.

"Marilyn, do you know my Stuart?"

Everyone knows Grace's Stuart. He is always the last one down the hall and into his classroom. Florence is always scolding him for losing his lunch ticket, and Nan drags his forgotten jacket in from the playground two or three times a week. After awhile Stuart comes asking if anyone's seen his jacket. "Look on the Lost & Found table,

Stuart." To Stuart's and no one else's surprise, it's always there. Whenever her class goes somewhere, Grace holds his hand, having learned from experience that, as often as not, he'll start off for the music room when everyone else is going to the gym.

"You know what he did yesterday?" Grace continues. "He learned to read right before my eyes. I'd about given up on the little guy. He's so nutty. I never thought he'd settle down enough to get it. But he did. I called him up to the table to read, and he just sat down and read the whole little book. Didn't miss a word. Then I had him read another one just to be sure, and he read that one, too. I was so happy I just grabbed him and cried. And then he grabbed me back and cried, too. He couldn't believe it either. After lunch, can I send him down so he can show you?"

"I'd love it."

"You know, Marilyn, there are lots of days when I think it's time for me to go. I've been at this for so long, but then I get a miracle like Stuart. There's no reason in the world why that kid would learn to read. He's just a mess—lives down in those awful, cramped little apartments with his two brothers and his mom. I know for a fact she leaves them alone all the time—tends bar, sleeps most of the day. I'd bet you my bottom dollar there's not a book in that house and that she's never read those kids a story. Probably doesn't talk to them either. Just lets them run. So you tell me, why did he learn to read with all those strikes against him?"

"Because of you. You gave him a classroom full of books and language, you loved him, and you really wanted him to read. You're the miracle, Grace."

"Well, he's not home free yet. The two of us have a long haul ahead. He's got to get some skills under his belt, and we don't have a lot of year left. Wish he'd caught on about 4 months ago."

Stuart brings his book down at 1:00. Marilyn watches him as he arranges himself in his chair. His straw-blond hair stands up every which way, the effect of a 4-month-old crew cut and the fact that he gets himself ready for school in the morning. He's wearing the same green sweatsuit that he's worn for a couple of weeks, and Marilyn half suspects that he's sleeping in it too. He stops wiggling and looks intently at the cover of his book. He pokes his tongue between his teeth and follows the author's name with his finger. "Brian Wild . . ." He stops to think. Then, in a rush, ". . . Brian Wildsmith!" He looks up at Marilyn and grins. He reads the title. "All Fall Down." And the rest of the book.

"That's terrific, Stuart! You read *every* word."

"I know. I've got the idea of reading now."

"I'll bet you're happy about that."

"So's Miss Johnson. She was so happy she cried."

"How did that make you feel, Stuart? "

"Like I was going to cry, too. And I did."

"I think Miss Johnson really loves you."

"We love each other." Stuart has had enough sentimentalizing. He asks Marilyn the question he has asked dozens of times before. "When are you going to do the August birthdays? My birthday's in August. There's no school then."

"In June, Stuart. The last week of school, we'll have cake for all the summer birthdays. OK?" Marilyn brushes Stuart's cheek lightly with her hand.

"OK."

The children went home a half an hour ago, and the office has fallen unnaturally quiet. The phone hasn't rung for 10 minutes, and it feels as if it won't ring again this afternoon. "I'm going down to see Lil for a few minutes," Marilyn says as she passes Rose's desk.

"OK," Rose says without looking up from counting change to take to the bank tomorrow.

The afternoon is warm, so Marilyn cuts through the courtyard. Mr. Schneider's daffodils have come into early bloom in this protected space. She slows her walk for a quick feast on the crowded yellows. As she comes through the back door, she hears a thud in Mr. Schneider's room, then muffled voices. She hesitates with her hand on the door knob for a second, then goes in. Mr. Schneider is behind his desk just inside the door. Nathan stands at the front of the room by the blackboard. Mona sprawls across the floor between him and the first row of desk chairs. She is just putting her hand on the floor to get up. "He pushed me," she pants as she gets up. "That kid knocked me down on the ground. He's violent. Crazy. Out of control. I don't know what I'm going to do with him."

Marilyn looks from Mona to Nathan to Mr. Schneider. Mr. Schneider finally finds his voice. "Mona came in to get Nathan's assignments. He was absent today."

Mona picks up the story. "You're damn right he was absent today. He skipped school. Did you know that, Ms. Wallace? Did you?" Marilyn shakes her head. "Well you should've. What's the matter with you people? Don't you even know who's in school? You know what he did? He stole 20 dollars outta my purse. When I found out the money was missing, I came up here to talk to him, and he wasn't here. You wasn't either. They said you went to a meeting or something. But I at least thought they'd tell you."

"Well, I haven't gone through all the notes on my desk yet, but I'm sure Rose left one for me. It's been a busy day." Marilyn makes the best excuse she can.

"Yeah, well I went looking for him. Finally found him playing video games at the mall. Shoulda known. Shoulda gone there first. That's always what he wants to do. Well, I can tell you one thing. He's not going to leave the house again 'til hell freezes over.

"I brought him up here to get a truckload of work for him. He's just going to sit there and do page after page of homework. No TV. No nothin'. I've had it with this kid. I've just had it. First my jewelry, now my money. Every week, it's something else. He pushes me around, too. This isn't the first time. He does it at home whenever he feels like it. I mean to tell you, I'm half scared."

"Mona, you need to get ahold of your caseworker right now. Tell her what's happening. You can't go on like this. It's not good for either one of you," Marilyn says.

"I can't talk to that woman. She's already looking to take Nathan away. She hears something like this, and it'll be curtains."

"A breather, Mona. You two need a breather. Maybe it would help if Nathan went to a foster home temporarily—just for a couple of weeks," Marilyn urges.

"They ain't into breathers. They'll want him for a long time, want to put him in one of those treatment centers."

Mona's afraid, Marilyn thinks. She's afraid that if Nathan starts to get well, she'll have to make some changes. She wants Nathan to be this sick. She says, "Well, do you have everything you need, Mona? I think Mr. Schneider has papers to correct."

"That's right," Mr. Schneider says.

Mona and Nathan walk out of the room together. "You two sure you'll be all right?" Marilyn asks after them as they leave.

"Yeah, sure. We'll be fine," Mona says over her shoulder, sarcasm running deep through her voice.

"That's just about the strangest thing I've seen in all my years of teaching," Mr. Schneider says. "What do you do? You wouldn't suspend a student for knocking his own mother down, I guess." Even Mr. Schneider, who is usually eager for Marilyn to suspend students, sees the complexity of the situation.

"I don't know," Marilyn says. "I don't think so. Besides, Mona would have raised holy hell if I'd tried to do that."

"Yeah, you're right. Well, I'll tell you one thing: I'm glad I'm close to retirement."

When Marilyn opens her door, Lil is sitting at the kidney-shaped table, where she works with small groups of children during the day. She looks up from a stack of their journals. "These are so wonderful! I'd never get to know the kids as well without them. I always kind of dread sitting down to read them. I think I'm too tired; then I get going, and I can't stop."

"Does Eddie write much in his?" Marilyn asks as she sits down.

"No. Just scribbles and scrawls. Maybe I'm wrong, but I let him sketch. I keep thinking that if he draws long enough, he'll begin to write," Lil says, a little reticent about her unorthodoxy.

"Just do what your gut tells you, Lil. It's not as if anyone has any answers. How's he doing in class?"

Lil hesitates as she answers. "You know children who have dozens of seizures every day, and you may not know it except that their eyes change and they lose track of what's going on around them for a few seconds? And then, once in awhile, they have a bigger seizure that everyone notices?" Marilyn nods. "Well," Lil goes on, "I think that's the way it is for Eddie. He's having continual small shocks of rage. Most of the time, I don't notice except when I see him shake his head hard, or he moves his chair away from someone, or picks up his things and goes to the table at the back of the room. And then someone bumps him or looks at him funny, and he's on his feet ready to fight. He's forgotten where he is or what's going on. He's literally blind with rage. Then we all have to back off and give him space."

"How long does it take for him to calm down?" Marilyn asks.

"If we get out of his way, probably only 3 or 4 minutes. Not long. You should see it, Marilyn. The children know exactly what to do. They just go about their business as calmly and quietly as anything. They know he's going through some kind of hell, and they're sorry."

"They're probably the best therapists he could have," Marilyn says. Lil nods. "How often does he have one of these spells?"

"It varies. Sometimes once a day. Sometimes he has a long stretch where he's pretty good, and then he'll only have one or two a week." Lil looks at Marilyn, trying to figure out what she's getting at.

"Eddie's having a lot of trouble around school—in the cafeteria, during recess, in the halls."

"I know," Lil says. "Tom and Marge and Christine have been complaining to me. Rachel. Estelle, too. She says she sees him tripping children and punching them in the hall. It's getting pretty bad, huh?"

"Yeah, it is. People are fed up with him."

"It's harder for them. They're not used to him. Maybe I should keep him with me more. He could eat lunch with me in the classroom and then draw instead of going out to play."

"That's really good of you to offer, Lil, but I don't think you should do that. You need your time without children. And, besides, we might just be delaying the inevitable," Marilyn says.

"What do you mean?" Lil is worried.

"Well, I think we need to talk about him in Screening Committee. It may be time to ask for an assessment. We've talked and talked about it and never done it." Marilyn tries to put this position forward as gently as she can.

Even so, alarm spreads across Lil's face. "You don't think he should go into a self-contained classroom, do you?"

"To tell you the truth, I don't know what I think. But I do think that he's maintaining as well as he is because you're making some pretty extraordinary efforts, Lil. I don't know what it will be like for him next year if we can't put him with someone as patient and wise as you are."

"But isn't that what we're here for?"

"Yeah, Lil, it is," Marilyn says sadly as she fingers her keys.

"Well, if you want me to refer him, I will," Lil says. "But I want to ask for an academic as well as a psychological. Something's wrong with his reading and writing. I don't know what it is, but it just doesn't seem right to me."

The next few days are hard going. Every day 3 or 4 first graders spill their lunch trays on the cafeteria floor for no apparent reason.

Children who are usually even-tempered get into squabbles and brawls on the playground. Jolene is working in the front hall before school putting up the new PTA schedule and hears Florence scolding children for scuffling around in the lunch ticket line. "I know it's none of my business, but that woman shouldn't yell at the kids like that." On Mondays and Fridays at least four or five teachers call in sick. "People sure are taking a lot of R&R," Rose says as she brings in payroll cards for Marilyn to sign.

After school on Friday, Nan is in the office getting a phone number out of the file. "Want a cup of tea? I'll put the water on," Marilyn offers.

Nan would rather have a cigarette and a coke, but she says, "Sure."

Marilyn hands Nan a mug and then slowly dunks the bag up and down in her mug. "What is it this week? Nothing's gone right."

Nan blows on her tea and looks up over the rim as she takes a slow sip. "It's the kids. They're upset, having a real hard time." Marilyn waits for Nan to go on. "I didn't even get time to talk to you about it, we've been so busy. Did you know Amy's baby sister died last weekend?"

"God. No. I can't even remember seeing Amy this week. What happened?"

"SIDS. Amy found her."

"Oh, Nan. That baby was only a month old. That's awful."

"I know it."

"Have you talked with her?"

"Yeah. A little bit. She's really in denial, though. You know how she gets. Then, the year-old brother of one of the kindergarten kids got meningitis and died. The whole block around where he lived is crazy, people afraid they'll get it and stuff. And then there's April's family. You remember them? They came in September. You put April in Jane's room."

"Sure. I remember April. Has a little brother in kindergarten and a baby sister—Cliff and Autumn. They've moved around a lot."

"Right. You're good with names. Well, they moved into a little house over on the other side of the park. It burned down Wednesday night. They lost everything. Jolene has been helping to get them clothes and stuff, but it's pretty bad."

"I didn't know *that,* either." Marilyn shakes her head slowly. "Don't you feel like we only see the smallest tip of the iceberg?"

"Yup. That's why we have such a hard time figuring out the kids sometimes. I know they've been so wild all week because this stuff is upsetting them."

"Do they know about it?"

"You betcha. They all talk about it in one way or another—even the kindergartners. It scares them. They think their little brother or sister might die in the night or that their house will catch on fire. It's too hard for them."

Half an hour after Rose leaves, Marilyn is still trying to get her paperwork done, but she can't concentrate. She walks down to Jane's room, and, as she expected, Jane is straightening up the shelves in her little classroom library. The two of them settle in the book corner, Marilyn in the rocking chair, Jane sitting on the floor in front of the bookshelf. "Why didn't you tell me about April?"

"I tried to a couple of times, Marilyn, but I couldn't get to you. Whenever I came by your office, you had someone in there. Besides, I figured you didn't need one more thing to deal with. You looked like you were having a hard week."

"Yeah. It was bad, but I still wish I'd known. How's she doing?"

"Poor baby. She's trying to be so grown-up about everything. Talks about helping her mom. About taking care of the baby. They're back living in a motel for now, and she says cooking off the hot plate is like camping. She lost most of her clothes. I thought I'd go get her a couple of outfits this weekend."

"I'll give you some money. Maybe you could get her a new jacket, too."

"Thanks, Marilyn. That'll help." Jane pauses for a long time. "Why do we do it, Marilyn? What's the point when all these children have such hard lives? No matter how much we do, it isn't enough. Does anything make any difference?"

Jane has asked the question that Marilyn tries not to ask herself. She is quiet for awhile. "I don't know, Jane. I guess we do it just because it's there to be done. And once in awhile we get a miracle. Grace had one this week. Her Stuart learned to read. Besides, you love them, Jane. I know you do."

"You do too, Marilyn."

"I just can't imagine doing anything else."

Jane is crying softly. She reaches her hand out toward Marilyn. Marilyn takes it and squeezes it.

23

Lil comes to the Screening Committee nervous and prepared. As the women settle in, she says to Marilyn, "I went over to talk to Tess about this meeting. I wanted her to come, but she just wouldn't. She kept saying, 'You guys go ahead. You do what you think is best.'"

"It would take an act of God to get her here, but thanks for trying."

"Are we ready to go?" Christine asks, staring the women around the table into silence. "We'll start out with Eddie Harris. He was last reviewed in December when he seemed to be functioning fairly well. In the last few weeks, though, problems have been developing." Christine nods to Lil to begin.

Lil goes through the background material everyone is used to hearing. "But I want to say something about Eddie. I know we always talk about his behavior and how bright he is, but I think there's something going on with his learning. He's not writing. I mean, not at all. And if you ask him to, he only prints a few letters and then gets so frustrated he gives up."

Marge interrupts. "But almost anything frustrates him."

"That's not really right. I watch him work through his frustration when he's doing math, and he has incredible discipline when he's drawing. No. It's something else. I notice too that it's just impossible for him to copy anything from the board. I think he's got some kind of perception problem. We need to get an academic evaluation on him. And a psychological, too, of course."

"Well, I think that's fine," Christine says. The main thing is to get him processed this year." You "process" cheese, Marilyn thinks. "It's almost March, you know, and these placements take forever. I don't think any of us wants to go through another year with Eddie."

"That's not true, Christine!" Lil blurts out. "The last thing I want is for him to be in a self-contained classroom. I want to know what's going on with him, but I don't want to give him up."

Christine shrugs her shoulders. "Well, let's get these papers signed. It's a step at a time, you know," she says trying to bring a little lightness to the moment. "And, Lil, we know how hard you're working with Eddie. You've really held him together this year."

"Thanks," Lil says, more out of politeness than out of any sense that Christine understands what she's been trying to say.

Whenever Marilyn sees Lil during the next couple of weeks, Lil looks worried, and is even quieter than usual. Marilyn spots her standing by the back of the cafeteria during an assembly. The children sit cross-legged on the floor gazing up at the storyteller and her elaborate and beautiful puppets that swoop and bounce and bob through "Billy Goat Gruff." Marilyn goes to stand beside Lil.

"Are you OK?"

Lil looks at her with some surprise. "Why?"

"I don't know. You've just seemed a little down lately."

"I guess I am . . . I'm worried about Eddie." They both watch the storyteller for awhile. Then she continues, "And I really think I offended Christine in the Screening Committee. She's hardly said a thing to me since then."

"Christine has some pretty strong opinions. She's really tied up with Eddie too. You know, she was Tess's teacher."

"Mmm. She told me. But does that make her an expert on Eddie?" Lil blurts out. Her lower lip quivers. Having Eddie is taking its toll. She's getting possessive of him in the way good teachers do when they have a difficult child and not enough help.

"Lil. Are you doing anything for yourself?" It is a trite question designed to give them both a polite end to this uncomfortable conversation. Lil looks at Marilyn and shrugs. Marilyn does not press the point.

Just before lunch on Monday, Rose comes into Marilyn's office. "Lil wants you to come down to her room." When Marilyn opens the door, Eddie is standing in the middle of the room. Three or four chairs and two desks are lying on their sides on the floor. The children are gathered in a wide circle on the edge of the room, and Lil stands between them and Eddie. "I don't know what happened. He started to kick Rob. Rob jumped out of the way, and Eddie went after him. I got between them, and Rob ran out of the room. I don't know where he is now. Then Eddie started kicking the chairs and tables over. He's never done anything like this before."

Marilyn goes and stands right beside Eddie. He is red and breathing hard. His eyes are moving quickly from face to face, threatening anyone who makes a move toward him, but he takes no notice of Marilyn.

"I want you to leave the room with me now, Eddie," Marilyn says. "Will you do that?" Eddie does not answer; neither does he make a lunge for her. She turns and starts to walk out of the room, and he follows.

As they walk toward the office, Eddie hugs the wall, staying as far away as possible. She does not look at him or talk to him. She has learned Eddie's rules to near perfection. When they get to the office, she says in a perfectly flat voice, "Please go on in and sit down in my office, Eddie. I'll be in just as soon as I've called Mrs. Wagner to let her know that we got here."

"We're here, Lil."

"Oh, good. Rob came back. He was hiding in the boys' bathroom. He saw you go by and knew it was safe. Are you going to send Eddie home?"

"Yeah, I'll call Tess and have her come up."

Marilyn makes the call. Tess says she'll be there as soon as she can pack up the baby.

Eddie has chosen not to sit down. He is standing by the windows looking out. "What happened, Eddie?"

Much to Marilyn's surprise, he answers. "He looked at me."

"Rob *looked* at you?" Eddie nods. "And that made you angry?" He nods again. "And you wanted to kick him because he looked at you?"

Eddie is panting; short, hot little pants. "No, I didn't want to kick him. But that's all you'd let me do."

"What did you want to do, Eddie?"

"I wanted to blind him."

"How would you have done that?" Marilyn asks quietly.

"Hairspray. I would have sprayed it in his eyes, and he would have been blind."

"But you didn't have any hairspray. Is that it, Eddie?"

"I knew where it was. I could have gotten it off Mrs. Wagner's shelf, and I could have sprayed it in his eyes."

"Why didn't you do that, Eddie?" Marilyn asks. She is riveted by this conversation.

"Because you would have kicked me out of Mrs. Wagner's room. You would have made me go back to Mrs. Douglas's room."

"I don't think so," Marilyn says.

"You would too. My mom says that if I'm bad, she'll call you up and tell you to give me back to Miss Douglas."

"No, Eddie. Miss Douglas teaches second grade. You're in third grade. It wouldn't help you to put you in Miss Douglas's room. I don't think you like school much now, and you really wouldn't like it if you were in Miss Douglas's room again. Do you like school at all, Eddie?"

Eddie says nothing for awhile, and Marilyn has nearly given up on his answering the question, when he says, very softly, "School is torture."

"Why? Why is it torture?" Marilyn asks, just as softly.

"Everyone looks at me. All the time. Even when they pretend not to, they look at me. Rob looks at me. He laughs at me with his eyes. Nobody's supposed to look at me."

"Thank you for telling me what happened, Eddie. I understand better now." Marilyn pauses and then makes a rough transition. "Eddie, I think you need to spend the rest of the day at home, just so that you can be quiet and let your anger go away a little bit. I called your mom. She'll be here to take you home in a few minutes."

The color rushes back into Eddie's face. Before Marilyn realizes what is happening, he grabs the largest of her violets from the windowsill and smashes it on the floor. He kicks a chair over, then makes a futile, almost comical, attempt to upend Marilyn's desk. He bolts out of the room. As he passes her desk, Rose looks up from the telephone in surprise. Marilyn follows on his heels. He breaks into a run. He passes the cafeteria door and sees the children lining up to go through the lunch line. He spots Rob across the room and runs toward him. Marilyn follows, dodging children as she tries to keep up with him. Eddie jumps on Rob's back, taking the boy by complete surprise.

At that moment, Marge Friedman comes into the cafeteria to begin her lunch duty. She pulls Eddie off of Rob. In the next instant, Marilyn is beside her. Marge, who is a large and strong woman, holds Eddie in front of her, arms around his chest. "I got him, boss. Whatcha want me to do with him?"

"Take him back into my office," Marilyn says, not knowing what good that will do. She just wants him out of the middle of the cafeteria.

Marge tightens her grip around his chest, lifts him an inch off the floor, and starts walking him toward Marilyn's office. "I've wrestled a lot of calves in my day. I can handle this puppy. No problem." Once inside, Marge eyes a chair, backs into it, sits down, and pulls Eddie with her onto her lap. "How's that, Eddie? You comfortable? I'll just sit here with you for a little while, if that's OK with you." She looks around the room. "You got a real mess. Our friend here do that?"

Marilyn nods. "He sure did."

"Well, I guess I'll just hold onto him a little while longer. Wouldn't want to see any more of your pretty flowers bite the dust."

At that moment, Tess walks into the room. She is holding Ricky on her hip. He dangles a bottle of juice from one hand. His face is expressionless. As Tess takes in the scene, her body sags, and—for the first time ever—Marilyn notices fear and sorrow in her eyes. "Eddie is angry, Tess, and he's having a hard time. He wants to hurt another boy in his class because the boy looked at him. He is angry with me, and you can see what he's done here. Ms. Friedman needed to hold him so that he wouldn't run away or hurt anyone. This is pretty serious, Tess."

"I know," Tess says softly. "I know. I don't know what to do."

"Well, right now, I think the three of you should just go home for the rest of the day. We'll start over in the morning."

"You mean you're going to let him come back to school?" Tess asks.

"Yes, I think so. You bring him to school tomorrow, Tess." Then she looks at Eddie. "Eddie, when you come, I want you to tell me and your mom and Mrs. Wagner that you won't try to hurt other children if someone looks at you." Eddie doesn't say anything. "OK, Ms. Friedman, I think you can let Eddie go now. And thank you for helping us."

"Glad to do it, boss. I need to get back to cafeteria duty. Take it easy, Eddie. See ya tomorrow, kiddo." Marge gives Eddie a wave as she leaves.

Eddie is quiet now. Tess puts her arm around his shoulder. He pulls away. "Let's go home, Eddie," she says, and he walks out of the office ahead of her. She follows with Ricky. Marilyn turns to look at her room. She picks up the chairs and sets them in their usual places. Then she goes to look at the smashed violet. She has potted and repotted the old purple violet until it crowded an 11-inch pot. She doesn't think she'll try to save it. She stops at Rose's desk. "After Chuck's through in the cafeteria, will you ask him to clean up the mess in my office?"

"That sure was a nice plant that kid ruined. You had it a long time, didn't you?" Rose asks with real sympathy in her voice.

"Ten years or so. I'll miss it. Well, I think I'm going to walk the halls a little while and then get some lunch."

"Sure thing," Rose says. "Take your time."

She walks down the long hall of the primary wing. A little boy comes out of the bathroom by the first-grade rooms. "There's some people in the bathroom. Nobody's supposed to be in there now," he tattles. Marilyn pushes though the heavy swinging door. The familiar smell of dampness, powdered soap, and unflushed toilets greets her. Something else, too—the sound of crying made louder by the tile, metal, and porcelain surfaces.

In the far corner, between a child-size urinal on one wall and a low sink on the other, Eddie, Tess, and Ricky sit on the floor. Marilyn kneels and puts her arm around Tess. Tears are streaming down her face. Tess looks up at the older woman and shakes her head. "I don't know what to do. I don't know." Marilyn looks at Eddie. She has never seen him cry, but he is crying now—deep, shaking crying.

"There's help, Tess. There's help," Marilyn says.

The testing on Eddie goes faster than anyone could have believed. By the first of April, the psychologist, the social worker, and the speech pathologist present detailed reports about Eddie to the Screening Committee. Christine is talking. "Are you saying that you don't know whether he's learning disabled or not?" she asks Dolores.

"That's about it. His IQ comes out at 142, and his performance in math bears that out. He resisted the entire language assessment, though, and I can't tell whether it was because he couldn't or wouldn't do what I wanted him to do. He became very frustrated. Broke a pencil and threw it across the room at one point. So we really don't have anything to explain why Lil can't get him to write. But we've got him qualified on the psychological. Looks like 'Seriously Disturbed.'"

"Will you be able to show that his disturbance is not environmentally induced?" Marilyn asks.

"Oh, yeah, I think so. It'll be tricky, but I think we can do it. And—with that IQ—we can easily show that he isn't working up to his potential," Dolores says quickly, not wanting to upset Marilyn.

"Does that mean he'll qualify for a behavior classroom?" Marge asks.

"Sure does," Dolores says, "but we've got a little problem there. The classes are all full and have waiting lists."

"He shouldn't go into a behavior classroom anyway," Lil says. "That would be the worst thing you could do for that child—to put him in a room with a lot of other children who are even worse off than he is. At least now he gets to see normal behavior. You can't do that to him."

"We can't *not* do that to him, if he qualifies." Dolores replies.

"That's just where he belongs, if you ask me," Marge offers. "Look, I care about that kid a lot. You all know that. I hate to send kids to behavior rooms, but after what I saw a couple of weeks ago, I don't think we have a choice."

"He isn't like that all the time, Marge," Lil says, "only once in awhile."

"But he's getting worse and worse. Think about what he'll be like next year."

Nan breaks in. "OK. I have an idea. The behavior classrooms are all full right now. Isn't that right, Dolores?" Dolores nods. "But we have to serve him. That's the law. Right?" Dolores nods again. Nan drives her idea home. "So, can we get Special Ed to pay for him to see a therapist? A good one? A hundred-dollar-an-hour type?"

"I don't know. It's a long shot, but we could try it. They'd be worried about setting precedent," Dolores says.

"Can't you tell them that it will save them money in the long run? It'll cost a hell of a lot less for him to see a shrink than to rot in a behavior classroom," Nan insists.

"I could work with the therapist," Lil says. "We could put together something that might really help him. I'd do it in a minute."

"You know, I think Tess is ready, too. I think she'd get involved," Marilyn says. "She's beginning to wake up to how much Eddie is hurting. This is the first time that she's really seen what's going on. But if we don't do something soon, she'll back off again."

"All right," Dolores says. I'll take the idea to my boss. Marilyn, would you call him too, and tell him that you support the idea? It helps when bosses talk to bosses."

"The minute we're out of here," Marilyn says.

Eddie begins seeing the therapist the next week. He goes once, and then Tess misses two appointments in a row. "What's going on?" Marilyn asks Nan over lunch. "She's not going to bail out on us?"

"God, I hope not," Nan says. "I'm going to call her. No. I'll go over there. Right after lunch."

She's back in half an hour. "Her car is broken, and Mitch is out of town. She was sick about missing, but she was too shy to call and explain. It's OK. I showed her how to get there on the bus. She can do it."

It's late in April, Run-for-the-Arts Day. Marilyn spends the morning outside with the children. They will raise money today to pay for 3 or 4 assemblies during the year. At Lincoln School, the children raised enough money for 10 or 12 assemblies, usually more than they could schedule in a year. But Marilyn is determined not to let the comparison spoil the fun. Just before 9:30, she changes into a T-shirt, sweatpants, and running shoes and walks out through the courtyard to join the children. Mr. Schneider's daffodils have given way to early azaleas and rhododendrons. Grace catches up with her. "Nice morning, Marilyn."

"Just about perfect."

"I gotta hurry. Catch up with the kids. I don't want to lose Stuart."

"How's he doing?"

"Reading like gangbusters. He's going to be fine in second grade," she calls over her shoulder as she hurries after her class. Everyone knows that Marilyn is beginning to work on class lists for next year.

They wait for Tom to shoot the starting pistol. A few other teachers have joined Marilyn at the starting line—Jane, Lil, Nan, Rachel, Marge. The children are amused and amazed. "Are you going to run, Ms. Wallace?" they ask.

"Yes, but not very fast. I'm slow," she answers.

"Just do your best," they encourage.

The children leave the starting line at a gallop. Halfway through the first lap, most of them have slowed to a walk. They run like the wind, walk, run again. Marilyn strikes a slow, steady pace in hopes that she will be good for six or eight laps. Every time she finishes a lap, the children shout, "Go, Principal, go!"

After three laps, Sylvia, who has been running very fast, overtakes Marilyn. "I think I'll run with you for awhile, Ms. Wallace. You're slow."

Marilyn laughs. "I know. I don't think I was ever as fast as you are."

"You're pretty old, aren't you, Ms. Wallace?"

"Yes. Pretty old."

"Are you as old as my grandmother?"

"Yes. I think I am."

"That's old," Sylvia concludes.

When Marilyn slows to a fast walk, the children like it better. Now they can hold her hand and talk. First one child and then another comes to walk with her for a little while before taking off to run again. Marilyn is glad when Leticia, La Shanda's cousin, comes to walk beside her.

"Leticia, I've been worried about you lately," Marilyn says.

"I been crying a lot, Ms. Wallace," Leticia acknowledges.

"Is something wrong?"

"There sure is. I got problems." Marilyn waits. "My father is getting out of jail."

"When?"

"Next week. I'm scared."

"Will he come to see you?"

"He's not s'posed to, but he might come anyway. My mother doesn't know what to do. She had one boyfriend, and now she's got another one, and now my father's getting out of jail. She don't want him to come see us either. He be mad that she got boyfriends."

"Has it been a long time since you saw your father, Leticia?"

"Yes. A long time. I don't remember his face."

"Why did your father go to jail?"

"He robbed someone and killed him. It was very bad what he did. He might do it again. Mebbe he would hurt me or my mother. Well, bye, Ms. Wallace. I got to go run some more."

As she watches Leticia break into her long, graceful run, Marilyn feels some of the joy leave the day.

Late that afternoon, Marilyn is working in her office. The windows are open. The lawn crew has just mowed, and the smell of cut grass fills her office. She has momentarily forgotten her conversation with Leticia and the residue of helplessness that it left as she remembers the pleasure on the children's faces as they ran in the sun. She looks up to see Gus standing in front of her desk.

"I don't like to complain, but it's been 3 days in a row now that there's been crap all over the boys' bathroom down in the intermediate wing," he says. "It's really bad. I shouldn't have to clean up messes like that."

"No, of course you shouldn't," Marilyn quickly agrees. "I'll tell the teachers what's happening and ask them to keep track of who goes to the bathroom when. Give us a week, Gus. We'll try to find out who's doing this."

Gus has a better idea. "I could lock the place up for you, Ms. Wallace. That'd show that kid."

"I hate to take the bathroom away from all the boys just because of one child. Besides, he could just go somewhere else and start doing the same thing."

Gus is not happy. He likes his solution better. "OK, but I don't like cleaning up crap. I can tell you that."

A few days later, Nan comes in to see Marilyn. "Well, we caught him?"

"Who?"

"The one who was messing in the bathroom." Marilyn looks at her. "It was Eddie."

"Are you kidding?" Marilyn is shocked and disappointed. "You sure it was him?"

"Yup. Lil had the time he was out of the classroom pinpointed exactly. It was him, all right."

"I thought he was getting better. What are we going to do?"

"Well, I called his therapist. He told me to talk to Eddie nice and straight. Tell him that we know what he's doing and that we want him to stop doing it. No scolding, no consequences. Just let him know. So I did. I called him in and told him."

"What'd he do?"

"Nothing. He just looked at me, but he had a kind of funny look. Connected. Like we were in on a secret together. I don't think he'll do it again."

Nan is right. Several weeks go by with no crapping in the bathroom, and everyone begins to breathe more easily on Eddie's account. One afternoon Lil asks to see Marilyn.

"I know that you're beginning to make assignments for next year, and I wanted to talk to you about me and Eddie."

Marilyn is puzzled.

"Well," Lil says, "you know . . ." She stops. She wants to say something important, and she wants to get it right. She starts again, "Well, you know how sometimes things have to get worse before they can get better?" Marilyn nods. "That's what I think happened to Eddie a while back with the bathroom business. He's getting some help now, so he can show us how sick he really is. He let us catch him."

Marilyn is listening carefully.

"I feel like I'm just beginning to understand him. The children are, too. We like Eddie, you know. We're not just putting up with him. We honestly like him." She gulps and plows ahead. "I've been thinking about this a lot, and I'd like to ask you something. I know it's unusual, but could I possibly keep my whole class another year? I think if we could stay together—like a family—we might be able to . . ." Her voice trails off. "I know this sounds corny. We might be able to save Eddie. With his mom's help, of course. And the therapist. And Nan. And you, too. But I think we could do it." She stops talking, embarrassed at her own earnestness, unsure of what Marilyn will say.

"Thank you, Lil. Thank you."

VI
A June Farewell

24

May is always like this. The tension began to build a couple of weeks ago with the contest to name the carnival. Sylvia won with "Carnival Capers," and her prize was $5.00 worth of tickets. It's a generous prize. Thirty tickets will buy a hot dog, pop, and cotton candy, and take her to enough games to get through the evening and still have a ticket left for the cakewalk. All the children from kindergarten through fifth grade have made Carnival Caper posters, and Jolene has been coming to school early every day to tape them along the halls. The children gaze at each others' posters while they talk about the games, the snow cones and popcorn, how many tickets their mom will let them have.

On Tuesday of the week before the carnival, Marilyn has a meeting downtown, so she doesn't get to school until late morning. When she comes through the cafeteria doors, Jolene is the first to catch her.

"Did you hear?" Marilyn looks at her blankly. "About Stuart?" Marilyn shakes her head. "He was in an accident last night. It's bad."

"What happened?"

"Well, you know he lives in those apartments up by the Interstate? Those kids that live in them found a little passageway to get up on the Interstate. They've been going up there and messing around. Yesterday after school, Stuart and his brother and Cory— they went. I guess they wanted to throw rocks at the cars. Anyway, they hit one, and it scared them. The two big boys ran across the highway. Then they called for Stuart to come and he ran. But he tripped over his shoelaces. A truck hit him. Maybe two."

"Oh, my God! That's awful. How is he?"

"They took him to St. Andrew's in the helicopter. He might not make it. "

Rose confirms Jolene's story. Marilyn checks with Nan to see what she knows. No more than anyone else. She stops by to see Grace. Fear and grief are written all over her face. "His book. I'd just finished making him his book. I was going to send him down to read it to you today. I don't know what to say to the class. What do I tell them? I can't tell them that he's going to be all right, can I?"

Grace's questions force Marilyn to face what she's been avoiding. "I'll call the hospital. See what I can find out and let you know. We want to be as concrete and as truthful as we can with them."

As much as she wishes otherwise, the hospital switchboard rings right through to Stuart's room. The flat voice that answers is Stuart's mother's. "Everything's broken—his legs, his arm, his chest is crushed, his head . . . "

"Is there anything we can do?"

"Just pray."

The next afternoon, Marilyn and Nan take a plant and box of food that Jolene and a few of the other mothers have put together over to the apartment where Stuart lived. His mother, his grand-mother, his aunt, and six or eight neighborhood children crowd the little space. They give way to let the women find the kitchen table to set down the box. The grandmother and the aunt are crying, Stuart's mother is stony-faced and dry-eyed. She stands along the hallway wall, almost as if she doesn't belong in the scene.

Marilyn goes over to her, feeling as if she wants to hug her but stretches out her hand instead. "We're so sorry. All of us. Stuart was . . ." Words fail her. The children have circled around Nan and are asking her questions, so Marilyn is left on her own with Stuart's mother.

"Thanks for coming, Ms. Wallace. I appreciate that. It's hard to know what to do."

"When is the funeral?"

"Tomorrow. I guess at 10:00. I'm waiting to see what my folks get worked out about the church."

On the way back to school, Nan asks the inevitable,"You going to the funeral?"

"I think I need to."

"Want me to pick you up?"

Marilyn appreciates the offer of Nan's company. "Sure. Sounds like it's going to be at 10:00? I guess we should get there around a quarter 'til."

"Did Stuart's mom belong to this church?" Marilyn wonders as she and Nan drive up to the fine old brick church in an established, middle-class neighborhood across town from Madison.

"Don't think so. It's his grandparents' church. Stuart and his brothers never saw the inside of it. Well, not unless she had them baptized or something."

Marilyn is slow climbing out of Nan's apple-red Blazer. She doesn't want to go in. She doesn't want to put on her polite face. She doesn't want to say the "right things." Nan stops and waits for her, shifting her bag from one shoulder to the other.

"I don't want to do this, Nan."

"No kidding! Well, it'll be over in 45 minutes."

As the women walk up the stairs, they see Cory huddled in the corner by the big double doors with wrought iron pulls. "You go on, Marilyn. I'd better see to Cory here. He's dealing with an awful lot."

Marilyn's grey silk dress and light sweater do not seem warm enough as she steps from the sunshine into the dark. She can smell the dust and the dampness and can imagine mold growing between the pages of the old hymnals. For a few seconds, all she can see is a cluster of people in a small, bright room on the other side of the dark sanctuary. She thinks she sees the back of Stuart's mother or maybe his aunt and wonders if she should go over to pay her respects. She has the impression that the casket may be there in the room with the people. No, she rationalizes. Not now. They want to be alone. Where's Nan? she wonders, half irritated that she has abandoned her for Cory.

Marilyn looks around the cavernous room with its gold paint peeling in long strips high along the ceiling. Twenty or 30 people scatter in the hard, flat pews. Grace is sitting alone about a third of the way down, and Marilyn takes a seat beside her. "Nan's on her way," she whispers as Grace scoots over to make more room.

"I can't talk. I'll just start crying again," Grace says as she draws a long sniff and pulls at the tissue in her hand.

A minute or two later Nan comes. "He was really scared. Hadn't ever been to a funeral. Didn't know what would happen. I think he's OK for now. It was nice of his mom to bring him. It's good that we came. The kids . . ." Two young men wheel the small particle-board casket down the aisle. Grace sobs into her tissue. Nan shifts in her seat.

An elder in a blue suit with pant legs short enough to reveal his thick white socks leads a long prayer. Marilyn stares at her hands and twists her gold ring set with coral, the only distraction available to her. She does not feel like singing or praying or crying with the others. Both she and Nan shift and glance at each other. Another serious old man begins to talk about being called home, something about Stuart's being too good to live in this world. "Who's that?" Marilyn whispers.

"Granddad, I think. What I want to know is, who's that man with Mom?" Marilyn looks forward to the second pew. Stuart's mother clasps both arms around the beefy neck of a large man, but Marilyn forms the clear impression that the two don't know each other well. Stuart's brothers sit at the end of the pew, talking and punching at each other.

Marilyn looks at her watch again. The grandfather is still talking. "Those of us who loved him knew from the beginning that Stuart was a free spirit, always in a hurry. He never had time to tuck in his shirt or tie his shoe laces. You could never keep track of him. If you took him to the store, he was gone the minute you looked away, crawling under a rack of clothes, taking down the toys and playing with them. When he was just a little guy, he'd take off for the park, never tell anyone. Stuart was like that—always on the run, always full of mischief. He just never was for this world. He was too precious, a little angel . . ."

Marilyn is suddenly aware of the ache from her clenched jaw. The air has left the room. There's nothing but the smell of the old hymnals, Nan's cigarettes, Grace's Skin-So-Soft. Marilyn is trapped. She feels a howl rising just below her shallow breathing and nudges Nan. "I've got to get out of here."

"You OK?"

"This is making me sick."

"Hang in there. Just one more song. Then it'll be over."

The song stops, and someone lifts the lid of the casket. No, not this, Marilyn thinks. Don't make us look. The front rows begin to file up. "You going up there?" Marilyn asks.

"Yeah, we gotta. We don't want to worry the kids. Come on."

How can they be making us look? Marilyn wonders. His head. His head was gone. The semi ran over his skull. It was crushed. Don't do this. Don't make the children see this. Nan has gotten up and out of the pew. Grace is standing, waiting for Marilyn to move.

The puffy, dull, powdered face has no more to do with Stuart than the singing and the praying did. Marilyn walks back out into the sunshine. She is cold. She wishes she could leave the face in the darkness, but she will see it always. Before she can get her bearings, Grace is in her arms. "He'll never get to read all those books. I wanted him to read, Marilyn. I wanted him to grow up. I loved that little guy."

"I know you did, Grace. You were probably the best thing in his whole life."

"You really think so? You really think I made a difference?"

"You made a difference."

"Thanks, Marilyn, and . . . thanks for coming. It helped a lot. Having you here."

The grandfather breaks in. "Dr. Wallace? You have our deepest gratitude for coming today. And for everything you did for little Stuart and his family. We loved him very much. He was our darling boy."

Marilyn waits for words. Then, ever-so-carefully, . . . she says, "We were all very fond of him at school. We'll miss him."

"You are a wonderful woman." Marilyn aims a tight smile at the old man, making sure that she doesn't see him. He turns away, and Marilyn scans the few people who are left. Stuart's mother stands across the lawn embracing her companion. Nan is talking to the brothers.

"You guys did a good job. Now, you're going to your grandma and grandpa's for the rest of today and tomorrow?" The boys nod. "That should be nice. You think you'll come back to school on Monday?" They nod again. "I'll be looking for you. I'll check in on you and see how you're doing."

Marilyn waits for Nan to finish up, feeling guilty that she isn't helping. Finally, Nan says, "Well, we gotta go now. See you guys Monday. You take care. Hear?"

As they walk away, Nan says, "This really got to you, didn't it? I thought you were going to drag me out of there halfway through."

"Did you hear him, Nan? Did you hear? That funeral wasn't about a little boy and what his life meant. That was about all the adults letting themselves off the hook because no one ever looked after Stuart. No one ever knew where he was. And they want to blame him, to say he was always in trouble, that it was *his* fault. The only one who ever really loved him was Grace. She taught him to read through sheer love and determination."

"I know it, but what're you going to do? We've got to believe they were doing the best they could. And think what they're going to live with—for the rest of their lives."

"Think of what Grace will live with. What we'll all live with."

In the days that follow, Marilyn and all the rest of the staff have little time to mourn Stuart. They minister to the children. They answer their questions as honestly as they can. They put up a bulletin board with pictures of Stuart and letters and drawings the children have made for him. They plant a little maple tree and tie yellow ribbons on it. And gradually the talk turns away from Stuart and back to the carnival.

25

Josh comes into the room. A crowd gathers around him. I tell him—as well as the other children—to sit down. It turns out he is giving away stickers, totally disrupting the beginning of our morning routine. I say, "Put them on my desk. You may get them after school." He refuses. Finally complies. Also he's loaded down with baseball cards. He gives me more back talk. We have been through this before several times. I am not putting up with this back talk! Absolutely not! I tell him to go out in the hall and cool off. Give *me* a chance to cool off. He grabs his stuff and announces he is leaving and going home! (Fine with me!) He heads down the hall and I follow him. He goes to the office. I don't really mind the stickers if he would choose an appropriate time to give them out. What I object to is all the *stuff* . . . It disrupts. The biggest issue is sassing back. Absolutely no way! I have really made an effort to build a relationship with Josh and feel we have one. But this mouth problem continues to come up over and over. It has to stop!

Marilyn sighs. It's Carnival Week all right. She puts the neon yellow referral down on top of a haphazard pile of paper. Five or six other yellows stand out among the bureaucratic white of memos and end-of-the-year surveys on her desk. She looks up at the clock—not yet 9:00. Even Jane's had it, she thinks as she looks out to the waiting chairs to see Josh watching her. "You want to come in and tell me about this?"

"I wanted to give the other kids some stickers. And she got mad."

"Come on, Josh. Mrs. Reed doesn't get mad for giving kids stickers. What about the talking?"

"I just told her . . ."

Marilyn runs over Josh's line. She's had it, too. "That wasn't all, Josh. You said a whole bunch of stuff. Didn't you?"

"Yeah, I guess."

"Mrs. Reed says it's fine by her if you don't come back to class today. She doesn't say that very often, does she?"

"Uh-uh. She never said that before, and I've been this bad before."

"Why do you think she said it this time?"

"She doesn't have any patience left?" Josh has been through this more than once.

"I guess that's it. Well, tell me this, Josh. Do you want to go back to class?" Josh nods vigorously. "Do you think you can handle it?" He nods again. Marilyn glances at her phone. It would be easier to call Jane, but she thinks she'd better walk down to her room to ask the question. Marilyn's legs are tired this morning, left over from walking the halls yesterday and the day before.

The room is a bright confusion of math. Children are working everywhere—on the tables, on the floor, in the book corner—with kidney beans, unifix cubes in primary colors, boxes of buttons and bolts, making their own sense out of number combinations. Jane walks over to the door to talk to Marilyn. "Some referral, huh?"

"It was long enough. Josh driving you crazy?"

"You could say that. It's his mouth. He just never shuts up."

"I know it. I just about lost it with him in the lunch line yesterday. Do you really want me to send him home?"

"It's OK. He can come back. If he'll just keep his mouth shut."

"Are you tired, Jane?"

"Yeah. The kids are *so* high this week. And it's only Wednesday. I don't know what it'll be like by Friday. All they're talking about is the carnival."

The children are restless; there's an undercurrent. They're too noisy in the cafeteria, play too hard outside. Every day after recess they're piled in the office—some for Band-Aids and ice because they've fallen down or bumped into someone; others because their "play-fighting" or name-calling turned into punches. Marilyn has the impression that every teacher in the school is sending children to the office, mostly for petty crimes. This is more than the excitement over the carnival, she thinks.

On Thursday Henry, one of the mildest of the fifth grade boys, punches Nathan on the cheek, leaving a red splotch that will turn into an ugly bruise. Henry sits silently through the interrogation. When Marilyn runs out of questions, she stops talking and looks at the boys—first Nathan, then Henry, then Nathan, then Henry. Nathan shifts in his chair and looks uneasily between her and Henry.

Henry stares straight ahead, saying nothing, admitting nothing. "You're still angry, aren't you, Henry?" Marilyn asks. Henry gives no sign that he has heard the question. "Why are you angry, Henry?"

Finally he says, "He said I was *poor.* He said I didn't have any money for tickets. So I hit him." The truth chunks into place. This is the worst insult, worse than any of the profanities or mother insults the children hurl back and forth. This is the worst insult of all because it is true.

Marilyn sends Henry and Nathan back to Mr. Schneider and calls Corine to have her send down Charlotte and Alicia. Charlotte is at least 5 feet 6 inches, the tallest girl in fourth grade. She was new in the fall and has yet to make a friend. Alicia is small and thin and is absent more days than not.

"What happened?"

"Charlotte kicked me. I was just standing there in the line . . ."

"She 'cut me,' " Charlotte interrupts.

"Is that right, Alicia? Did you 'cut' Charlotte?"

"Katrina gave me 'cuts.' She said I could be by her."

"What's the 'cuts' rule, Alicia?"

"Don't give 'cuts'?"

"That's right. Don't give 'cuts.' So I guess you set Charlotte up, didn't you?" Alicia nods.

"But you kicked Alicia. Is that right, Charlotte?"

"She kicked me hard. Just bam. Her foot came up and she knocked me down with it."

"Alicia, did I ask you to talk right then?" Alicia shakes her head and stops talking. She has made her point.

"Charlotte, did you kick Alicia?" Charlotte looks straight at Marilyn and nods.

"Why?"

"I don't know. Something just came over me. I guess it was PMS."

Marilyn suddenly comes to attention. For the first time in weeks, she's heard a new excuse. This will be fuel for a good laugh between her and Nan, but for now, she takes Charlotte entirely seriously.

"Well, Charlotte, PMS is a problem for a lot of women, but it's not a good reason for kicking someone. You're going to have to learn how to handle your PMS. It's your body, and you're responsible for it. When the nurse comes next week, would you like to talk with her? She can give you some good suggestions."

Both Alicia and Charlotte are listening raptly to what Marilyn has to say. They have forgotten their fight in the face of this much more interesting subject.

An hour later, Marilyn is walking down to Mr. Schneider's class when she meets Lacey coming out of the girls' bathroom. They walk together until Lacey peels off at Miss Johnson's room. "Are you coming to the carnival tomorrow?"

"I guess not."

"How come?"

"My dad was gonna get his overtime pay, but he didn't," Lacey says matter-of-factly. "He says we'll do something to make up for it when he gets his money."

They're all worried about not having the money for the carnival, Marilyn thinks. The girls will talk about it. The boys won't talk, so they fight.

When she gets back from Mr. Schneider's room, she unlocks her closet and pulls a bill out of her purse. Florence gives her 20 one-dollar bills out of the change from selling lunch tickets. At noon, Marilyn finds Lacey. "How many tickets would it take to have fun at the carnival?"

Lacey thinks about the question. "I don't know. Probably five or something." Lacey's first-grade estimating won't get her through the carnival.

Marilyn takes $3.00 out of her pocket. "Here you go. You can buy 18 tickets for this many dollars. That will be enough for a hot dog and some pop and still play 15 games."

"That's a lot. That's a real lot. Thank you." Lacey hugs Marilyn.

"You go find Jolene. She's in the hall by the office . She'll sell you 18 tickets for your dollars."

Lacey runs off down the hall, and Marilyn doesn't call the usual, "Walk! Don't run!" after her. Then Marilyn looks for Henry. For the rest of the day she quietly doles out dollar bills. Most of the teachers are doing the same thing, but they aren't talking about it. Neither are the children. These are silent agreements so that nobody will know that someone else doesn't have enough money to go to the carnival.

26

It is raining lightly on the morning of the carnival, but the weather report promises clearing and sunshine later on. Even in the rain-muted light, the day is extravagant with rhododendrons in red, pink, and cream; peonies, lilacs, and iris; the beginning of roses. Mr. Schneider's plum tree has faded from its coral pink of 2 weeks ago to shell white. Wet petals lie heavy on the ground this morning.

Marilyn forgot last night to buy a cake for the cakewalk, so she stops at her neighborhood bakery on her way to school. She points to the first cake that catches her eye, asks what kind it is—chocolate mint—and how much it costs—$15—and hurriedly buys it. By the time she merges onto the Interstate, she is far enough behind schedule that the traffic is much heavier than usual. It annoys her that she has to concentrate on her driving rather than spend her precious 15 minutes ordering the day ahead. She pulls into the school parking lot late for her first meeting. She carries in the cake and plunks it down with all the other cake boxes on the counter in the workroom. She sinks into the meeting without taking time to pour a cup of coffee. Fortunately, it is already so well underway that no one notices that she spends a few minutes gathering her thoughts before she jumps into the discussion. It will be a long day.

The scent of flowers, warm and dry from the afternoon sun, lightly fills the evening. A night like this will bring a big crowd, she thinks. When the carnival officially opens at 6:30, she is pleased by the promising scatter of people in the cafeteria. The PTA volunteers blow up the last of the balloons, and the smells of hot dogs and popcorn fill the room. Marilyn savors the early evening light coming through the high windows. Its softness gives a feeling of memory to the scene. She stops at the ticket booth to load up on another $20 worth of tickets. The cut rate still holds for her. She stuffs the tickets in the pocket of her jeans skirt along with her keys and the combination to the safe. She will meet Jolene every half an hour to put the money from the ticket sales in the little safe on the floor of her closet. She goes down to see how things are going in the gym.

The cakewalk is set up just inside the door. "Did you see the cake someone brought?" Jolene asks, pointing to Marilyn's cake box. "It's from 'Justine's.' Have you ever had one of them cakes? They're good! It's going to be our Grand Prize. We'll give it away at 8:00. You'll draw the number, won't you?"

"Sure," Marilyn laughs. She is ashamed for being so annoyed by the inconvenience of getting the cake.

The teachers are beginning to take their places at the concession stands. They will work shifts at the various games throughout the evening. They're simple games—Floating Ducks, Fish Pond, Basketball Toss, and Number Spin. Nan already has a long line at her fortune-telling booth. She is dressed for the part in an old purple velour bathrobe and a red turban with a rhinestone pin at its center. Susan and Melanie have the face-painting booth, one of the most popular. Within the last 10 minutes, the ticket line by the front door has grown long and eager.

Because she knows how tired they are on Friday nights this time of the year, Marilyn does not pressure the teachers to attend, and so she is pleased so many are here. But it's hard for Jolene to think of the teachers as having lives and interests beyond the school, and she can't understand why they don't all *want* to come. "It's for the kids, you know," Jolene explains to Marilyn as if all Marilyn has to do is explain the same thing to the teachers.

Marilyn takes another walk to the gym. This is the swing that she'll make at least a dozen times over the the next 2 hours—stopping to talk, checking on the booths, pointing the way to one concession or another, letting someone use the phone, opening the safe for Jolene. She notices Cheryl Stevens standing off to one side in the hall. April and Cliff stand beside her; Autumn sits in her stroller. Marilyn has never seen the man who is standing with them. He wears a black baseball cap backwards over his long, straight hair. "Hi, Cheryl. Good to see you," Marilyn says.

"Oh, hi, Ms. Wallace. The kids really wanted to come tonight. Do you know how many tickets the games cost?"

"They're one ticket per game. The PTA tries to keep things as reasonable as they can for the kids. They don't try to make a lot of money off the carnival."

Marilyn is talking too much, and Cheryl isn't interested in the information. Cheryl turns to April. "You're only going to get to play five games. That's just all there is to it. You can have a dollar. That's all."

"Are you short on money, Cheryl?" Marilyn asks.

"Yeah. First we had the fire. Then Clyde hurt his back. He was pulling out a big motor. We're hard-up right now." Clyde stands by, saying nothing, while the women discuss him.

Marilyn pulls a handful of tickets out of her pocket, puts some of them in April's hand and gives the rest to Cliff. "Here you go. You have fun with them. If you run out, come back and find me."

"Thanks, Ms. Wallace. That was real nice of you," Cheryl says and pauses. "Ms. Wallace? That worked out. Having April go to second grade. We've had a bad year with getting burned out and all, but she's done good anyway. And I did like you said. I made sure that she came to school. Just except for a few days there right after the fire when we was getting resettled. Mrs. Reed is a good teacher. I feel like she can get kids to where they should be."

"Yes. Mrs. Reed is one of the best," Marilyn agrees. "I'm glad that April has done so well. You must be proud."

"I am proud. She's gonna do better in school than I did. I think you got better teachers here than I had. It sure makes a difference."

When Marilyn steps back into the cafeteria, it feels stuffy from all the people who have crowded in during the last 10 minutes. Six long tables are set up at the far end of the room close to the kitchen where Florence presides over the food.

"Glad to help out," she says. "I like to see the kids having a good time." People line up to get their hot dogs from her. There's another line for soda, and a still longer one for popcorn. The snow cone and cotton candy machines are up by the stage. This is the extent of the food. Marilyn remembers the elaborate fare from the carnival at Lincoln School—pizza, hamburgers, fried chicken, salads, Dove ice cream bars, Mrs. Field's cookies. But no one else makes the comparison, so it doesn't matter.

The men and women sitting on the benches do not say much to each other. They have no easy small talk to share. Although they are neighbors, they do not know one another and are not likely to make each other's acquaintance tonight. They have come to the carnival because their children nagged and because they didn't want to disappoint them.

Marilyn doesn't want to add to the uneasiness hanging in the room, so she is careful not to bully the parents with smiles and small talk. The children, however, are here to have a good time. Sylvia comes from across the room, holding her mother's hand, pulling ahead. Marilyn smiles and steps toward her small wise friend. "Mom, this is Ms. Wallace. She's our principal."

"Hi! I'm Marilyn. I'm glad to meet you."

"Hi. Sylvia told me a lot about you," the woman says shyly.

"Well, you have a special little girl. She has wonderful ideas. We really appreciate her around here. What's your name?"

"Maria."

"You and Sylvia sure look alike." Maria smiles. She is proud of Sylvia. "Is she your only one?"

Maria nods, then says hesitantly, "Could I ask you a question?"

"Sure."

"Well, could you give Sylvia a hard teacher next year? She has Mrs. Conrad this year, and I guess she's strict but I don't think she's hard. Sylvia's got to have a hard teacher."

"Why do you say that, Maria?"

"I don't think she reads good enough, and she's just got to learn to read. I know because I couldn't read for a long time. Then, when Sylvia was a baby, I knew I couldn't be like that no more, so I taught myself to read. But it was real hard."

"How did you do that? Did you go to school?"

"Naw, I couldn't get to school. I watched 'Sesame Street' with her. Everyday I watched, and I learned my letters and sounds. After awhile I could read simple things, and I just kept at it. Now I can read most of what I want to. Slow, but I get the idea. I don't want it to be like that for Sylvia That's why she has to have a hard teacher."

"Why do you think you didn't learn to read in school?" Marilyn asks, genuinely curious.

"It was my mom. She didn't speak English. She didn't know what was going on. And she never went to the school; she couldn't go up there not speaking English or nothin'. So us kids just fooled her all the time."

Marilyn looks puzzled.

"The teacher would send home notes telling her to come to school or telling her we weren't doing our work or that we were late or absent all the time. She'd ask us what the notes said, and we'd tell her that they said how nice we were or that our work was good. She'd believe us, and we wouldn't learn anything. And I've had it real hard because of that."

"Well, you've really done a wonderful job of making up, and you're sure doing right by Sylvia. She's really reading very well," Marilyn says. She is afraid that she sounds fatuous and hopes Maria hasn't heard her in the noise of the carnival.

But she has heard, and she is pleased. "I did my best," she says.

"I'll make sure that Sylvia has a good reading teacher next year."

"Thank you," Maria says. "Thank you very much."

"Come on, Mom," Sylvia says, "I want to get my face painted, then Nan will tell my fortune. She could tell yours, too."

Marilyn watches them as they walk off. She's heard a rumor that Mr. Schneider might retire. If he really does this time, maybe she can hire a strong, new teacher for fifth grade and for Sylvia.

Joey comes toward her with his two little brothers in tow. She suddenly realizes how tall and "cool" he has grown this year. His blond hair is spiked all over his head and shaved close at the back of his neck. He wears a small earring and has carefully rolled up his pant legs. He holds the 3-year-old's hand tightly, and the 6-year-old runs ahead of him. "Come here, Dustin. You stay beside me and Duane. If you get lost, you have to stay here all night. The janitor'll lock you in."

"Hi, Joey. You in charge of your brothers tonight?"

"Yeah. Dad wanted to go down to Slippery Sue's, so he told me to bring the little kids on over here for awhile."

"That's a big job for you, Joey."

"Naw. I do it all the time. They're good kids. Ms. Wallace, will they take food stamps for some tickets? That's all I got. They'd probably take them for sure for the hot dogs, wouldn't they?"

"Don't use your food stamps, Joey. You need them." She pulls a wad of tickets out of her pocket. "Here. You take these. If they aren't enough, you come back and find me."

Joey breaks into a wide grin. "Wow! Thanks *a lot*, Ms. Wallace!"

"You have fun!" Joey doesn't hear. He strides after Dustin who has wandered off again, grabs his hand, and brings him back, gently scolding him. He forms a caucus of three in the middle of the cafeteria to negotiate which booth they'll to go to next. The Market Place is their clear choice just as it is with most of the other children.

The idea of the Market Place is simple. The children line up to throw darts at the balloons that Mr. Schneider blew up and tacked to a board between the time school was out and the carnival opened. Whenever a child hands him a ticket, he gives the child three darts. The children throw their darts at close range, so their chances are good. Whenever one is popped, Mr. Schneider goes to the long table and picks out a bag of donated groceries. The little boys' arms are still a little weak and their aim unsteady, but Joey is a sure marksman. He pops a big red balloon right in the middle of the board on this first try.

"Let's see, Joey. It's you and your dad and the two little ones, isn't it? You could probably use a gallon of milk, couldn't you? And you'd probably like some peanut butter and bread."

He hands a bag to Joey. The little boys start grabbing at it to see what's inside, so Joey sets it down on the floor and lets them take out its contents for inspection. They're excited about the chunky peanut butter, the cans of chicken noodle soup, and the little ham. The potato chips go without comment. "OK, you guys. Put it all back in there. You're getting in the way. The other people want to get by you so they can have their turn," Joey says as he realizes they're creating a traffic jam. He helps the little boys stuff the food back in the bag—a much more haphazard job than Mr. Schneider's expert packing.

Emily and Patty Halloran come up to Marilyn. "I don't suppose you remember me, Ms. Wallace. I came to talk to you about Emily and Mrs. Bannister."

"Sure I remember you. Hi, Emily. Having fun?" Emily nods. "I haven't heard from you for a long time, Patty. How did the rest of the year go with Mrs. Bannister?"

"Well, I learned a lot from that whole thing. I was so mad and so afraid for Emily. I really wanted her out of that room. But Emily didn't want to transfer to another class. The idea was just killing her. I just kept watching. And things would get me upset. Mrs. Bannister can't spell. She really can't. Papers kept coming home with mistakes—her newsletters and everything. But Emily liked her, and it seemed like she was learning. I just decided, finally, that I was a good speller and that I could take care of that department. And a year with a teacher who couldn't spell probably wouldn't ruin Emily. It would have been a lot worse for her to have had a really mean teacher for a whole year. Then she might have ended up hating school. It's so hard figuring out what's best for your child." Patty squeezes Emily. "She's my only one."

"She's lucky to have you, Patty. You're her best advocate and don't ever forget that."

"Let's go get our faces painted, Mom," Emily urges.

Amy is sitting at the face-painting booth in front of the stage. She watches intently in the mirror as Susan Parrish paints a delicate butterfly high on her cheek. Marilyn stops to marvel. She hadn't realized that Susan was so artistic. As she finishes up, she smiles at Amy. "There you go, sweetheart. You're beautiful."

I don't know this side of Susan, Marilyn thinks. Why can't she be like this in the classroom? She does care about the children. Maybe what she hates is teaching reading. Maybe that's what makes her so wretched about the phonics. Maybe if I had her team with someone else so that she didn't have to . . . Amy interrupts the thought.

"Did you see, Ms. Wallace? Did you see what Mrs. Parrish made for me?"

"Yes. I was watching her. It's lovely, Amy." The butterfly sits just where the bruise had been a few months before. "Are you having fun?"

"I sure am."

"Where's your mom?"

"She was tired. She told me to go by myself. It's OK. I can go around with my friends," Amy reassures Marilyn.

"Do you have enough tickets?"

"George gave me a dollar."

"Well, here're some more." Marilyn pulls out more tickets and hands them to Amy without counting them.

Boys hardly ever stop at the face-painting booth, but Susan is painting Tino's face now. She is creating an intricate geometric design on his cheek, and he sits so still that he hardly seems to breathe. Marilyn watches. The scar along his forehead has lost most of its redness. Someone grabs her arm from behind.

"Have you seen Nathan?"

Marilyn turns and almost bumps into Mona. "No, I haven't seen him. Why?"

"You sure he's not here? He's gotta be here," Mona insists.

"No, I don't think so, Mona. I've been everywhere, and I haven't seen him."

"You coulda missed him. This place's awful crowded. He might be slinking somewhere—hiding. You know."

"Well, maybe. You want me to check the bathrooms?"

"Yeah. Would you do that? He stole my money. All of it. I'm not kidding. I had $60 put away, and he got it. It was for the rest of the month. I can't believe he got it. I thought sure he come up here with it."

"Let's look around, Mona. We'll see if we can find him." Marilyn is sure that they won't find him. If he had $60, he wouldn't come to the carnival. A whole evening's worth of tickets couldn't possibly amount to more than $5 or $6.

Twenty minutes later Marilyn and Mona agree that Nathan isn't here. "Can I use the phone? I'm gonna call the cops on that kid. I'll have the cops go after him."

"You can call, Mona. But they won't do anything about it yet. He hasn't been gone long enough to be a missing person."

"He's no *missing person.* He's a thief. I'm going to have them pick him up for stealing. They can just lock him up for a night. See how he likes that."

Marilyn unlocks the office so that Mona can make her call. "Just pull the door shut when you leave, Mona. It'll lock behind you."

"Will do. Me and that kid's just about got to the end of the road. I've had it with him."

Marilyn walks back out into the hall. Lacey is standing with her dad, talking to Grace who has just finished her shift at the ticket table.

"Hi, Jeff. Aren't you proud of Lacey?" Marilyn asks. "She's just done wonderfully this year." Grace nods in enthusiastic agreement.

"She's a good girl," Jeff says quietly and pulls Lacey close.

"Are you two having fun?" Marilyn wants to know.

"Oh, yeah," Jeff says. "I always like the carnivals and events. You know, I was wondering, did you guys ever think about having a social club here at school? Dances and stuff for the adults. There are a lot of us who are alone. I sure have a hard time meeting anyone with my schedule and keeping up with the housework." Marilyn shakes her head and starts to give an explanation, but Jeff doesn't want to put her on the spot. "Just thought I'd ask. And thanks for letting Lacey have them tickets. That was nice of you."

The crowd in the cafeteria has thinned, and the sense of empti-
ness suddenly reminds Marilyn of the children who haven't come
tonight. It has been a month or more since she and Pam McBride
have talked about Jewel. Have they just forgotten in the press of
other matters or has Jewel disappeared from school again? She's
heard no word of Star. No other school has requested her records.
They've had calls about Eli; he's still at Webster School, but next year
he'll be placed in a self-contained classroom. The classroom will be
of no help to Eli. It will only keep him from disrupting the rest of
the school. And Stuart. He learned to read this year and what it felt
like to love his teacher and have his teacher love him. Tears form
behind Marilyn's glasses and the room blurs around her.

She jumps as Gus touches her arm. "Hey, Ms. Wallace. They
want you down in the gym. They're going to do the last cakewalk, and
they want you to draw the number.

"Thanks, Gus. I'll get down there. How do things look? You think
you'll have to work real late?"

"So far it ain't too bad. They've got a mess over by the soda where
they've spilled a lot. But not much else. We haven't had many of them
teenagers. They must have a game or a dance or something over at
the high school. So they ain't coming around and tearing up the
place. I should be outta here by midnight."

The gym is still crowded. Children are taking their last turns at
the games, and a small crowd has gathered to see who'll win the last
cakewalk. The children's faces are flushed from the fun of the
evening. The adults have relaxed into the children's pleasure and are
smiling themselves. Marilyn feels welcome, a part of the crowd.
"They're waiting for you, Ms. Wallace. This is the big one," someone
says. People fall back so that she can make her way easily toward the
center of the circle. Jolene hands her a coffee can with numbers
inside. Marilyn's cake box is the last one left on the table—a big
square box with red writing on top, tied with red string. The top flap
is bent and smudged from an evening of peeking inside. When
Jolene walks over to the old school-issue record player, the gym falls
quiet.

Marilyn knows everyone in the circle. Lillian stands with Leticia
and La Shanda who are nudging at each other, trying to get their feet
squarely planted on a number. "You girls stand still!" Lillian snaps at
them. She has had enough fussing. Tess and Eddie stand together on

their squares. Marilyn can't remember that Tess has ever brought Eddie to a carnival before. Tonight they have come and have stayed the evening through. Cody looks back over his shoulder at Lynette. She runs her hand lightly down the side of his face and winds one of his blond curls around her finger. She bends to whisper something to him.

The scratchy music begins. The players step solemnly from number to number, their eyes on their feet. Step. Step. Step. They make their way once around, and then another quarter of a circle. The music stops. Everyone looks at Marilyn. She holds up the coffee can and reaches in for the number. "Number 10." There is a breathless moment while the players look at their feet.

Then Lillian nudges Leticia. "Go on. It's your number. Go get the cake." Jolene stands beside Marilyn holding the cake box. Leticia comes up to the two women, and Jolene hands the little girl the box. She carries it carefully over to the table where Jolene has set out paper plates and a knife. Leticia watches as Jolene lifts the cake out of the box. She gives the knife to Leticia and gently guides her hand as she makes the first cut. Then Jolene takes the knife and makes another cut and another one. With perfect concentration she cuts the cake into slices so thin that she has to hold her hand under them as she slides them onto the plates.

She passes the plates to Leticia who hands them to Tess, who stands nearest her in the circle. When each player in the circle has a piece, they pass plates out to the children and adults standing along the outside. Marilyn could not have imagined that one cake could be cut into so many slices. People stand quietly, slowly eating the cake with their fingers, agreeing that it's very good—one of the best cakes they've ever had. "This has been a good carnival," they say. "The kids had fun." Everyone feels a little closer.

Next year, Marilyn thinks, I'll bring a bigger cake.

27

The next days and weeks pass as quickly as all the other days and weeks of the year have passed. It is late in the afternoon of a long June day. The school is empty. When the bell rang an hour and a half ago, Marilyn went out into the hall to watch the children leave for the last time this year. They came in a throng, seven and eight abreast, parents walking along beside them, teachers saying good-bye and wishing them happy summers. The children were loaded down with papers and art projects, sweaters, sweatshirts, and an assortment of caps—all of which had been forgotten in lockers and at the back of classroom cubbies until today's clean out.

Marilyn walked out the front door along with the children. She stopped at the bike rack to make sure that the boys walked their bikes to the edge of the school grounds. She didn't need to remind them. They had learned the rule to habit long ago. April gave Jane a long hug, and Jane smoothed the little girl's hair as she reassured her that they would see each other again in September.

Marilyn walked on out to the sidewalk where the buses were loading. Someone grabbed her from behind, and she twisted around far enough to catch a glimpse of Cody's head.

"Come on around, buddy. Let's have a look." Cody grinned up at her. His new teeth are almost in now.

"B-B-bye, Ms. Wallace."

"Bye, Cody. You have a good summer. I'll see you in September." Cody nodded. "I-I'll miss you."

"I'll miss you too, Cody. But I'll remember you. Every day."

She watched as he hurried off to Lynette who was waiting across the street in her pickup. Sylvia caught up with Marilyn as she walked along with the children toward the bus. "Hi, Sylvia. Are you ready for vacation?"

"I don't want school to be out. It's no fun in the summer. There's nothing to do. It's better when we have to come to school."

"You read this summer, just like you did last summer, Sylvia. Tell your mother, 'Hi'!"

The safety patrol was at the corner in their yellow hats. For the last time, they lowered their poles with the orange flags to let the younger children cross. Amy nudged Eddie to tell him something. Instead of pulling away, Eddie turned to talk to her. Lacey crossed the street and climbed into her dad's car, and Jeff waved at Marilyn and Grace as he pulled away. Grace had been standing a little behind Marilyn. Now she moved beside her. "Lacey is one of the best readers that I've had in years, but Stuart was my miracle. Before the accident, I had decided that just having had the two of them could keep me going another year. I guess I still think that. I know he's gone, but there'll be another Stuart. And another miracle. We just have to believe that, don't we?"

"I think so, Grace. Please go on believing that. Please stay. The children need you. They need miracles."

"I guess I need them, too," Grace said quietly.

Leticia and La Shanda waited over by the plum tree for Lillian.

Marilyn stood at the edge of the sidewalk as the last of the children climbed on board and scrambled into their seats. The driver slowly pulled away from the curb, and Marilyn waved as the bus ambled down to the end of the block and stopped at the corner. Waving children filled the back window. She still waved, now with her arm high as the bus pulled across the intersection. Soon it was so far away that she could no longer see the children's faces. Marilyn hated losing the children to summer. As she walked back into the school, Marge came up beside her. Usually Marilyn was happy to share small talk with Marge, but at this moment she would rather have been alone.

"Well, that about wraps it up," Marge declared.

"It's funny about the years. They go so fast. Last September seems a lifetime away. Already I can't remember half of it."

"I know what you mean. Well, we sure can use the break. I don't know about the kids, but I'm ready."

"Doing anything special this summer?" Marilyn asked.

"As little as I can. That's my idea of a *real* vacation."

Nan joined them. "Did I tell you that I got Eddie a great campership? Two weeks at a chess camp. Sure hope he doesn't blow it."

"He'll be OK. He can always hold it together when he wants to. And he'll love chess. Besides, the kids at chess camp won't set him off. There won't be any Joeys there. It's perfect for him," Marge said.

"You know, we ought to get him into Talented and Gifted next year.
I'll bet he'll qualify."

"I'll check his spring test scores," Marilyn said, but the scores are
the easy part. The hard part will be whether he can manage his
behavior. "How many camperships did you get, Nan?"

"Gosh, I don't know anymore. Maybe around 30. I wish I could
get more. I hate these kids having all summer with nothing to do."

They walked back into the school, dark in contrast with the June
afternoon, and waded into a sea of discarded worksheets, math
papers, crayon drawings, bright squares of construction paper. Gus
had moved his cart and one of the big garbage cans into the vestibule. Marilyn pulled a dangling carnival poster the rest of the way
off the wall.

"Looks like a cyclone hit in here," she said to Gus as she stuffed
the poster into his garbage can.

"You can say that again."

"Well, no hurry cleaning it up. What you don't get done today
will be here tomorrow."

Within half an hour, the school fell into empty silence. Jane and
Lil were the last ones to leave. As they put their keys on their hooks
in the key box, they called, "Come on, Marilyn. Hang it up. Everyone's gone over to Handy's for summer beer. You too. You need to
come."

"I hear you. I'll try to get over there. I just have a little bit to
finish up."

That was an hour ago. The hush of the empty school has spread
out into neighborhood. The plum tree's leaves are red and full,
glistening in their newness. They move dance-like in the small
breeze that has come up. There are no cars, no people. The only
noise that comes through the open windows is the high whine of the
"semis" on the Interstate. In the warm quiet of the afternoon, it
seems very close. Marilyn wonders for how many years this hum will
bring Stuart back to her—and the other children. In one way or
another, so many of them play on the edge of the Interstate.

Without having acknowledged it to herself, Marilyn has decided
not to join the celebrating teachers. Not this afternoon. Another time
maybe. She picks up a bundle of computer printouts, spreads them
in front of her and flicks her tongue over her forefinger as she leafs

through the pages to Lil's class. She scans the green and white bands, two names to a band, until she comes to Eddie. He is in the 90th percentile in reading and 97th in math. He easily qualifies for TAG. She scribbles notes to Marge and Nan giving them the good news.

This is about the only good news Marilyn has from her spring test scores. Yet again Madison is among the lowest of the schools—not the very lowest, but close. She has had the results for over a week now, but she hasn't told anyone. It isn't the right time. The teachers are as tired as she is; they don't need to be as discouraged.

Frank called as soon as he got his copy of the scores. "You see those scores, Marilyn? They're not a pretty picture, are they?"

"No. I'm disappointed. I think it's just going to take long . . ."

"The board isn't going to be interested in taking longer, Marilyn. It wants results. Madison is always in the basement. This thing isn't turning around. If anything, it's worse."

"I don't know about that, Frank. I don't think we're worse. We're holding our own."

"Well, the board is going to be asking for an explanation. I want you to get me something in writing by the end of the week. You give me a nice tight analysis of those scores and a point-by-point plan for how you're going to bring them up. I want that memo in my pocket in time for the Monday night board meeting. Think you can do that, Marilyn?" She murmured an affirmative. "Good," Frank said, and the dial tone hummed in her ear. She slowly put the phone back on its receiver.

Marilyn wrestled with the assignment 2 nights in a row. The scores made no sense that she could talk about in a report. She could see what she expected to see: Lil's class had grown from far below the district average to just a little above; Corine's students had shown no growth; neither had Mr. Schneider's for all his presidents' reports. This is news that cannot be shared; but Marilyn knows, from years of looking at the scores, that it is also the news that tells the most truth.

Finally, she found something that she could put in her memo. For the first time in 3 years, every grade equalled—and sometimes exceeded—the average growth for the district. The words began to snake across her monitor, and her courage surprised her as she wrote,

We do not expect to make major changes in our program. We
will continue to keep our curriculum tightly aligned with district goals and to develop and refine instructional strategies that
support the curriculum. Our strongest emphasis, however, will
be on creating a child-centered environment that is safe, consistent, and structured yet nurturing, where children can become available for learning.

Even though she wrote in the jargon-ridden language of the bureaucracy, she felt as if her words expressed a truth for herself. Frank
was not likely to take her meaning, but that was just as well. Her fight
had gone underground long ago.

Her memo came back from Frank a day later with red words
scrawled across it: "Come on, Marilyn. You can do better than this. I
can't take this kind of soft stuff to the board. I told you that I wanted
hard analysis, and that's what I meant. Tell me, grade by grade, goal
by goal, how you're going to pull up those scores. BE SPECIFIC!!"
Marilyn had underestimated Frank. He *had* taken her meaning.

She still remembers the headline after last year's report to the
board: "Alarm Rises Among School Officials Over Fall in Test Scores."
Will the headline be even more grim after Frank's Monday night
report? It seems as if every time she picks up a newspaper, she
stumbles on an article about her failures. "Surveys Find U.S. School
Children Doing Better but not Good Enough." "Scores in Math Add
to Worries of State Schools." The editors and columnists pour out a
never-ending stream of advice to Marilyn: "Phonics Should Again
Be A-e-i-o-used."

She knows what "they" want her to do. She takes their meaning.
They want her to shape up, to bear down, to get hard-nosed, to line
those little children up in neat rows in tidy schools, and to teach
phonics, to teach addition, subtraction, multiplication, and division,
to teach the facts—the names, the dates, the battles, the wars. They
want it clean and simple and to the point. They want results that can
be measured. They can't understand why something so straightforward as that can't be done easily and well.

Marilyn takes off her glasses and rubs her eyes. She swings her
chair around—away from her cluttered desk and the test scores. She

looks out beyond the windowsill of violets, beyond Mr. Schneider's plum tree, across the lawn. The neighborhood is absolutely still under the spell of this last day; still, except for Joey. Joey, who couldn't wait to bound out of school into the freedom of summer, is back. He rides his bike in long, wide, slow circles in the middle of the empty street. He peddles intently, first bending low over the handlebars, steering with absolute concentration, staring at the pavement in front of him. Then he straightens, takes his hands off the handle bars and puts them on the back of his seat, and coasts through the turn. He squints far out into the afternoon sun. When he was shepherding his little brothers around the carnival he seemed large and old for his age, but now he seems small, and, from this distance, his near-white hair gives him an otherworldly look.

He circles, and circles again, until he has made 12 or 13 loops. Then, as if signalled by something or someone unknown to Marilyn, he breaks the circle and takes off down the street, picking up speed as he goes. In an instant, he has sped off out of sight. She sits looking out the window at the empty street. Then she hears voices somewhere far away. The children no longer crowd the playground; she cannot see where they are now. They are lost to her.

She turns back to her desk and folds the printout in on itself. She opens her bottom desk drawer and gathers up five or six old lunch sacks. She will take nothing else home tonight. She locks her office and stands looking down the hall. The the old maroon tile is scuffed and dull from a year of footsteps. Gus's cart stands abandoned at the far end of the hall.

She walks through the cafeteria, dim now in the late afternoon light. The smell of the last hot lunch of the year lingers. She pushes open the back door and walks past Stuart's tree with its yellow ribbons fluttering in the breeze. She will try again to look at the test scores on Monday. Maybe then she will be able to make Frank's sense out of them. But she will never be able to make them tell the truth about the children. Frank doesn't know the stories that Marilyn knows.